ADVANCED COOPERATIVE LEARNING

David W. Johnson

Roger T. Johnson

Edythe Johnson Holubec

Interaction Book Company

7208 Cornelia Drive

Edina, Minnesota 55435

(612) 831-9500

This book is dedicated to the thousands of teachers who have taken our training in cooperative learning and created classroom environments where students care about each other and each other's learning.

TABLE OF CONTENTS

PREFACE

How students interact with each other as they learn has been a relatively ignored variable in teaching despite its powerful effects on a wide range of instructional outcomes. Learning situations may be structured so that students compete with each other, ignore each other and work independently, or work together cooperatively. The extensive research comparing these student-student interaction patterns clearly suggests that cooperation among students produces higher achievement, greater motivation to learn, more positive relationships among students, greater acceptance of differences, higher self-esteem, and a number of other outcomes than do competition or working individualistically. At the same time, teachers have been taught and encouraged to prevent students from helping each other, talking to each other, or encouraging each other. Rather, teachers have been taught to ensure that students work alone.

This book is about structuring learning situations cooperatively, so that students work together. Cooperative learning is an old idea. Shifting the emphasis from working alone to caring about whether classmates are learning is a relatively simple idea. Implementing it is not. This book contains a set of practical strategies for structuring cooperative learning groups and specific suggestions for teaching collaborative skills to students. Gaining a high level of expertise in implementing cooperative learning strategies is not easy. It will take some training, perseverence, and support. The training that has been planned to go with these chapters should provide a good start, but it may take a year or two before cooperative learning becomes an integrated and natural part of your teaching. Persisting until you can use cooperative learning procedures and strategies at a routine-use level will benefit your students in numerous ways. It is well worth your efforts.

If students are to learn and master the procedures and skills required for working cooperatively with others, they must do so in the classroom. First, they must have the opportunity to do so. This is much more than simply placing them in groups. Teachers must carefully structure learning situations cooperatively. Doing so requires implementing the five basic elements of a well-structured cooperative lesson (i.e., positive interdependence, face-to-face promotive interaction, individual accountability, social skills, and group processing). Having the opportunity to cooperate with classmates does not guarantee that students will be competent in doing so. Teachers must instruct students in how to provide the leadership, communication, trust, decision-making, and conflict management required for learning groups to be effective. This book includes many practical strategies as well as specific suggestions for teaching cooperative procedures and skills to students.

It has taken us nearly 25 years to build the theory, research, and practical experience required to write this book. In the 1960's we began reviewing the research conducting our intial research studies, and training teachers in the classroom use of cooperation. Since then our work has proliferated. Previous writings on cooperative learning include **Cooperation In The Classroom** (Johnson, Johnson, & Holubec, 1984/1991), **Learning Together and Alone** (Johnson & Johnson, 1975/1991), **Circles of Learning** (Johnson, Johnson, & Holubec, 1986/1990), and **Active Learning: Cooperation in the College Classroom** (Johnson, Johnson, & Smith, 1991). Related work on interpersonal skills may be found in our books such as **Reaching Out** (Johnson, 1972/1990), **Joining Together** (Johnson & F. Johnson, 1975/1991), and **Human Relations and Your Career** (Johnson, 1978/1991). Recently we have published **Teaching Students To Be Peacemakers** (Johnson & Johnson, 1991) and **Creative Controversy: Intellectual Challenge In The Classroom** (Johnson & Johnson, 1992) on the classroom use of conflict to teach students how to manage conflicts within cooperative learning groups constructively. Yet the concept of cooperative learning is much, much older than our work. Our roots reach back to Morton Deutsch and then to Kurt Lewin. We wish to acknowledge our indebtedness to the work of both of these social psychologists.

Many teachers have taught us procedures for implementing cooperative learning and have field tested our ideas in their classrooms with considerable success. We have been in their classrooms and we have sometimes taught beside them. We appreciate their ideas and celebrate their successes. In addition, we have had many talented and productive graduate students who have conducted research studies that have made significant contributions to our understanding of cooperation. We feel privileged to have worked with them.

This is not a book you can read with detachment. It is written to involve you with its contents. By reading this book you will not only be able to learn the theoretical and empirical knowledge now available on cooperative learning, but you will also learn to apply this knowledge in practical ways within your classroom and school. Often in the past, practitioners concerned with cooperative learning did not pay attention to the research literature, and cooperation researchers neglected to specify how their findings could be applied. Thus, the knowledge about effective use of cooperation was often divided. In this book we directly apply existing theory and research to the learning and application of effective cooperative learning procedures and skills. In other words, this book combines theory, research, and practical application to the classroom. In using this book, diagnose your present knowledge and skills, actively participate in the exercises, reflect on your experiences, read the chapters carefully, discuss the relevant theory and research provided, and integrate the information and experiences into your teaching repertoire. In doing so, you will bridge the gap between theory and practice. You should then plan how to continue your skill- and knowledge-building activities after you have finished this book. Most important of all, you should systematically plan how to implement the material covered in each chapter into your classroom.

Our debt to Judy Bartlett is unmeasurable. Her talents, her dedication, and her work beyond the call of duty have all contributed to the completion of this book. We are continually impressed with and are grateful for her work. She also believes in cooperative learning and often works beyond the call of duty to ensure that it is shared with students in the classroom. We wish to thank Thomas Grummett and Nancy Valin for most of the drawings in this book.

COOPERATIVE LEARNING

Introduction

Beginning in 1492 with the discovery of America, Spain acquired an empire that was one of the most vast and richest the world has ever known. The royal standard of Spain was proudly flown from California and Florida in the north to Chile in the south, in the Philippine Islands across the Pacific, and at scattered outposts along the coast of Africa. Never before had a country controlled such far-flung territories or gained such great wealth. Spain was able to build such an empire through being the greatest naval power in the world.

In 1588 Spain decided to invade England, conquer it, and end its challenge to Spain's dominance of the seas. An armada of more than 130 ships sailed into the English Channel. A naval battle ensued, Spain suffered heavy casualties and retreated, and a storm came up and sank several more Spanish ships. Only about half of the great Armada returned home to Spain and the back of Spain's empire was broken. Amazingly, the English ships suffered almost no damage. The question is, "How did the English sink all those Spanish ships while suffering very little damage to their ships?"

A number of hypotheses have been advanced to answer this question. One hypothesis was that the armada ships were too large and slow. In fact, the largest and slowest ship in the battle was the Triumph, an English ship. A second hypothesis was that the Armada was too lightly armed. In fact, they did have one-third fewer cannons than the English, but all the cannons were of equivalent size and power and there were lots of them on the Spanish ships. A third hypothesis was that the armada ran out of ammunition. In fact, the research indicates that the Spanish had plenty of ammunition. The most interesting finding is that the Spanish cannons were fired on an average of one to two times a day during the battle.

Here is a sufficient explanation for the Spanish's remarkable failure to inflict serious damage on the English fleet. The Spanish simply did not fire their cannons, especially their heaviest cannons, often enough. Why? The answer appears to be that the Spanish had not planned to fire their cannon at sea. The cannons were to be used primarily for land artillery once the Spanish had landed in England.

Until that fateful day, naval battles consisted mostly of capturing enemy ships by maneuvering close, tying the two ships together, firing one round of grape-shot to clear the deck of the enemy ship, and then boarding and fighting it out hand-to-hand until the enemy ship was captured. The last thing you would want to do is blow a hole in the side of the enemy ship because if it sank while you were tied to it, it would take you down with it. The English changed the rules. Instead of tying their ships to Spanish ships, the English kept their distance and blew holes in the sides of Spanish ships, which then sank.

The Spanish did not know what to do. They could not adapt quickly enough to save themselves due to their highly specialized procedures and battle drills. They had no procedure for disciplined reloading on board ship: The cannons could not be withdrawn and run out, reloading crews were drawn from many different stations, cannons of different calibers and metrics were on the same ship which made it difficult to load the right cannon ball in the right cannon, and the Spanish crews were largely captured sailors pressed into service who spoke many different languages and could not understand each other. Given these problems, the Spanish could not respond to the English's change of paradigms of naval warfare.

The lesson to learn from the armada's failure is not to hang onto the past, trying to make do with slight modifications in the status quo, when faced with a need to change paradigms. And sometimes paradigms have to change quickly.

Changing Paradigms Of Teaching

A **paradigm** is a theory, perspective, or frame of reference that determines how you perceive, interpret, and understand the world. It is a **map** of certain aspects of the world. To deal with the world effectively, you need the right map. Suppose, for example, you wanted to find a specific location in central Minneapolis. If you were given a map of Seattle by mistake, you would be frustrated and your efforts would be futile. You might decide that the problem is your **behavior**. You could try harder, be more diligent, or double your speed. But your efforts would still be ineffective. You might decide that the problem is your **attitude**. You could think more positively. But you still would not find your destination. The fundamental problem has nothing to do with your behavior or your attitude. It has everything to do with having a wrong map. Your behavior and attitude only affect your outcomes when you have the right map.

Almost every significant breakthrough in the field of scientific endeavor is first a break with traditional old ways of thinking--with old paradigms (Kuhn, 1962). There are a number of classic examples. For Ptolemy, the great Egyptian astronomer, the earth was the center of the universe. But Copernicus created a paradigm shift (and a great deal of resistance and persecution as well) by placing the sun at the center. Suddenly, everything took on a different interpretation. Until the germ theory was developed, a high percentage of women and children died during childbirth, and no one could understand why. In military skirmishes, more men were dying from small wounds and diseases than from the major traumas on the front lines. No one knew what to do. But as soon as the germ theory was developed, dramatic medical improvement became possible due to the paradigm shift.

In teaching a paradigm shift is taking place. Minor modifications in current teaching practices will not solve the current problems with instruction. Teaching success in today's world requires a new approach to instruction.

Old Paradigm

Pardon him, Theodotus: he is a barbarian, and thinks that the customs of his tribe and island are the laws of nature.

G. B. Shaw, **Caesar and Cleopatra**

The old paradigm of teaching is based on John Locke's assumption that the untrained student mind is like a blank sheet of paper waiting for the teacher to write on it. Student minds are viewed as empty vessels into which teachers pour their wisdom. Because of these and other assumptions, faculty think of teaching in terms of these principal activities:

1. **Transferring knowledge from faculty to students.** The faculty's job is to give it. The student's job to is get it. Faculty transmit information that students are expected to memorize and then recall.

2. **Filling passive empty vessels with knowledge.** Students are passive recipients of knowledge. The faculty **own** the knowledge that students memorize and recall.

3. **Classifying students** by deciding who gets which grade and **sorting students into categories** by deciding who does and does not meet the requirements to be graduated, go on to college, and get a good job.

4. **Conducting education within a context of impersonal relationships among students and between faculty and students**. Based on the Taylor model of industrial organizations, students and faculty are perceived to be interchangeable and replaceable parts in the "education machine."

5. **Maintaining a competitive organizational structure** in which students work to outperform their classmates and teachers work to outperform their colleagues.

6. **Assuming that anyone with expertise in their field can teach without training to do so.** This is sometimes known as the content premise--if you have a PhD or work experience in the field, you can teach.

The **old paradigm** is to transfer the faculty's knowledge to a passive student so that faculty can classify and sort students in a norm-referenced, competitive way. The assumption was that if you have content expertise, you can teach.

Many educators consider the old paradigm the only alternative. They have no vision of what could be done instead. Lecturing while requiring students to be passive, silent, isolated, and in competition with each other seems the only way to teach. For such teachers it may be helpful to review Hans Christian Andersen's tale of **The Emperor's New Clothes**. An emperor invests substantial time and money in order to be well-dressed. One day two dishonest men arrive at court. Pretending to be weavers, they claim that they are able to create garments so fine that they are not visible to people who are either unfit for the office that they hold, or stupid. The emperor's vanity and desire to test the competence of his staff leads him to be duped. The weavers are supplied with silk, gold thread, and money, all of which they keep for themselves while pretending to weave the emperor's new clothes.

When the weavers announce that the clothes are ready the emperor sends a succession of trusted ministers to see them. Not wanting to appear unfit for office or stupid, they all report that the new clothes are lovely. Finally, the emperor himself goes to see the clothes which were so heartily praised by his subordinates. Although he sees nothing, he proclaims, "Oh! The cloth is beautiful! I am delighted with the clothes!"

On the day of a great procession the emperor disrobes, dons his "new clothes," and marches through his kingdom, warmed only by the ooh's and ah's emitted by his subjects. Never before had any of the emperor's clothes caused so much excitement! Then, with an innocent persistence, a small child said, "But the emperor has nothing on at all!" The child was not yet constrained by the forces that silenced the adult crowd and caused them, despite the evidence of their senses, to validate their superior's false judgment.

This story is an example of events that all too often occur in schools: **Not wanting to appear unfit or stupid, faculty members conform to the current consensus about instruction and are afraid to challenge the collective judgment of how best to teach.** The tradition of the old paradigm is carried forward by sheer momentum, while almost everyone persists in the hollow pretense that all is well.

All is not well. Students often do not learn what faculty think they are teaching. Student performance on exams or students' questions may indicate that they do not understand the material in the way or to the extent that faculty would like them to. Furthermore, students often ask boring questions, such as "What do I have to do to get an A?" or "Will it be on the final exam?" Students ask the latter question to determine if the material is important. **What matters, of course, is not whether or not it will be on the exam but rather do professionals in practice use the concept or procedure regularly.** Such problems wear teachers down. There is a way to break out of the old paradigm of teaching and define in more creative ways what it means to be an teacher. The way is known as the new paradigm of teaching.

New Paradigm Of Teaching

It is time for us to reaffirm that education--that is, teaching all its forms--is the primary task of higher education.

Stanford University President Donald Kennedy

Teaching is changing. We are dropping the old paradigm of teaching and adopting a new paradigm based on theory and research that has clear applications to instruction. Faculty ought to think of teaching in terms of several principal activities.

First, knowledge is constructed, discovered, transformed, and extended by students. Faculty create the conditions within which students can construct meaning from the material studied by processing it through existing cognitive structures and then retaining it in long-term memory where it remains open to further processing and possible reconstruction.

Second, students actively construct their own knowledge. Learning is conceived of as something a learner does, not something that is done to a learner. Students do not passively accept knowledge from the teacher or curriculum. Students activate their existing cognitive structures or construct new ones to subsume the new input. The failure of schools to involve students actively in the learning process has been consistently criticized by recent national commissions and scholarly reports (Association of American Colleges, 1985; Bok,

Table 1.1 Comparison Of Old And New Paradigms Of Teaching

	Old Paradigm	New Paradigm
Knowledge	Transferred From Faculty To Students	Jointly Constructed By Students And Faculty
Students	Passive Vessel To Be Filled By Faculty's Knowledge	Active Constructor, Discoverer, Transformer Of Own Knowledge
Faculty Purpose	Classify And Sort Students	Develop Students' Competencies And Talents
Relationships	Impersonal Relationships Among Students And Between Faculty And Students	Personal Transaction Among Students And Between Faculty And Students
Context	Competitive/ Individualistic	Cooperative Learning In Classroom And Cooperative Teams Among Faculty
Assumption	Any Expert Can Teach	Teaching Is Complex And Requires Considerable Training

1986; Boyer, 1987; National Institute of Education, 1984; Task Group on General Education, 1988). Teaching is criticized as being focused on transmitting fixed bodies of information while ignoring (a) the preparation of students to engage in a continuing acquisition of knowledge and understanding and (b) the careful supervision of students reasoning about challenging problems. The continuing acquisition of knowledge and monitoring reasoning require students to be active participants in discussions with classmates.

Despite the academic advantages of involving students in active discussions, many teachers do not do so. Probably the most frequent strategy used is to involve students in whole-class discussions. Frequently, however, students are so socialized into a "spectator" role that it is difficult to get them to participate in class. Barnes (1980) found in an observational study of teacher-student interaction that even when teachers attempted to solicit student participation through whole-class questioning, students responded only 50 percent of the time. Even when teachers manage to obtain student participation, a very small minority of students tends to dominate. Karp and Yoels (1988) documented that in classes of less than 40 students, four to five students accounted for 75 percent of all interactions and, in classes with more than 40 students, two to three students accounted for over half of the exchanges. Stones (1970) surveyed over 1,000 college students and found that 60 percent stated that a large number of classmates listening would deter them from asking questions, even if the teacher encouraged them to do so.

Third, faculty effort is aimed at developing students' competencies and talents. Student effort should be inspired and schools must "add value" by cultivating talent. James Duderstadt, President of the University of Michigan, noted that colleges and universities have focussed on selection processes in the recruitment of students and faculty and have given little or no attention to developing human potential (Sheahan & White, 1990). Astin (1985) has challenged the four traditional models of excellence in education--reputation, content, resources, outcome--and advocated a talent-development model in which the development of student and faculty talent is primary. Within schools, a "cultivate and develop" philosophy must replace a "select and weed out" philosophy.

In the old paradigm of teaching, students are classified and sorted into categories that are considered more or less permanent. In the new paradigm, the emphasis is on the development of student competencies and talents which are considered dynamic and always susceptible to change. The implications of this difference may be seen in the history of the IQ test (Davison, 1991). When Benet built his IQ test, he conceived of a measure that would facilitate student development through the promotion of effort. Just as children matured physically, Benet was convinced that children matured mentally. He wanted to be able to show students through IQ scores that they are smarter this year than they were last year. Each year a student's IQ score would increase, and the teacher could say, "If you work hard and learn a great deal, next year you will have an even higher IQ." What Terman at Stanford University did to the IQ was to reverse the emphasis from effort and development to classifying and sorting students. By dividing IQ by chronological age, Terman created a situation in which IQ does not change. Thus, a teacher says to a student, "No matter how hard you work, no matter how much you learn, your IQ will stay the same. You will never get smarter." In the new paradigm, with its emphasis on student development, it is important for students to associate effort with achievement and intelligence. Schools want students to go to bed each night celebrating the fact that they are smarter today than they were yesterday.

The schools that produce the most knowledgeable graduates are not necessarily doing the best job in educating their students. Why? Because under the old paradigm the management of quality within American schools has generally focused on (a) selecting only the most intelligent students for admission to advanced classes and then (b) inspecting continually to weed out defective students. Under such a system, the "value added" by some schools is questionable. Gifted and advanced-placement programs may produce the most knowledgeable graduates because they attracted and admitted the highest achieving students and provided a holding ground. Quality is managed in the admission process, not in the educational process. Little or no attention is given to the developing human potential. Marginal students who, with a little development effort, could be transformed into superstars are ignored. Similarly, when only the most productive teachers are hired schools can ignore the faculty-development process. Thus, the true "value added" by the school must be questioned.

The second part of quality control under the old paradigm is constant inspection to "weed out" any defective students. One of the mistakes that American industry made was trying to "inspect" quality into its products by identifying and throwing out all defective parts. The ineffective practices were left in place while more and more effort was put into better inspection procedures. American schools are making the same mistake by using stand-ardized and nonstandardized tests to "inspect" quality into the school's product. Those students who fail and, therefore, who are obviously defective, are weeded out so that only the most high quality students are graduated and sent on for further education. The educational practices that resulted in the failure are not questioned and only the student pays the penalty. Quality control in American industry is changing. The new focus is on curing the cause of defects rather than to continue to reject defective parts. Likewise, schools may wish to focus its attention on identifying the source of its "failures." Under the new paradigm, (a) student performance is monitored and when students falter, help and support is provided and (b) when a student fails the educational practices are examined and modified to prevent such a failure occurring again in the future.

The old paradigm classifies and sorts students into categories under the assumption that ability is fixed and unaffected by effort and education. The new paradigm develops students' competencies and talents under the assumption that with effort and education they can be improved. The old paradigm controls quality through emphasizing selection and weeding-out processes. The new paradigm controls quality through continually refining the educa-tional process to cultivate and develop students' competencies and talents. Under the old paradigm schools (and especially advanced-placement programs) are holding grounds for carefully selected students. Under the new paradigm schools add value by developing students' potential and transforming students into more knowl-edgeable and committed individuals.

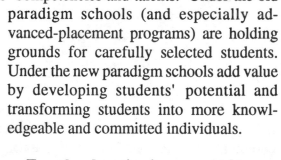

Fourth, education is a personal trans-action among students and between the faculty and students as they work to-gether. All education is a social process that cannot occur except through interper-sonal interaction (real or implied). Learn-

1 : 8

ing is a personal but social process that results when individuals cooperate to construct shared understandings and knowledge. Faculty must be able to build positive relationships with students and to create the conditions within which students build caring and committed relationships with each other. The school then becomes a learning community of committed scholars in the truest sense.

Within the new paradigm, faculty recognize that (a) long-term, hard, persistent efforts to achieve come from the heart, not the head, and (b) the fastest way to reach a student's heart is through peer relationships (Johnson & Johnson, 1989b). Students work together to construct their knowledge and as they succeed in doing so, they become committed to and care about each other's learning and each other as people. Caring about how much a person achieves and caring about him or her as a person go hand-in-hand; academic and personal support tend to be closely related (Johnson & Johnson, 1989a). Within learning situations, it is acts of caring that draw students together and move them forward. Love of learning and love of each other (as well as the faculty) are what inspire students to commit more and more of their energy to their studies.

Striving for increased expertise is an arduous and long-term enterprise. Individuals become exhausted, frustrated, and disenchanted. They are tempted to give up. Caring relationships encourage the heart to continue improving expertise year after year after year. What sustains students' efforts is the knowledge that classmates care about, and are depending on, their progress. Students' commitment to learning is nurtured by their knowing that (a) their contributions to classmates' learning and (b) their own progress in gaining knowledge and expertise, are perceived, recognized, appreciated, and celebrated by their classmates and the faculty. Caring and committed relationships provide meaning and purpose to learning. They contribute to achievement and productivity, physical health, psychological health, and constructive management of stress (Johnson & Johnson, 1989a).

The more difficult and complex the learning, the harder students have to struggle to achieve, the more important the social support students need. There is a general rule of instruction: **The more pressure placed on students to achieve and the more difficult the material to be learned, the more important it is to provide social support within the learning situation.** Challenge and social support must be balanced if students are to cope successfully with the stress inherent in learning situations.

In summary, learning is a social process that occurs through interpersonal interaction within a cooperative context. Individuals, working together, construct shared understandings and knowledge. Learning proceeds more fruitfully when relationships are personal as well as professional. Long-term, persistent efforts to achieve come from the heart, not the head, and the heart is reached through relationships with peers and faculty. Love of learning and love of each other are what inspire students to commit more and more of their energy to their studies. The more difficult and complex the learning, the more important are caring relationships to provide the needed social support.

Fifth, all of the above can only take place within a cooperative context. When students interact within a competitive context, communication is minimized, misleading and false information is often communicated, helping is minimized and viewed as cheating, and classmates and faculty tend to be disliked and distrusted. Competitive and individualistic learning situations, therefore, discourage active construction of knowledge and the development of talent by isolating students and creating negative relationships among classmates and with teachers. Classmates and faculty need to be viewed as collaborators rather than as obstacles to students' own academic and personal success. Faculty, therefore, structure learning situations so that students work together cooperatively to maximize each other's achievement. Ideally, administrators would in turn create a cooperative, team-based organizational structure within which faculty work together to ensure each other's success. There is considerable data indicating that higher achievement, more positive relationships, and better psychological adjustment results from cooperative than from competitive or individualistic learning (Johnson & Johnson, 1989a).

Ensuring that students are active in class usually requires the use of cooperative learning groups. It takes two or more people interacting within a cooperative context to think creatively in divergent ways so that **new** ideas, solutions and procedures are generated and conceptual frameworks are constructed (i.e., process gain) (Johnson & Johnson, 1989a). Much of the evidence on active learning comes from research on college teaching. McKeachie and his associates (1986, 1988) have recently reviewed the research on methods of college teaching and found that students learning strategies such as self-monitoring and learning-how-to-learn skills from discussions with groupmates. Bligh (1972) reviewed close to 100 studies of college teaching that were conducted over 50 years. He found that students who participated in active discussions of their ideas with classmates had fewer irrelevant or distracting thoughts and spent more time synthesizing and integrating concepts than students who listened to lectures. Bligh concluded that during discussion students tended to be more attentive, active, and thoughtful than during lectures. Kulik and Kulik (1979) concluded from a review of research on college teaching that student discussion groups were more effective than lectures in promoting students' problem-solving abilities. Smith (1977, 1980) conducted an observation study of college classes in a variety of academic subjects and found student-student interaction to be related to critical thinking outcomes and study habits characterized by more active thinking and less rote memorization.

Sixth, teaching is assumed to be a complex application of theory and research that requires considerable teacher training and continuous refinement of skills and procedures. Becoming a good teacher takes at least one life time of continuous effort to improve.

The **new paradigm of teaching** is to help students construct their knowledge in an active way while working cooperatively with classmates so that students' talents and competencies are developed. The assumption is that teaching requires training and skill in and of itself.

Implementing The New Paradigm: Cooperative Learning

The primary means of achieving the new paradigm of teaching is to use cooperative learning. Cooperative learning provides the means of operationalizing the new paradigm of teaching and provides the context within which the development of student talent is encouraged. Carefully structured cooperative learning ensures that students are cognitively, physically, emotionally, and psychologically actively involved in constructing their own knowledge and is an important step in changing the passive and impersonal character of many classrooms.

One intent of this book is to provide teachers with the knowledge required for beginning the journey of gaining expertise in using cooperative learning. To gain this expertise faculty must **first** understand what cooperative learning is and how it differs from competitive and individualistic learning. **Second**, they must be confident that using cooperative learning is the most effective thing to do. Confidence in the use of cooperative learning in the classroom is based on the 90 years of research that has produced over 600 studies demonstrating that cooperative learning experiences result in higher achievement, more positive relationships among students, and healthier psychological adjustment than do competitive or individualistic learning experiences. **Third**, faculty must realize that simply placing students in discussion groups will **not** magically produce these outcomes. For cooperation to be effective, five essential elements must be structured within the learning situation. **Fourth**, faculty must know that there are many different ways to use cooperative learning. The various operationalizations of cooperative learning may be subsumed under formal cooperative learning groups, informal

cooperative learning groups, and base groups. **Finally**, what is good for students is even better for faculty. It is just as important to structure the school so faculty work in cooperative teams as it is to use cooperative learning within the classroom. In essence, the organizational structure of schools must change from competitive-individualistic to cooperative.

Student-Student Interaction

In every classroom, no matter what the subject area, teachers may structure lessons so that students:

1. Work cooperatively in small groups, ensuring that all members master the assigned material.

2. Engage in a win-lose struggle to see who is best.

3. Work independently on their own learning goals at their own pace and in their own space to achieve a preset criterion of excellence.

There are three ways student-student interaction may be structured: competitively, individualistically, and cooperatively. When students are required to **compete** with each other for grades, they work against each other to achieve a goal that only one or a few students can attain. Students are graded on a norm-referenced basis, which requires them to work faster and more accurately than their peers. In doing so, they strive to be better than classmates, work to deprive others (*My winning means you lose*), to celebrate classmates' failures (*Your failure makes it easier for me to win*), view resources such as grades as limited (*Only a few of us will get "A's"*), recognize their negatively linked fate (*The more you gain, the less for me; the more I gain, the less for you*), and believe that the more competent and hard-working individuals become "haves" and the less competent and deserving individuals become the "have nots" (*Only the strong prosper*). In **competitive situations** there is a negative interdependence among goal achievements; students perceive that they can obtain their goals if and only if the other students in the class fail to obtain their goals (Deutsch, 1962; Johnson & Johnson, 1991). Unfortunately, most students perceive school as predominantly competitive enterprises. Students either work hard to do better than their classmates, or they take it easy because they do not believe they have a chance to win.

When students are required to work **individualistically** on their own, they work by themselves to accomplish learning goals unrelated to those of the other students. Individual goals are assigned and students' efforts are evaluated on a criteria-referenced basis. Each

Table 1.2 Characteristics Of Social Interdependence

Characteristic	Interdependence		
	Positive	**Negative**	**None**
Fate	Mutual	Opposite	Individual
Benefit	Mutual	Differential	Self
Time Perspective	Long-Term	Short-Term	Short-Term
Identify	Shared	Relative	Individual
Causation	Mutual	Relative	Self
Affiliation Motives	Enhance	Oppose	Oppose

student has his or her own set of materials and works at his or her own speed, ignoring the other students in the class. Students are expected and encouraged to focus on their strict self-interest (*How well can I do*), value only their own efforts and own success (*If I study hard, I may get a high grade*), and ignore as irrelevant the success or failure of others (*Whether my classmates study or not does not affect me*). In **individualistic learning situations**, students' goal achievements are independent; students perceive that the achievement of their learning goals is unrelated to what other students do (Deutsch, 1962; Johnson & Johnson, 1991).

Cooperation is working together to accomplish shared goals. Within cooperative activities individuals seek outcomes that are beneficial to themselves **and** beneficial to all other group members. **Cooperative learning** is the instructional use of small groups so that students work together to maximize their own and each other's learning. The idea is simple. Class members are split into small groups after receiving instruction from the teacher. They then work through the assignment until all group members have successfully understood and completed it. Cooperative efforts result in participants striving for mutual benefit so that all group members benefit from each other's efforts (*Your success benefits me and my success benefits you*), recognizing that all group members share a common fate (*We all sink or swim together here*), recognizing that one's performance is mutually caused by oneself and one's colleagues (*We can not do it without you*), and feeling proud and jointly celebrating when a group member is recognized for achievement (*You got an A! That is terrific!*). In cooperative learning situations there is a positive interdependence among students' goal attainments; students perceive that they can reach their learning goals if and only if the other students in the learning group also reach their goals (Deutsch, 1962; Johnson & Johnson, 1991).

In summary, students' learning goals may be structured to promote cooperative, competitive, or individualistic efforts. In every classroom, instructional activities are aimed at accomplishing goals and are conducted under a goal structure. A **learning goal** is a desired future state of demonstrating competence or mastery in the subject area being studied. The **goal structure** specifies the ways in which students will interact with each other and the teacher during the instructional session. Each goal structure has its place (see Johnson & R. Johnson, 1991). In the ideal classroom, all students would learn how to work collaboratively with others, compete for fun and enjoyment, and work autonomously on their own. The teacher decides which goal structure to implement within each lesson.

After half a century of relative neglect, cooperative learning procedures are increasingly being used throughout public and private schools and colleges. Cooperative learning is the most important of the three types of learning situations, yet currently it is the least used. This has not always been the case. Cooperative learning is a tradition within education.

Types of Cooperative Learning Groups

These problems are endemic to all institutions of education, regardless of level. Children sit for 12 years in classrooms where the implicit goal is to listen to the teacher and memorize the information in order to regurgitate it on a test. Little or no attention is paid to the learning process, even though much research exists documenting that real understanding is a case of active restructuring on the part of the learner. Restructuring occurs through engagement in problem posing as well as problem solving, inference making and investigation, resolving of contradictions, and reflecting. These processes all mandate far more active learners, as well as a different model of education than the one subscribed to at present by most institutions. Rather than being powerless and dependent on the institution, learners need to be empowered to think and learn for themselves. Thus, learning needs to be conceived of as something a learner does, not something that is done to a learner.

Catherine Fosnot (1989)

Students often feel helpless and discouraged, especially when facing a difficult class. Giving them cooperative learning partners provides hope and opportunity. Perhaps the most important aspect of faculty life is empowering students by organizing them into cooperative teams. It is social support from and accountability to valued peers that motivates committed efforts to achieve and succeed. Cooperative learning groups empower their members by making them feel strong, capable, and committed. If classrooms are to be places where students care about each other and are committed to each other's success in academic endeavors, a cooperative structure must exist. A cooperative structure consists of the integrated use of three types of cooperative learning groups.

Cooperative learning groups may be used to teach specific content (**formal cooperative learning groups**), to ensure active cognitive processing of information during a lecture (**informal cooperative learning groups**), and to provide long-term support and assistance for academic progress (**cooperative base groups**). Any assignment in any curriculum may be done cooperatively. In **formal cooperative learning groups** the teacher structures the learning groups (deciding on group size and how to assign students to groups); teaches the academic concepts, principles, and strategies that the students are to master and apply; assigns a task to be completed cooperatively; monitors the functioning of the learning groups and intervenes to (a) teach collaborative skills and (b) provide assistance in academic learning when it is needed; and then evaluates student learning and guides the processing by learning groups of their effectiveness.

During a lecture **informal cooperative learning groups** can be used to focus student attention on the material to be learned, set a mood conducive to learning, help set expectations as to what will be covered in a class session, ensure that students cognitively process the material being taught, and provide closure to an instructional session. Students can summarize in three-to-five minute discussions what they know about a topic in focused discussions before and after a lecture. Short three-to-five minute discussions in cooperative pairs can be interspersed throughout a lecture. In this way the main problem of lectures can be countered: The information passes from the notes of the teacher to the notes of the student without passing through the mind of either one.

Finally, **cooperative base groups** can be used to provide each student the support, encouragement, and assistance he or she need to make academic progress. Base groups meet daily (or whenever the class meets). They are permanent (lasting from one to several years) and provide the long-term caring peer relationships necessary to influence members consistently to work hard in school. The use of base groups tends to improves attendance, personalizes the work required and the school experience, and improve the quality and quantity of learning. The larger the class or school and the more complex and difficult the subject matter, the more important it is to have base groups.

The coordinated use of all three types of cooperative learning groups provides a structure to courses. A typical class period, for example, may start with a base group meeting, move to a short lecture utilizing informal cooperative learning groups, give an assignment that is completed in formal cooperative learning groups, and end with a base group meeting.

Basic Elements Of Cooperative Learning

> *The best answer to the question, "What is the most effective method of teaching?" is that it depends on the goal, the students, the content, and the teacher. But the next best answer is, "Students teaching other students." There is a wealth of evidence that peer teaching is extremely effective for a wide range of goals, content, and students of different levels and personalities.*
>
> McKeachie, et al. (1986, p. 63)

It takes far more to create a cooperative learning group than placing a number of people in physical proximity and telling them to work together. There are many ways in which group efforts may be ineffective. Less able members sometimes "leave it to George" to complete the group's tasks thus creating a **free rider** effect (Kerr & Bruun, 1983) whereby group members expend decreasing amounts of effort and just go through the team-work motions. At the same time, the more able group member may expend less effort to avoid the **sucker effect** of doing all the work (Kerr, 1983). High ability group members may be deferred to and may take over the important leadership roles in ways that benefit them at the expense of the other group members (**rich-get-richer** effect). In a learning group, for example, the more able group member may give all the explanations of what is being learned. Since the amount of time spent explaining correlates highly with the amount learned, the more able member learns a great deal while the less able members flounder as a captive audience. The time spent listening in group brainstorming can reduce the amount of time any individual can state his or her ideas (Hill, 1982; Lamm & Trommsdorff, 1973). Group efforts can be characterized by self- induced helplessness (Langer & Benevento, 1978), diffusion of responsibility and social loafing (Latane, Williams, & Harkin, 1979), ganging up against a task, reactance (Salomon, 1981), dysfunctional divisions of labor ("I'm the thinkist and you're the typist") (Sheingold, Hawkins, & Char, 1984), inappropriate dependence on authority (Webb, Ender, & Lewis, 1986), destructive conflict (Collins, 1970; Johnson & Johnson, 1979), and other patterns of behavior that debilitate group performance. Cooperation often goes wrong due to a lack of understanding of the critical elements that mediate its effectiveness.

It is only under certain conditions that cooperative efforts may be expected to be more productive than competitive and individualistic efforts. Those conditions are:

1. Clearly perceived positive interdependence.

2. Considerable promotive (face-to-face) interaction.

3. Clearly perceived individual accountability and personal responsibility to achieve the group's goals.

4. Frequent use of the relevant interpersonal and small group skills.

5. Frequent and regular group processing of current functioning to improve the group's future effectiveness.

Positive Interdependence

All for one and one for all.

Alexandre Dumas

Within a football game, the quarterback who throws the pass and the receiver who catches the pass are positively interdependent. The success of one depends on the success of the other. It takes two to complete a pass. One player cannot succeed without the other. Both have to perform competently if their mutual success is to be assured. They sink or swim together.

The first requirement for an effectively structured cooperative lesson is that students believe that they "sink or swim together." Within cooperative learning situations students have two responsibilities: learn the assigned material and ensure that all members of their group learn the assigned material. The technical term for that dual responsibility is positive interdependence. **Positive interdependence** exists when students perceive that they are linked with groupmates in a way so that they cannot succeed unless their groupmates do (and vice versa) and/or that they must coordinate their efforts with the efforts of their groupmates to complete a task. Positive interdependence promotes a situation in which students (a) see that their work benefits groupmates and their groupmates' work benefits them and (b) work together in small groups to maximize the learning of all members by sharing their resources, providing mutual support and encouragement, and celebrating their joint success. When positive interdependence is clearly understood, it highlights:

1. Each group member's efforts are required and indispensable for group success (i.e., there can be no "free- riders").

2. Each group member has a unique contribution to make to the joint effort because of his or her resources and/or role and task responsibilities.

There are a number of ways of structuring positive interdependence within a learning group:

1. **Positive Goal Interdependence:** Students perceive that they can achieve their learning goals if and only if all the members of their group also attain their goals. The group is united around a common goal--a concrete reason for being. To ensure that students believe "they sink or swim together" and care about how much each other learns, you (the teacher) have to structure a clear group or mutual goal such as "learn the assigned material and make sure that all members of your group learn the assigned material." The group goal always has to be a part of the lesson.

2. **Positive Reward/Celebration Interdependence:** Each group member receives the same reward when the group achieves its goals. To supplement goal interdependence, you may wish to add joint rewards (if all members of the group score 90 percent correct or better on the test, each will receive 5 bonus points). Sometimes teachers give students a group grade for the overall production of their group, individual grades resulting from tests, and bonus points if all members of the group achieve up to the criterion on the tests. Regular celebrations of group efforts and success enhances the quality of cooperation.

3. **Positive Resource Interdependence**: Each group member has only a portion of the resources, information, or materials necessary for the task to be completed and the members' resources have to be combined in order for the group to achieve its goals.

You may wish to highlight the cooperative relationships by giving students limited resources that must be shared (one copy of the problem or task per group) or giving each student part of the required resources that the group must then fit together (the jigsaw procedure).

4. **Positive Role Interdependence:** Each member is assigned complementary and interconnected roles that specify responsibilities that the group needs in order to complete the joint task. You create role interdependence among students when you assign them complementary roles such as reader, recorder, checker of understanding, encourager of participation, and elaborator of knowledge. Such roles are vital to

high-quality learning. The role of checker, for example, focuses on periodically asking each groupmate to explain what is being learned. Rosenshine and Stevens (1986) reviewed a large body of well-controlled research on teaching effectiveness at the pre- collegiate level and found "checking for comprehension" to be one specific teaching behavior that was significantly associated with higher levels of student learning and achievement. While the teacher cannot continually check the understanding of every student, the teacher can engineer such checking by having students work in cooperative groups and assigning one member the role of checker.

There are other types of positive interdependence. **Positive task interdependence** exists when a division of labor is created so that the actions of one group member have to be completed if the next member is to complete his or her responsibility. **Positive identity interdependence** exists when a mutual identity is established through a name or motto. **Outside enemy interdependence** exists when groups are placed in competition with each other. **Fantasy interdependence** exists when a task is given that requires group members to imagine that they are in a hypothetical situation.

The authors have conducted a series of studies investigating the nature of positive interdependence and the relative power of the different types of positive interdependence (Hwong, Caswell, Johnson, & Johnson, 1990; Johnson, Johnson, Stanne, & Garibaldi, 1990; Johnson, Johnson, Ortez, & Stanne, in press; Lew, Mesch, Johnson, & Johnson, 1986a, 1986b; Mesch, Johnson, & Johnson, 1988; Mesch, Lew, Johnson, & Johnson, 1986). Our research indicates that positive interdependence provides the context within which promotive interaction takes place, group membership and interpersonal interaction among students do not produce higher achievement unless positive interdependence is clearly structured, the combination of goal and reward interdependence increases achievement over goal interdependence alone, and resource interdependence does not increase achievement unless goal interdependence is present also.

Face-To-Face Promotive Interaction

In an industrial organization it's the group effort that counts. There's really no room for stars in an industrial organization. You need talented people, but they can't do it alone. They have to have help.

John F. Donnelly, President, Donnelly Mirrors

Positive interdependence results in promotive interaction. **Promotive interaction** may be defined as individuals encouraging and facilitating each other's efforts to achieve, complete tasks, and produce in order to reach the group's goals. While positive interdependence in and of itself may have some effect on outcomes, it is the face-to-face promotive interaction among individuals fostered by the positive interdependence that most powerfully influences efforts to achieve, caring and committed relationships, and psychological adjustment and social competence. Promotive interaction is characterized by individuals providing each other with efficient and effective help and assistance, exchanging needed resources such as information and materials and processing information more efficiently and effectively, providing each other with feedback in order to improve their subsequent performance, challenging each other's conclusions and reasoning in order to promote higher quality decision making and greater insight into the problems being considered, advocating the exertion of effort to achieve mutual goals, influencing each other's efforts to achieve the group's goals, acting in trusting and trustworthy ways, being motivated to strive for mutual benefit, and a moderate level of arousal characterized by low anxiety and stress.

Individual Accountability/Personal Responsibility

What children can do together today, they can do alone tomorrow.

Vygotsky

Among the early settlers of Massachusetts there was a saying "If you do not work, you do not eat." Everyone had to do their fair share of the work. The third essential element of cooperative learning is **individual accountability**, which exists when the performance of each individual student is assessed, the results given back to the individual and the group, and the student is held responsible by groupmates for contributing his or her fair share to the group's success. It is important that the group knows who needs more assistance, support, and encouragement in completing the assignment. It is also important that group members know they cannot "hitch-hike" on the work of others. When it is difficult to identify members' contributions, when members' contributions are redundant, and when members are not responsible for the final group outcome, members sometimes seek a free ride (Harkins & Petty, 1982; Ingham, Levinger, Graves, & Peckham, 1974; Kerr & Bruun, 1981; Latane, Williams & Harkins, 1979; Moede, 1927; Petty, Harkins, Williams, & Lantane, 1977; Williams, 1981; Williams, Harkins, & Latane, 1981). This is called social loafing.

The purpose of cooperative learning groups is to make each member a stronger individual in his or her own right. Individual accountability is the key to ensuring that all group members are in fact strengthened by learning cooperatively. After participating in a cooperative lesson, group members should be better prepared to complete similar tasks by themselves.

To ensure that each student is individually accountable to do his or her fair share of the group's work you need to assess how much effort each member is contributing to the group's work, provide feedback to groups and individual students, help groups avoid redundant efforts by members, and ensure that every member is responsible for the final outcome. Common ways to structure individual accountability include:

1. Keeping the size of the group small. The smaller the size of the group, the greater the individual accountability may be.

2. Giving an individual test to each student.

3. Randomly examining students orally by randomly calling on one student to present his or her group's work to you (in the presence of the group) or to the entire class.

4. Observing each group and recording the frequency with which each member contributes to the group's work.

5. Assigning one student in each group the role of checker. The **checker** asks other group members to explain the reasoning and rationale underlying group answers.

6. Having students teach what they learned to someone else. When all students do this, it is called simultaneous explaining.

There is a pattern to classroom learning. **First**, students learn knowledge, skills, strategies, or procedures in a cooperative group. **Second**, students apply the knowledge or perform the skill, strategy, or procedure alone to demonstrate their personal mastery of the material. Students learn it together and then perform it alone.

Interpersonal and Small Group Skills

I will pay more for the ability to deal with people than any other ability under the sun.

John D. Rockefeller

The fourth essential element of cooperative learning is the appropriate use of **interpersonal and small group skills**. In order to coordinate efforts to achieve mutual goals,

Constructing a T-Chart

1. *Write the name of the skill to be learned and practiced at the top of the chart and draw a large T below it.*

2. *Label the left side of the T "Looks Like" and the right side "Sounds Like."*

3. *Think of an example for each of the columns and write that below the crossbar.*

4. *Ask students for other behaviors that operationalize the skill and list those on the left side.*

5. *Ask students for further phrases that operationalize the skill and list those on the right side.*

6. *Have group members practice both **Looks Like** and **Sounds Like**.*

7. *Observe the groups working on a lesson and record the frequency with which the skill is used in each group.*

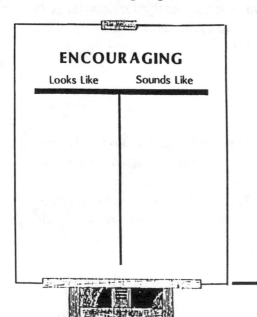

students must (1) get to know and trust each other, (2) communicate accurately and unambiguously, (3) accept and support each other, and (4) resolve conflicts constructively (Johnson, 1990, 1991; Johnson & F. Johnson, 1991). Placing socially unskilled students in a group and telling them to cooperate does not guarantee that they are able to do so effectively. We are not born instinctively knowing how to interact effectively with others. Interpersonal and small group skills do not magically appear when they are needed. Students must be taught the social skills required for high quality collaboration and be motivated to use them if cooperative groups are to be productive. The whole field of group dynamics is based on the premise that social skills are the key to group productivity (Johnson & F. Johnson, 1991).

The more socially skillful students are, and the more attention teachers pay to teaching and rewarding the use of social skills, the higher the achievement that can be expected within cooperative learning groups. In their studies on the long-term implementation of cooperative learning, Lew and Mesch (Lew, Mesch, Johnson & Johnson, 1986a, 1986b; Mesch, Johnson, & Johnson, 1988; Mesch, Lew, Johnson, & Johnson, 1986) investigated the impact of a reward contingency for using social skills as well as positive interdependence and a contingency for academic achievement on performance within cooperative learning groups. In the cooperative skills conditions students were trained weekly in four social skills and each member of a cooperative group was given two bonus points toward the quiz grade if all group members were observed by the teacher to demonstrate three out of four cooperative skills. The results indicated that the combination of positive interdependence, an academic contingency for high performance by all group members, and a social skills contingency promoted the highest achievement. One way to define a social skill for students is through the use of a **T-Chart**.

Group Processing

> *Take care of each other. Share your energies with the group. No one must feel alone, cut off, for that is when you do not make it.*
>
> Willi Unsoeld, Renowned Mountain Climber

The fifth essential component of cooperative learning is group processing. Effective group work is influenced by whether or not groups reflect on (i.e., process) how well they are functioning. A **process** is an identifiable sequence of events taking place over time, and **process goals** refer to the sequence of events instrumental in achieving outcome goals (Johnson & F. Johnson, 1991). **Group processing** may be defined as reflecting on a group session to (a) describe what member actions were helpful and unhelpful and (b) make decisions about what actions to continue or change. The purpose of group processing is to clarify and improve the effectiveness of the members in contributing to the collaborative efforts to achieve the group's goals.

Stuart Yager examined the impact on achievement of (a) cooperative learning in which members discussed how well their group was functioning and how they could improve its effectiveness, (b) cooperative learning without any group processing, and (c) individualistic learning (Yager, Johnson, & Johnson, 1985). The results indicate that the high-, medium-, and low-achieving students in the cooperation- with-group-processing condition achieved higher on daily achievement, post-instructional achievement, and retention measures than did the students in the other two conditions. Students in the cooperation-without-group-processing condition, furthermore, achieved higher on all three measures than did the students in the individualistic condition. Johnson, Johnson, Stanne, and Garibaldi (1990) conducted a follow-up study comparing cooperative learning with no-processing, cooperative learning-with-teacher processing (teacher specified cooperative skills to use, observed, and gave whole-class feedback as to how well students were using the skills), cooperative learning with teacher and student processing (teacher specified cooperative skills to use, observed, gave whole-class feedback as to how well students were using the skills, and had learning groups discuss how well they interacted as a group), and individualistic learning. Forty-nine high ability Black American high school seniors and entering college freshmen at Xavier University participated in the study. A complex computer-assisted problem-solving assignment was given to the students. All three cooperative conditions performed higher

Figure 1.1 Group Processing And Achievement

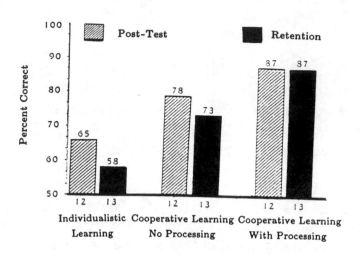

Source: Yager, Johnson, & Johnson (1985). Data summarized by Ted Graves.

than did the individualistic condition. The combination of teacher and student processing resulted in greater problem- solving success than did the other cooperative conditions.

While the teacher systematically observes the cooperative learning groups he or she attains a "window" into what students do and do not understand as they explain to each other how to complete the assignment. Listening in on the students' explanations provides valuable information about how well the students understand the instructions, the major concepts and strategies being learned, and the basic elements of cooperative learning. Wilson (1987, p.18) conducted a three-year, teaching- improvement study as part of a college faculty development program. Both faculty and students agreed that faculty needed help on knowing if the class understood the material or not. Listening to students explain how to complete the assignment to groupmates provides better information about what students do and do not know than do correct answers on a test or homework assignments handed in.

There are two levels of processing--small group and whole class. In order to ensure that **small group processing** takes place, teachers allocate some time at the end of each class session for each cooperative group to process how effectively members worked together. Groups need to describe what member actions were helpful and unhelpful in completing the group's work and make decisions about what behaviors to continue or change. Such processing (1) enables learning groups to focus on maintaining good working relationships among members, (2) facilitates the learning of cooperative skills, (3) ensures that members receive feedback on their participation, (4) ensures that students think on the meta-cognitive as well as the cognitive level, and (5) provides the means to celebrate the success of the group and reinforce the positive behaviors of group members. Some of the keys to successful small group processing are allowing sufficient time for it to take place, providing a structure for processing (such as "List three things your group is doing well today and one thing you could improve"), emphasizing positive feedback, making the processing specific rather than general, maintaining student involvement in processing, reminding students to use their cooperative skills while they process, and communicating clear expectations as to the purpose of processing.

In addition to small group processing, the teacher should periodically engage in **whole-class processing**. When cooperative learning groups are used, the teacher observes the groups, analyzes the problems they have working together, and gives feedback to each group on how well they are working together. The teacher systematically moves from group to group and observes them at work. A formal observation sheet may be used to gather specific data on each group. At the end of the class period the teacher can then conduct a whole-class processing session by sharing with the class the results of his or her observations. If each group has a peer observer, the results of his or her observations may be added together to get overall class data.

An important aspect of both small-group and whole-class processing is group and class celebrations. It is feeling successful, appreciated, and respected that builds commitment to learning, enthusiasm about working in cooperative groups, and a sense of self-efficacy in terms of subject-matter mastery and working cooperatively with classmates.

Summary: Seeing The Beauty In The Beast

There is a fairy tale about the beautiful daughter of a wealthy merchant who, to rescue her father, agreed to live with a beast. When seeing the beast for the first time she let out a cry of horror and fainted. When she awoke she heard the beast sobbing as if its heart would break. Ashamed and sorry she said, "Do not weep, my friend, your ugly shape is not your doing. True beauty lies within, not in what is without." When at last she embraced the beast in love and commitment, the beast was transformed to a handsome price. And she lived in love and luxury forever after.

The inner beauty of cooperative efforts lies in seeing beyond students talking to each other to the five essential components described in this chapter. The inner beauty of cooperation comes from feeling bonded to others through a mutual interdependence, providing help and encouragement out of a true commitment to each other's success and well-being, striving to do one's personal best to help the team, providing leadership and enhancing communication, and reflecting jointly on how members may work together even more effectively.

Many educators who believe that they are using cooperative learning are, in fact, missing its essence. There is a crucial difference between simply putting students in groups to learn

Structuring the Five Basic Elements Is Like Using Pulleys to Lift Weights

Using the five basic elements of cooperation skillfully increases an instructor's power to increase student achievement, build a more caring and supportive learning community, and enhance students' psychological adjustment and social competencies. The power that each of the five elements adds is like using ropes and pulleys to lift weights. Putting students in groups and having them interact face to face gives little advantage over having each student work alone. Adding each of the five essential elements, however, doubles the amount of weight a person can lift with the same amount of effort. Thus, with two pulleys 100 pounds of effort lifts 200 pounds of weight, with three pulleys 100 pounds of effort lifts 300 pounds, and with five pulleys 100 pounds of effort lifts 500 pounds. Whenever instructors want learning groups to be more powerful, they only needs to operationalize the five basic elements in more precise and refined ways.

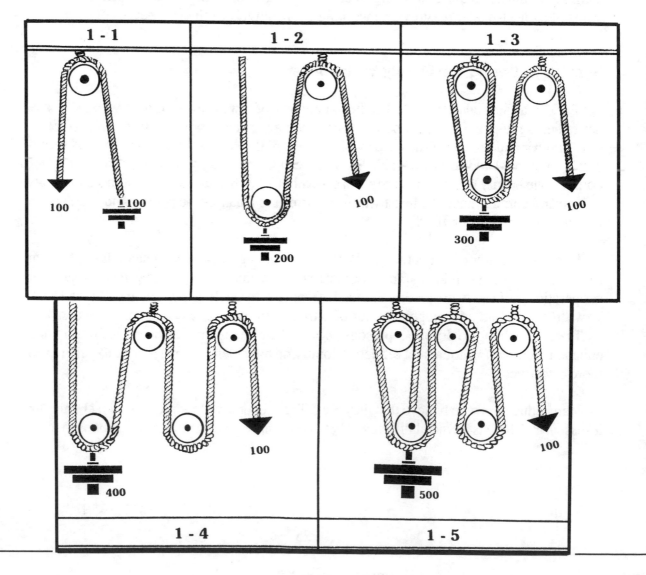

and in structuring cooperation among students. Cooperation is **not** having students sit side-by-side at the same table to talk with each other as they do their individual assignments. Cooperation is **not** assigning a report to a group of students where one student does all the work and the others put their names on the product as well. Cooperation is **not** having students do a task individually with instructions that the ones who finish first are to help the slower students. Cooperation is much more than being physically near other students, discussing material with other students, helping other students, or sharing material among students, although each of these is important in cooperative learning.

To be cooperative a group must have clear positive interdependence, members must promote each other's learning and success face-to-face, hold each other personally and individually accountable to do his or her fair share of the work, appropriately use the interpersonal and small group skills needed for cooperative efforts to be successful, and process as a group how effectively members are working together. These five essential components must be present for small group learning to be truly cooperative. There are four types of cooperative learning groups within which these five essential elements must be structured: formal, informal, base groups, and academic controversy. They are discussed in in Chapters 2, 3, 4, and 5. The integrated use of the four types of cooperative learning is discussed in Chapter 6. Once the use of cooperative learning is mastered, it must be integrated with other instructional procedures. Chapter 7 focuses on the integrated use of cooperative, competitive, and individualistic learning. The social skills involved in leadership, trust, and communication are then covered in Chapters 8, 9, and 10. The management of student diversity within the classroom is covered in Chapter 11. Chapter 12 focuses on cooperative teams of faculty members and working with colleagues to improve their expertise in using cooperative learning.

Leaving The Ivy Tower For The "Real World"

Self-managing teams in business and industry are teams of 5 to 15 employees who produce an entire product or provide an entire service. Team members learn all tasks and rotate from job to job. The teams take over managerial duties, including work and vacation scheduling, the ordering of supplies and materials, and the hiring of new members. Self-managing teams can increase productivity 30 percent or more and substantially raise quality. They fundamentally change the way work is organized, giving employees control over their jobs, wiping out tiers of managers, and tearing down bureaucratic barriers between departments. A flatter organization results. Self-managing teams were used by a few companies in the 1960s and 1970s and have rapidly spread in the mid-to-late 1980s. They appear to be the wave of the future.

This new organizational structure of self-managing teams stands in opposition to the principles developed by Frederick W. Taylor. Taylor advocated divisions of labor in which simple, repetitive tasks were performed by low skilled workers under close supervisory control. In the new organizational model work is handed over to small teams of highly skilled employees who make incremental improvements in products and services. Products must continually change, as current products can become obsolete quickly. **Where before companies sold a "product," now they sell a team "process."**

The keys to today's and tomorrow's workplace are the team and the employee. To flourish, companies will need involved and committed employees, who are self-directed and creative thinkers, who continuously seek to upgrade their knowledge and skills, who rapidly and continuously improve products and services, and who are willing to move from job to job. Teamwork makes this possible because the employees usually are "cross-trained" to perform all tasks. They can fill in for absent coworkers and respond quickly to changes. They can teach knowledge and skills to each other. They can monitor coworkers' actions and ensure high quality of work and products.

It is time for faculty to leave the ivy tower of placing students in rows to see who is best and enter the modern world of team- based cooperative organizational structures. Life in classrooms should match more closely the real world of work for which students are supposedly being trained. In many modern corporations, a school graduate can only be employed if he or she can work as part of a team.

Preparing students to live in the real world includes making classroom experiences (a) more similar to career situations, (b) more reflective of the increased interdependence in the world, and (c) more realistically aimed at building a high quality of life within and after school.

Career Success

> *Everyone has to work together; if we can't get everybody working toward common goals, nothing is going to happen.*
>
> Harold K. Sperlich, President, Chrysler Corporation

For an individual, piloting a Boeing 747 is impossible. For the three-person crew, it is straightforward. The crew, furthermore, does not work in isolation. Large numbers of mechanics, service personnel, cabin attendants, air traffic controllers, pilot educators (who keep crew members abreast of the latest developments and sharp in their responses to problem situations), and many others are necessary to the flying of the plane. From the demands of repairing a flat tire on a dark highway ("You hold the light while I...") to the complex requirements of flying a modern passenger jet, teamwork is the most frequent human response to the challenges of coping with otherwise impossible tasks.

The importance of cooperative learning goes beyond maximizing outcomes such as achievement, positive attitudes toward subject areas, and the ability to think critically, although these are worthwhile outcomes. Knowledge and skills are of no use if the student cannot apply them in cooperative interaction with other people. It does no good to train an engineer, accountant, or teacher if the person does not have the cooperative skills needed to apply the knowledge and technical skills in cooperative relationships on the job.

Much of what students have traditionally learned in school is worthless in the real world. Schools teach that work means performing tasks largely by oneself, helping and assisting others is cheating, technical competencies are the only things that matter, attendance and punctuality are secondary to test scores, motivation is up to the teacher, success depends on performance on individual tests, and promotions are received no matter how little one works. In the real world of work, things are altogether different. Most employers do not expect people to sit in rows and compete with colleagues without interacting with them. The heart of most jobs, especially the higher-paying more interesting jobs, is teamwork. Teamwork involves getting others to cooperate, leading others, coping with complex power and influence issues, and helping solve people's problems in working with each other. Teamwork involves communication, effective coordination, and divisions of labor.

Within the real world, cooperation is pervasive on many levels. Individuals join together in a group that is structured around a mutual goal. The group fits into the larger mosaic of groups working toward a larger goal. Those groups also form a mosaic working toward even a larger superordinate goal. Thus, there are individuals who work within teams that work within departments that work within divisions that work

Workplace Basics

A recent survey of major businesses and industrial firms concluded that the workplace basics to learn in school are:

1. *Learning to learn.*

2. *Listening and oral communications.*

3. *Competence in reading, writing and computation.*

4. *Adaptability based on creative thinking and problem solving.*

5. *Personal management characterized by self-esteem, goal-setting motivation, and personal/career development.*

6. *Group effectiveness characterized by interpersonal skills, negotiation skills and teamwork.*

7. *Organizational effectiveness and leadership.*

American Society for Training and Development and the U.S. Department of Labor (1988)

within organizations that work within a societal economic system that works within the global economic system.

Life in the real world is characterized by layers of positive interdependence that stretch from the interpersonal to the international. Current life in schools is dominated by competitive and individualistic activities that ignore the importance of positive interdependence. It is time for schools to leave the ivy tower of working alone to see who is best and ensure that classroom experiences realistically reflect the realities of adult life.

World Interdependence

Students increasingly live in a world characterized by interdependence, pluralism, conflict, and rapid change. Because of technological, economic, ecological, and political interdependence, the solution to most problems cannot be achieved by one country alone. The major problems faced by individuals (e.g., contamination of the environment, global warming, world hunger, violence toward women and children, international terrorism, nuclear war) are increasingly ones that cannot be solved by actions taken only at the national level. Our students will live in a complex, interconnected world in which cultures collide every minute and dependencies limit the flexibility of individuals and nations. The internationalization of problems will increase so that there will be no clear division between domestic and international problems. Students need to learn the competencies involved in managing interdependence, resolving conflicts within cooperative systems made up of parties from different countries and cultures, and personally adapting to rapid change.

Quality Of Life

Quality of life depends on having close friends who last a lifetime, building and maintaining a loving family, being a responsible parent, caring about others, and contributing to the well-being of the world. These are things that make life worthwhile. Grades in school do not predict which students will have a high quality of life after they are graduated. The ability to work cooperatively with others does. The ability of students to work collaboratively with others is the keystone to building and maintaining the caring and committed relationships that largely determine quality of life.

Summary

In teaching a paradigm shift is taking place. Minor modifications in current teaching practices will not solve the current problems with instruction. Teaching success in today's world requires a new approach to instruction. Teaching in the old way harder and faster with more bells and whistles will not do. The "select and weed out" approach to teaching must be replaced with the "development" approach. While academia has a number of purposes, including discovering and formulating knowledge through research and theory, teaching is one of their most important activities. Schools must refocus on teaching in order to develop student potential and talents. Faculty must "add value" through their teaching. The new paradigm of teaching may only be operationalized and implemented through the use of cooperative learning procedures.

Cooperative learning is the instructional use of small groups so that students work together to maximize their own and each other's learning. There is considerable research demonstrating that cooperative learning produces higher achievement, more positive relationships among students, and healthier psychological adjustment than do competitive or individualistic experiences. These effects, however, do not automatically appear when students are placed in groups. To be cooperative, learning groups must be carefully structured to include five basic elements. There are, furthermore, many different ways to structure cooperative learning. Three broad categories of cooperative learning strategies are formal cooperative learning groups, informal cooperative learning groups, and cooperative base groups. Finally, cooperation is just as powerful among faculty as it is among students. There needs to be an organizational restructuring from the existing competitive-individualistic school structure to a cooperative team-based organizational structure.

Final Note

The recent Carnegie Foundation study of student life revealed growing social separations and divisions in schools, increased acts of incivility, and a deepening concern that the spirit of community has diminished. In response, schools from coast to coast are searching for ways to affirm diversity. Issues like the quality of school life for students, however, are not considered by the old paradigm. The work of the faculty needs to be defined in ways that enrich, rather than restrict, the quality of school life. Cooperative learning provides a procedure for doing so. In choosing between the old and new paradigms of teaching, faculty may wish to remember how to broil a frog.

If you place a frog in a pot of boiling water, it will immediately jump out with little damage to itself. But if you place a frog in a pot of cold water, and slowly raise the temperature, the frog seems to adapt well to the new conditions, and stays in the pot until the water reaches 212 degrees Fahrenheit - boiling - and then the frog quickly dies. The frog does not have the sensors needed to detect the gradual rise in water temperature. Schools may be in danger of making the same mistake. They may make incremental changes to their dynamic environment until they suddenly realize that there has been a fundamental change and they are obsolete and out of date.

⊱[Cooperative Learning Contract]⊰

Major Learnings	Implementation Plans

Date _____   Date of Progress Report Meeting _____

Participant's Signature _____

Signatures of Other Group Members _____   _____

_____   _____   _____

Cooperative Learning
Progress Report

NAME _____ SCHOOL _____

AGE LEVEL _____ SUBJECT _____

DAY AND DATE	DESCRIPTION of TASKS and ACTIVITIES PERFORMED	SUCCESSES EXPERIENCED	PROBLEMS ENCOUNTERED

Description of critical or interesting incidents:

✑ COOPERATIVE LEARNING LOG SHEET ✑

WK.	LESSONS PLANNED AND/OR TAUGHT	COLLAB. SKILL STRESSED	PLANNED WITH	OBSERVED BY	GIVEN AWAY TO
1					
2					
3					
4					
5					
6					
7					
8					
9					
10					
11					
12					
13					
14					
15					
GRP					
TOTAL					

EXERCISE

MATERIALS

Fundamentals of Cooperative Learning

1. The learning goals of any lesson (in any subject area, in any curriculum, with any age student) may be structured in three ways. The three **goal structures** are (list and define):

   a.

   b.

   c.

   No more fuzzies. Whenever a lesson is taught, it should be clearly structured in one of these three ways.

2. To structure lessons cooperatively, you must know its **essential components** (basic elements) that differentiate it from traditional classroom grouping. The essential components are (list and define):

   a.

   b.

   c.

   d.

   e.

3. Conceptually understanding cooperative learning is not enough. You must be able to teach cooperative lessons. The overall **teacher's role** in conducting cooperative lessons may be divided into five parts (list and define):

   a.

   b.

c.

d.

e.

4. To become committed to using cooperative learning you must understand why it is so powerful--what it does for students and what it does for you. The three categories of **research outcomes** are (list and define):

a.

b.

c.

5. The heart of cooperation is **positive interdependence**. To be cooperative, the type of positive interdependence a lesson must clearly contain is (name and define):

a.

The other ways in which positive interdependence may be structured are (list and define):

b.

c.

d.

e.

f.

g.

h.

i.

6. Once positive interdependence is established, each student must be personally responsible to learn and to help groupmates learn. The purpose of cooperative learning groups is to make each member a stronger individual in his or her own right. Ways to structure **individual accountability** include (list and define):

   a.

   b.

   c.

   d.

7. Positive interdependence results in **promotive interaction** as students help, assist, encourage, and support each other's efforts to learn. This requires social skills. The four categories of **social skills** are (list and define):

   a.

   b.

   c.

   d.

8. The steps of teaching students social (or cognitive) skills are (list and define):

   a.

   b.

   c.

   d.

e.

9. In order for students to master social skills and for groups to improve their effectiveness, members must discuss how effectively they are working together. To help student do so, the teacher monitors the learning groups and provides them with specific feedback about their functioning. The procedures for **monitoring and processing** are (list and define):

a.

b.

c.

d.

e.

f.

g.

10. You now have a conceptual understanding of the fundamentals of using cooperative learning. The next step is perfecting your skills in actually teaching cooperative lessons. Gaining expertise takes (a) years of practice and (b) the help and assistance of colleagues who are also using cooperative learning. This assistance is provided within a **colleagial support group**.

a. What is a colleagial support group?

b. What are its three major activities (list and define)?

1.

2.

3.

d. When will your weekly meeting be (day and hour)?

11. You progressively refine your **expertise** in implementing cooperative learning by (list and define):

a.

b.

c.

d.

12. Verify that you are increasing your expertise in using cooperative learning by having two members of your colleagial support group sign the following statement.

We, the undersigned, have coplanned two cooperative learning lessons with _____ and observed him/her teach the lessons. We verify that he/she conceptually understands cooperative learning and can successfully apply that knowledge by using cooperative learning to teach his/her students.

_____   _____

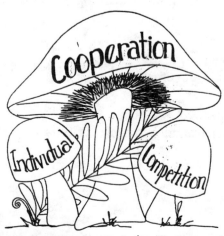

GOAL STRUCTURES

A learning **goal** is a desired future state of competence or mastery in the subject area being studied. A **goal structure** specifies the type of interdependence among students as they strive to accomplish their learning goals. Interdependence may be positive (cooperation), negative (competition), or none (individualistic efforts).

Cooperation: We Sink Or Swim Together

Teachers structure lessons so that students work together to maximize their own and each other's learning. Students work together to achieve shared goals.
- Work in small, often heterogeneous groups
- Strive for all group members' success
- What benefits self benefits others
- Joint success is celebrated
- Rewards are viewed as unlimited
- Evaluated by comparing performance to preset criteria

Competition: I Swim, You Sink; I Sink, You Swim

Teachers structure lessons so that students work against each other to achieve a goal only one or a few can attain.
- Work alone
- Strive to be better than classmates
- What benefits self deprives others
- Own success and others' failure is celebrated
- Rewards are limited
- Graded on a curve or ranked from "best" to "worst"

Individualistic: We Are Each In This Alone

Students work by themselves to accomplish learning goals unrelated to those of other students.
- Work alone
- Strive for own success
- What benefits self does not affect others
- Own success is celebrated
- Rewards are viewed as unlimited
- Evaluated by comparing performance to preset criteria

asic Elements Of Cooperative Learning

Positive Interdependence

Students perceive that they need each other in order to complete the group's task ("sink or swim together"). Teachers may structure positive interdependence by establishing **mutual goals** (learn and make sure all other group members learn), **joint rewards** (if all group members achieve above the criteria, each will receive bonus points), **shared resources** (one paper for each group or each member receives part of the required information), and **assigned roles** (summarizer, encourager of participation, elaborator).

Face-to-Face Promotive Interaction

Students promote each other's learning by helping, sharing, and encouraging efforts to learn. Students explain, discuss, and teach what they know to classmates. Teachers structure the groups so that students sit knee-to-knee and talk through each aspect of the assignment.

Individual Accountability

Each student's performance is frequently assessed and the results are given to the group and the individual. Teachers may structure individual accountability by giving an individual test to each student or randomly selecting one group member to give the answer.

Interpersonal And Small Group Skills

Groups cannot function effectively if students do not have and use the needed social skills. Teachers teach these skills as purposefully and precisely as academic skills. Collaborative skills include leadership, decision-making, trust-building, communication, and conflict-management skills.

Group Processing

Groups need specific time to discuss how well they are achieving their goals and maintaining effective working relationships among members. Teachers structure group processing by assigning such tasks as (a) list at least three member actions that helped the group be successful and (b) list one action that could be added to make the group even more successful tomorrow. Teachers also monitor the groups and give feedback on how well the groups are working together to the groups and the class as a whole.

Cooperative Learning
Classroom Observation

Teacher Observed: _____ Date: _____

Observer: _____

My focus as an observer for this lesson is: _____

		COMMENTS
Subject Matter Objective:		
Social Skills Objective:		
Positive Interdependence	☐ Group goal ☐ Group reward (e.g., bonus points) ☐ Division of labor ☐ Materials shared/jigsawed ☐ Roles assigned ☐ Group celebration of success ☐ Other:	
Group Composition	☐ Homogeneous ☐ Heterogeneous	
Seating Arrangement	☐ Clear view/access to others ☐ Clear view/access to materials	
Individual Accountability	☐ Each student evaluated (own work) ☐ Students check each other ☐ Random student evaluated ☐ Other:	
Teach Social Skill	☐ Rationale ☐ Defining social skill, e.g., T chart ☐ Intervening to correct and/or encourage	
Observation • task help • systematic • focused/systematic	**By:** ☐ Teacher ☐ Student(s) ☐ Observation form used ☐ Informal (anecdotal, etc.)	
Teacher Feedback: Social Skills	**To:** ☐ Class as a whole ☐ Group by group ☐ Individual	
Group Processing • first appears • specific processing	**Of:** ☐ Observation data ☐ Social skills ☐ Academic skills ☐ Positive feedback ☐ Goal setting (for next time)	
General Climate	☐ Group products displayed ☐ Group progress displayed ☐ Aids to group work displayed	1:44

ADVANCED LESSON PLANNING I

Structure a lesson you will soon teach cooperatively. Make sure it includes:

1. A creative twist.

2. Four ways of structuring positive interdependence ("sink or swim together").

3. Two ways of structuring individual accountability ("Everyone needs to understand/know").

4. Five specific collaborative skill behaviors you will observe for. Make an observation sheet to help you observe.

5. A "T-Chart" for the skill you are going to review with your class before the lesson begins.

6. Specific ways of having students process their use of the skill emphasized.

Advanced Lesson Planning II

1. In a group of three identify of instructional outcomes you wish to affect with cooperative learning. Work cooperatively to generate one list from the group.

2. Choose three variables, such as:

   a. Higher-level reasoning (critical thinking).

   b. Self-esteem.

   c. Civic pride in classroom and school.

3. Count off by 1, 2, and 3. Join a preparation group of 2 (2 1's, 2 2's, and 2 3's). One variable will be assigned to your pair. Your task is to plan a number of ways of structuring cooperative learning to effect directly that variable. Work cooperatively to generate one list from the pair.

   a. Make a list of roles, activities, requirements, rewards, and procedures that will influence (promote) the variable.

   b. Circle the three you like best.

4. Rejoin your triad. Teach your plan to the other two members. Learn their plans.

5. Work cooperatively in your triad to plan how to implement the plans into an upcoming cooperative lesson.

FORMAL **C**OOPERATIVE LEARNING

Sisyphus And The Old Paradigm

And I saw Sisyphus at his endless task, raising his prodigious stone, with both his hands. With hands and feet he tried to roll it up to the top of the hill, but always, just before he could roll it over onto the other side, its weight would be too much for him, and the pitiless stone would come thundering down again onto the plain. Then he would begin trying to push it uphill again, as the sweat ran off him and steam rose after him.

Homer (Oddyessy, Book 11)

Repetitive but futile efforts were personified by the ancient Greeks in the person of Sisyphus. Sisyphus was the legendary king of Corinth who was punished in Hades by having to roll a stone uphill eternally. As he neared the top of the hill, the stone always slipped from his grasp, and he had to start again. It is easy to feel that way while teaching in the old paradigm. The old paradigm of teaching assumes that the way you impart knowledge is to pour it into students' heads. What we have found is that telling students what we know feels like rolling a boulder up a hill with the students bored and uninterested. In essence we felt like Sisyphus.

Our next step was to break their knowledge up into small parts and take it up the hill a few parts at a time. This did not seem to increase the intellectual interest or involvement of students. If anything, it may have made the class even more boring. At that point we had to ask ourselves, **Who is doing the hard intellectual work in the course?** Who is doing the conceptualizing, the organizing, the elaborating, the presenting, the summarizing, the synthesizing, and the reconceptualizing? If the answer is, "The teacher," you know that everything is backwards. It is the students who are supposed to be doing the hard intellectual work in their courses. At that point we had to ask, **Who is having the most fun?** The answer may be, "No one." But if the answer is, "The Teacher," you know that everything is backwards. It is the students who are supposed to be enjoying the class.

We did not obtain the results we wanted with our teaching until we directly involved students in the learning process through cooperative learning groups. Instead of our rolling

the rock up the hill only to have it slip from our grasp when we analyzed the results of midterms and finals, we structured our courses so that all students helped to roll the boulder up the hill. When everyone, students as well as faculty, works together to roll it up the hill, then it does not slip from our grasp--it stays. As was reviewed in Chapter 2, structuring lessons cooperatively results in a number of advantages for achievement, interpersonal relationships, and psychological well-being. In addition, cooperative learning makes the classroom more realistic by making learning situations more similar to the real world of work.

Formal Cooperative Learning Groups

Howard Eaton, an English professor at Douglas College in Vancouver, British Columbia introduces his course, **Argumentative Writing for College Students**, by stating to the students, "You have bought an opportunity to learn something, not a service. This is not a prison and it is not social entertainment of the useless and unemployable. This is work. Your tuition, furthermore, only pays for 15 percent of the cost for this course. The taxpayers fund the other 85 percent. You have, therefore, a social obligation that translates into two responsibilities:

1. You are responsible for your own learning. It is up to you to get something useful and interesting from this course.

2. You are **equally** responsible for the learning of your groupmates. It is up to you to ensure that they get something useful and interesting from this course."

This introduction prepares students to do much of their work in formal cooperative learning groups. **Formal cooperative learning groups** have fixed membership, usually last from a few days to a few weeks, and have a well-defined task to accomplish. There is a wide variety of ways to structure formal cooperative learning groups. They may be structured specifically for learning of information, concept learning, problem solving, or composition. Before exploring each of these structures, the aspects of the teacher's role common to all are described.

The Teacher's Role: Being "A Guide On The Side"

Each class session teachers must make the choice of being "a sage on the stage" or "a guide on the side." In doing so they might remember that the challenge in teaching is not **covering** the material **for** the students, it's **uncovering** the material **with** the students.

One of Roger's favorite demonstration science lessons is to ask students to determine how long a candle burns in a quart jar. He assigns students to groups of two, making the pairs as heterogeneous as possible. Each pair is given one candle and one quart jar (resource interdependence). He gives the instructional task of timing how long the candle will burn and the cooperative goal of deciding on one answer that both pair members can explain. Students are to encourage each other's participation and elaborate what they are learning to previous lessons (social skills). Students light their candle, place the quart jar over it, and time how long the candle burns. The answers from the pairs are announced. Roger then gives the pairs the task of generating a number of answers to the question, "How many factors make a difference in how long the candle burns in the jar?" The answers from the pairs are written on the board. The pairs then repeat the experiment in ways that test which of the suggested factors do in fact make a difference in how long the candle burns. The next day students individually take a quiz on the factors affecting the time a candle burns in a quart jar (individual accountability) and their scores are totaled to determine a joint score that, if high enough, earns them bonus points (reward interdependence). They spend some time discussing the helpful actions of each member and what they could do to be even more effective in the future (group processing).

Science experiments are only one of the many places cooperative learning may be used. Cooperative learning is appropriate for any instructional task. Whenever the learning goals are highly important, the task is complex or conceptual, problem solving is required, divergent thinking or creativity is desired, quality of performance is expected, higher level reasoning strategies and critical thinking are needed, long-term retention is desired, or when the social development of students is one of the major instructional goals--cooperative learning should be used (Johnson & Johnson, 1989a).

Within cooperative learning situations, the teacher forms the learning groups, teaches the basic concepts and strategies, monitors the functioning of the learning groups, intervenes to teach small group skills, provides task assistance when it is needed, evaluates students' learning using a criterion-referenced system, and ensures that the cooperative groups process how effectively members worked together. Students look to their peers for assistance, feedback, reinforcement, and support.

The teacher's role in using formal cooperative learning groups includes five parts (Johnson & Johnson, 1991; Johnson, Johnson, & Holubec, 1990):

1. Specifying the objectives for the lesson.

2. Making decisions about placing students in learning groups before the lesson is taught.

3. Explaining the task and goal structure to the students.

4. Monitoring the effectiveness of the cooperative learning groups and intervening to provide task assistance (such as answering questions and teaching task skills) or to increase students' interpersonal and group skills.

5. Evaluating the students' achievement and helping students discuss how well they collaborated with each other.

Specifying the Instructional Objectives

There are two types of objectives that an teacher needs to specify before the lesson begins. The **academic objective** needs to be specified at the correct level for the students and matched to the right level of instruction according to a conceptual or task analysis. The **social skills objective** details what interpersonal and small group skills are going to be emphasized during the lesson. A common error many teachers make is to specify only academic objectives and to ignore the social skills objectives needed to train students to cooperate effectively with each other.

Preinstructional Decisions

Deciding on the Size of the Group

Once the objectives of the lesson are clear, the teacher must decide which size of learning group is optimal. Cooperative learning groups typically range in size from 2 to 4. In selecting the size of a cooperative learning group remember that the shorter the amount of time available, the smaller the group should be; the larger the group, the more resources available for the group's work but the more skills required to ensure that the group works productively. Sometimes the materials or equipment available or the specific nature of the task may dictate a group size.

Assigning Students to Groups

Teachers often ask four basic questions about assigning students to groups:

1. **Should students be placed in learning groups homogeneous or heterogeneous in member ability?** There are times when cooperative learning groups homogeneous in ability may be used to master specific skills or to achieve certain instructional objectives. Generally, however, we recommend that teachers maximize the heterogeneity of students, placing high-, medium-, and low-achieving students within the same learning group. More elaborative thinking, more frequent giving and receiving of explanations, and greater perspective taking in discussing material seems to occur in heterogeneous groups, all of which increase the depth of understanding, the quality of reasoning, and the accuracy of long-term retention.

2. **Should nontask-oriented students be placed in learning groups with task-oriented peers or be separated?** To keep nonacademically-oriented students on task it often helps to place them in a cooperative learning group with task-oriented peers.

3. **Should students select whom they want to work with or should the teacher assign students to groups?** Teacher-made groups often have the best mix since teachers can put together optimal combinations of students. Random assignment, such as having students "count off" is another possibility for getting a good mix of students in each group. Having students select their own groups is often not very successful. Student-selected groups often are homogeneous with high-achieving students working with other high-achieving students, white students working with other white students,

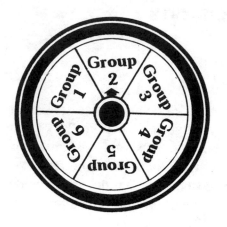

minority students working with other minority students, and males working with other males. Often there is less on-task behavior in student-selected than in teacher-selected groups. A useful modification of the "select your own group" method is to have students list whom they would like to work with and then place them in a learning group with one person they choose and one or two or more students that the teacher selects.

4. **How long should the groups stay together?** Actually, there is no formula or simple answer to this question. Some teachers keep cooperative learning groups together for an entire year or semester. Other teachers like to keep a learning group together only long enough to complete a task, unit, or chapter. Sooner or later, however, every student should work with every other classmate. Our best advice is to allow groups to remain stable long enough for them to be successful. Breaking up groups that are having trouble functioning effectively is often counterproductive as the students do not learn the skills they need to resolve problems in collaborating with each other.

Arranging the Room

How the teacher arranges the room is a symbolic message of what is appropriate behavior and it can facilitate the learning groups within the classroom. Members of a learning group should sit close enough to each other that they can share materials, maintain eye contact with all group members, and talk to each other quietly without disrupting the other learning groups. The teacher should have a clear access lane to every group. Within each learning group students need to be able to see all relevant task materials, see each other, converse with each other without raising their voices, and exchange ideas and materials in a comfortable atmosphere. The groups need to be far enough apart so that they do not interfere with each other's learning.

Planning the Instructional Materials to Promote Interdependence

Materials need to be distributed among group members so that all members participate and achieve. When a group is mature and experienced and group members have a high level of interpersonal and small group skills, the teacher may not have to arrange materials in any specific way. When a group is new or when members are not very skilled, however, teachers may wish to distribute materials in carefully planned ways to communicate that the assignment is to be a joint (not an individual) effort and that the students are in a "sink or swim together" learning situation. Three of the ways of doing so are:

1. **Materials Interdependence**: Give only one copy of the materials to the group. The students will then have to work together in order to be successful. This is especially effective the first few times the group meets. After students are accustomed to working cooperatively, teachers can give a copy of the materials to each student.

2. **Information Interdependence**: Group members may each be given different books or resource materials to be synthesized. Or the materials may be arranged like a jigsaw puzzle so that each student has part of the materials needed to complete the task. Such procedures require that every member participate in order for the group to be successful.

3. **Interdependence from Outside Enemies**: Materials may be structured into a tournament format with intergroup competition as the basis to promote a perception of interdependence among group members. Such a procedure was introduced by DeVries and Edwards (1973). In the teams-games-tournament format students are divided into heterogeneous cooperative learning teams to prepare members for a tournament in which they compete with the other teams. During the intergroup competition the students individually compete against members of about the same ability level from other teams. The team whose members do the best in the competition is pronounced the winner by the teacher.

All of these procedures may not be needed simultaneously. They are alternative methods of ensuring that students perceive that they are involved in a "sink or swim together" learning situation and behave collaboratively.

Assigning Roles to Ensure Interdependence

Positive interdependence may also be structured through the assignment of complementary and interconnected roles to group members. In addition to their responsibility to learn, each group member can be assigned a responsibility to help groupmates work together effectively. Such roles include a **summarizer** (who restates the group's major conclusions or answers), a **checker of understanding** (who ensures that all group members can explicitly explain how to arrive at an answer or conclusion), an **accuracy coach** (who corrects any

mistakes in another member's explanations or summaries), an **elaborator** (who relates current concepts and strategies to material studied previously), a **researcher-runner** (who gets needed materials for the group and communicates with the other learning groups and the teacher), a **recorder** to write down the group's decisions and edit the group's report, an **encourager of participation** who ensures that all members are contributing, and an **observer** who keeps track of how well the group is cooperating. Assigning such roles is an effective method of teaching students social skills and fostering positive interdependence.

Roles such as checking for understanding and elaborating are vital to high-quality learning but are often absent in classrooms. The role of checker, for example, focuses on periodically asking each groupmate to explain what is being learned. From their research review, Rosenshine and Stevens (1986) concluded that "checking for comprehension" was significantly associated with higher levels of student learning and achievement. Wilson (1987) conducted a three-year, teaching- improvement study as part of a college faculty development program and found that the teaching behavior faculty and students perceived faculty needing the most help on was "knows if the class is understanding the material or not." Wilson found that checking for understanding was highly correlated with overall effectiveness as an teacher. While the teacher cannot continually check the understanding of every student in the class (especially if there are 300 students in the class), the teacher can engineer such checking by having students work in cooperative groups and assigning one member the role of checker.

Structuring The Task And Positive Interdependence

Explaining the Academic Task

Teachers explain the academic task so that students are clear about the assignment and understand the objectives of the lesson. Direct teaching of concepts, principles, and strategies may take place at this point. Teachers may wish to answer any questions students have about the concepts or facts they are to learn or apply in the lesson. Teachers need to consider several aspects of explaining an academic assignment to students:

1. **Set the task so that students are clear about the assignment.** Most teachers have considerable practice with this already. Instructions that are clear and specific are crucial in warding off student frustration. One advantage of cooperative learning groups is that they can handle more ambiguous tasks (when they are appropriate) than can students working alone. In cooperative learning groups students who do not

understand what they are to do will ask their group for clarification before asking the teacher.

2. **Explain the objectives of the lesson and relate the concepts and information to be studied to students' past experience and learning to ensure maximum transfer and retention.** Explaining the intended outcomes of the lesson increases the likelihood that students will focus on the relevant concepts and information throughout the lesson.

3. **Define relevant concepts, explain procedures students should follow, and give examples to help students understand what they are to learn and do in completing the assignment.** To promote positive transfer of learning, point out the critical elements that separate this lesson from past learnings.

4. **Ask the class specific questions to check the students' understanding of the assignment.** Such questioning ensures thorough two-way communication, that the assignment has been given effectively, and that the students are ready to begin completing it.

Explaining Criteria for Success

Evaluation within cooperatively structured lessons needs to be criterion-referenced. Criteria must be established for acceptable work (rather than grading on a curve). Teachers may structure a second level of cooperation by not only keeping track of how well each group and its members are performing, but also by setting criteria for the whole class to reach. Improvement (doing better this week than one did last week) may be set as a criterion of excellence.

Structuring Positive Interdependence

Communicate to students that they have a group goal and must work cooperatively. We cannot overemphasize the importance of communicating to students that they are in a "sink or swim together" learning situation. In a cooperative learning group students are responsible for learning the assigned material, making sure that all other group members learn the assigned material, and making sure that all other class members successfully learn the assigned material, in that order. Teachers can do this in several ways.

1. **Structure positive goal interdependence by giving the group the responsibility of ensuring that all members achieve a prescribed mastery level on the assigned materials.** Teachers may wish to say, "One answer from the group, everyone has to agree, and everyone has to be able to explain how to solve the problem or complete the assignment." Teachers may establish the prescribed mastery level as (a) individual levels of performance that each group member must achieve in order for the group as a whole to be successful (the group goal is for each member to demonstrate 90 percent mastery on a curriculum unit) or (b) improvement scores (the group goal is to ensure that all members do better this week than they did last week).

2. **Structure positive reward interdependence by providing group rewards.** Bonus points may be added to all members' academic scores when everyone in the group achieves up to criterion. Or bonus points may be given to each member when the total of all group members' scores is above a preset criterion of excellence.

Positive interdependence creates peer encouragement and support for learning. Such positive peer pressure influences underachieving students to become academically involved. Members of cooperative learning groups should give two interrelated messages, "Do your work--we're counting on you!" and "How can I help you to do better?"

Structuring Individual Accountability

One of the purposes of a cooperative group is to make each member a stronger individual in his or her own right. This is usually accomplished by maximizing the learning of each member. A group is not truly cooperative if members are "slackers" who let others do all the work. To ensure that all members learn, and that groups know which members to provide with encouragement and help, teachers need to assess frequently the level of performance of each group member. Observing the participation patterns of each group member, giving practice tests, randomly selecting members to explain answers, having members edit each other's work, having students teach what they know to someone else, and having students use what they have learned on a different problem are ways to structure individual accountability.

Structuring Intergroup Cooperation

The positive outcomes found within a cooperative learning group can be extended throughout a whole class by structuring intergroup cooperation. Bonus points may be given if all members of a class reach a preset criteria of excellence. When a group finishes its work, the teacher should encourage the members to find other groups who are finished and compare and explain answers and strategies.

Specifying Desired Behaviors

The word **cooperation** has many different connotations and uses. Teachers will need to define cooperation operationally by specifying the behaviors that are appropriate and desirable within the learning groups. There are beginning behaviors, such as "stay with your group and do not wander around the room," "use quiet voices," "take turns," and "use each other's names." When groups begin to function effectively, expected behaviors may include:

1. Having each member explain how to get the answer.

2. Asking each member to relate what is being learned to previous learnings.

3. Checking to make sure everyone in the group understands the material and agrees with the answers.

4. Encouraging everyone to participate.

5. Listening accurately to what other group members are saying.

6. Not changing your mind unless you are logically persuaded (majority rule does not promote learning).

7. Criticizing ideas, not people.

Teachers should not make the list of expected behaviors too long. One or two behaviors to emphasize for a few lessons is enough. Students need to know what behavior is appropriate and desirable within a cooperative learning group, but they should not be subjected to information overload.

Monitoring And Intervening

Monitoring Students' Behavior

The teacher's job begins in earnest when the cooperative learning groups start working. Resist that urge to go get a cup of coffee or grade some papers. Much of your time in cooperative learning situations should be spent observing group members in order to (a) obtain a "window" into students' minds to see what they do and do not understand and (b) see what problems they are having in working together cooperatively. Through working cooperatively students will make hidden thinking processes overt and subject to observation and commentary. You will be able to observe how students are constructing their understanding of the assigned material. A variety of observation instruments and procedures that can be used for these purposes can be found in Johnson and F. Johnson (1991) and in Johnson, Johnson, and Holubec (1991a, 1991b).

Providing Task Assistance

In monitoring the groups as they work, teachers will wish to clarify instructions, review important procedures and strategies for completing the assignment, answer questions, and teach task skills as necessary. In discussing the concepts and information to be learned, teachers will wish to use the language or terms relevant to the learning. Instead of saying, "Yes, that is right," teachers will wish to say something more specific to the assignment, such as, "Yes, that is one way to find the main idea of a paragraph." The use of the more specific statement reinforces the desired learning and promotes positive transfer by helping the students associate a term with their learning. One way to intervene is to interview a cooperative learning group by asking them (a) What are you doing?, (b) Why are you doing it?, and (c) How will it help you?

Intervening to Teach Social Skills

While monitoring the learning groups teachers will also find students who do not have the necessary social skills and groups where problems in cooperating have arisen. **In these cases the teacher will wish to intervene to suggest more effective procedures for working together and more effective behaviors for students to engage in.** Teachers may also wish to intervene and reinforce particularly effective and skillful behaviors that they notice. The social skills required for productive group work, along with activities that may be used in teaching them, are covered in Johnson and F. Johnson (1991) and Johnson (1990, 1991).

Teachers should not intervene any more than is absolutely necessary in the groups. Most of us as teachers are geared to jumping in and solving problems for students to get them back on track. With a little patience we would find that cooperative groups can often work their way through their own problems (task and maintenance) and acquire not only a solution, but also a method of solving similar problems in the future. Choosing when to intervene and when not to is part of the art of teaching. Even when intervening, teachers can turn the problem back to the group to solve. Many teachers intervene in a group by having members set aside their task, pointing out the problem, and asking the group to create three possible solutions and decide which solution they are going to try first.

Evaluating Learning And Processing Interaction

Providing Closure to the Lesson

At the end of the lesson students should be able to summarize what they have learned and to understand where they will use it in future lessons. Teachers may wish to summarize the major points in the lesson, ask students to recall ideas or give samples, and answer any final questions students have.

Evaluating the Quality and Quantity of Students' Learning

Tests should be given and papers and presentations should be graded. The learning of group members must be evaluated by a criterion-referenced system for cooperative learning to be successful.

Processing How Well the Group Functioned

An old observational rule is, **if you observe, you must process your observations with the group.** Even if class time is limited, some time should be spent in **small group processing** as members discuss how effectively they worked together and what could be improved. Teachers may also wish to spend some time in **whole-class processing** where they give the class feedback and have students share incidents that occurred in their groups.

Discussing group functioning is essential. A common teaching error is to provide too brief a time for students to process the quality of their cooperation. Students do not learn from experiences that they do not reflect on. If the learning groups are to function better tomorrow than they did today, members must receive feedback, reflect on how their actions may be more effective, and plan how to be even more skillful during the next group session.

Cooperative Learning Structures

Any assignment in any subject area may be structured cooperatively. The teacher decides on the objectives of the lesson, makes a number of preinstructional decisions about the size of the group and the materials required to conduct the lesson, explains to students the task and the cooperative goal structure, monitors the groups as they work, intervenes when it is necessary, and then evaluates student learning and ensures groups process how effectively they are functioning.

One of the things we have been told many times by teachers who have mastered the use of cooperative learning is, "Don't say it is easy!" We know it's not. It can take years to become an expert. There is a lot of pressure to teach like everyone else, to have students learn alone, and not let students look at each other's papers. Students will not be accustomed to working together and are likely to have a competitive orientation. You may wish to start small by taking one topic or one class and use cooperative learning until you feel comfortable, and then expand into other topics or classes. In order to implement cooperative learning successfully, you will need to teach students the interpersonal and small group skills required to collaborate, structure and orchestrate intellectual inquiry within learning groups, and form collaborative relations with others. **Implementing cooperative learning in your classroom is not easy, but it is worth the effort.** The following ways in which formal cooperative learning groups may be structured within classrooms may prove helpful.

Cooperative Reading Pairs

Donald Dansereau (1987) defines **cooperative reading** as an activity which "typically involves two or more students working together to improve their understanding and retention of text material." Dansereau (1985) calls his strategy for cooperative reading MURDER and states it is effective for students learning procedural, technical, and narrative text while working in cooperative dyads. The roles of recaller and listener/facilitator are given to each student interacting as equal partners. The steps in MURDER are for the teacher to set the **mood** to study (creating a supportive environment) and for the students to read for **understanding** (marking important and difficult ideas); **recall** the material without referring to the text; correct recall and amplify and store it so as to **digest** the assigned material; **expand** knowledge by self-inquiry; and finally, **review** mistakes (learning from tests).

Conclusions

At this point you know what cooperative learning is and how it is different from competitive and individualistic learning. You know that there are three types of cooperative learning groups--formal cooperative learning groups, informal cooperative learning groups, and cooperative base groups. You know that **the essence of cooperative learning is positive interdependence** where students recognize that "we are in this together, sink or swim." Other essential components include individual accountability (where every student is accountable for both learning the assigned material and helping other group members learn), face-to-face interaction among students within which students promote each other's success, students appropriately using interpersonal and group skills, and students processing how effectively their learning group has functioned. These five essential components of cooperation form the conceptual basis for constructing cooperative procedures. You know that the research supports the propositions that cooperation results in greater effort to achieve, more positive interpersonal relationships, and greater psychological health and self-esteem than do competitive or individualistic efforts. You know the teacher's role in implementing formal cooperative learning. What is covered in the next chapter is the teacher's role in implementing informal cooperative learning groups.

EXERCISE

MATERIALS

INK

The Teacher's Role in Cooperation

Make Decisions

Specify Academic and Collaborative Objectives. What academic and/or collaborative skills do you want students to learn or practice in their groups? Start with something easy.

Decide on Group Size. Students often lack collaborative skills, so start with groups of two or three students; later advance cautiously to fours.

Assign Students to Groups. Heterogeneous groups are the most powerful, so mix abilities, sexes, cultural backgrounds, and task orientations. Assign students to groups randomly or select groups yourself.

Arrange the Room. The closer the students are to each other, the better they can communicate. Group members should be "knee to knee and eye to eye."

Plan Materials. Materials can send a "sink or swim together" message to students if you give only one paper to the group or give each member part of the material to learn and then teach the group.

Assign Roles. Students are more likely to work together if each one has a job which contributes to the task. You can assign work roles such as Reader, Recorder, Calculator, Checker,Reporter, and Materials Handler or skill roles such as Encourager of Participation, Praiser, and Checker for Understanding.

Set the Lesson

Explain the Academic Task. Prepare students by teaching them any material they need to know, then make certain they clearly understand what they are to do in the groups. This might include explaining lesson objectives, defining concepts, explaining procedures, giving examples, and asking questions.

*Structure Positive Interdependence. Students must feel that they need each other to complete the group's task, that they "sink or swim together." Some ways to create this are by establishing mutual goals (students must learn the material and make certain group members learn the material), joint rewards (if all group members achieve above a certain percentage on the test, each will receive bonus points), shared materials and information, and assigned roles.

*Structure Individual Accountability. Each student must feel responsible for learning the material and helping the group. Some ways to ensure this feeling include frequent oral quizzing of group members picked at random, giving individual tests, having everyone in the group write (pick one paper at random to grade), or having students do work first to bring to the group.

Structure Intergroup Cooperation. Having groups check with and help other groups and giving rewards or praise when all class members do well can extend the benefits of cooperation to the whole class.

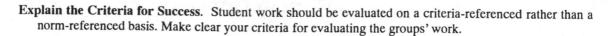

Explain the Criteria for Success. Student work should be evaluated on a criteria-referenced rather than a norm-referenced basis. Make clear your criteria for evaluating the groups' work.

Specify Expected Behaviors. The more specific you are about the behaviors you want to see in the groups, the more likely students will do them. Make it clear that you expect to see everyone contributing, helping, listening with care to others, encouraging others to participate, and asking for help or clarification. Younger students may need to be told to stay with their group, take turns, share, ask group members questions, and use quiet voices.

*Teach Collaborative Skills. After students are used to working in groups, pick one collaborative skill they need to learn, point out the need for it, define it carefully, have students give you phrases they can say when using the skill, post the phrases (praise, bonus points, stars), and observe for and encourage the use of the skill until students are doing it automatically. Then teach a second skill. Consider praising, summarizing, encouraging, checking for understanding, asking for help, or generating further answers.

Monitor and Intervene

*Arrange Face-to-Face Interaction. The beneficial educational outcomes of cooperative learning groups are due to the interaction patterns and verbal exchanges that take place among students. Make certain there is oral summarizing, giving and receiving explanations, and elaborating going on.

Monitor Students' Behavior. This is the fun part! While students are working, you circulate to see whether they understand the assignment and the material, give immediate feedback and reinforcement, and praise good use of group skills.

Provide Task Assistance. If students are having trouble with the task, you can clarify, reteach, or elaborate on what they need to know.

Intervene to Teach Collaborative Skills. If students are having trouble with group interactions, you can suggest more effective procedures for working together or more effective behaviors for them to engage in. You can ask students to figure out how to work more effectively together. If students are learning or practicing a skill, record on an observation sheet how often you hear that skill, then share your observations with the groups.

Evaluate and Process

Evaluate Student Learning. Assess how well students completed the task and give them feedback.

*Process Group Functioning. In order to improve, students need time and procedures for analyzing how well their group is functioning and how well they are using collaborative skills. Processing can be done by individuals, small groups, or the whole class. To start, have groups routinely list three things they did well in working together today and one thing they will do better tomorrow. Then summarize as a whole class.

Provide Closure. To reinforce student learning you may wish to have groups share answers or paper, summarize major points in the lesson, or review important facts.

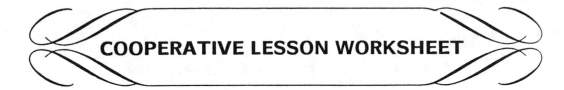

COOPERATIVE LESSON WORKSHEET

Grade Level: _____   Subject Area: _____

Step 1.   Select a lesson: _____

_____

Step 2.   Make Decisions.

    a. Group size: _____

    b. Assignment to groups: _____

_____

    c. Room arrangement: _____

_____

    d. Materials needed for each group:

_____

_____

    e. Assigning roles: _____

_____

_____

Step 3.   Set the Lesson. State, in language your students understand:

    a. Task: _____

_____

    b. Positive interdependence: _____

_____

_____

    c. Individual accountability: _____

_____

    d. Criteria for success: _____

_____

    e. Specific behaviors expected: _____

_____

Step 4.   Monitor and Process

   a. Evidence of expected behaviors (appropriate actions):

   _____

   _____

   b. Observation form: _____

   Observer(s): _____

   c. Plans for processing (feedback): _____

   _____

Step 5.   Evaluate Outcomes

   a. Task achievement: _____

   _____

   b. Group functioning: _____

   _____

   c. Notes on individuals: _____

   _____

   d. Suggestions for next time: _____

   _____

   _____

   _____

   _____

   _____

Problem Solving Lesson

Math

Geometry

TASK: Solve the problem(s) correctly.

COOPERATIVE: One set of answers from the group, everyone has to agree, everyone has to be able to explain the strategies used to solve each problem.

EXPECTED CRITERIA FOR SUCCESS: Everyone must be able to explain the strategies used to solve each problem.

INDIVIDUAL ACCOUNTABILITY: One member from your group will be randomly chosen to explain (a) the answer and (b) how to solve each problem. Alternatively, use the simultaneous responding procedure of having each group member explain the group's answers to a member of another group.

EXPECTED BEHAVIORS: Active participating, checking, encouraging, and elaborating by all members.

INTERGROUP COOPERATION: Whenever it is helpful, check procedures, answers, and strategies with another group.

Jigsaw Procedure

When you have information you need to communicate to students, an alternative to lecturing is a procedure for structuring cooperative learning groups called **jigsaw** (Aronson, 1978).

Task: Think of a reading assignment you will give in the near future. Divide the assignment in three parts. Plan how you will use the jigsaw procedure. Script out exactly what you will say to your class in using each part of the jigsaw procedure.

Procedure: One way to structure positive interdependence among group members is to use the jigsaw method of creating resource interdependence. The steps for structuring a "jigsaw" lesson are:

1. **Cooperative Groups**: Distribute a set of materials to each group. The set needs to be divisible into the number of members of the group (2, 3, or 4 parts). Give each member one part of the set of materials.

2. **Preparation Pairs**: Assign students the cooperative task of meeting with someone else in the class who is a member of another learning group and who has the same section of the material and complete two tasks:

   a. Learning and becoming an expert on their material.

   b. Planning how to teach the material to the other members of their groups.

3. **Practice Pairs**: Assign students the cooperative task of meeting with someone else in the class who is a member of another learning group and who has learned the same material and share ideas as to how the material may best be taught. These "practice pairs" review what each plans to teach their group and how. The best ideas of both are incorporated into each's presentation.

4. **Cooperative Groups**: Assign students the cooperative tasks of:

   a. Teaching their area of expertise to the other group members.

   b. Learning the material being taught by the other members.

5. **Evaluation**: Assess students' degree of mastery of all the material. Reward the groups whose members all reach the preset criterion of excellence.

PEER EDITING: Cooperative Learning In Composition

Whenever you assign a paper or composition to be written by students, cooperative learning groups should be used. Whenever we give an assignment that requires students to write a paper, for example, we ask them to hand in a paper revised on the basis of two reviews by members of their cooperative learning group. In other words, we use a process writing procedure requiring a cooperative group.

Task: Write a composition.

Cooperative: All group members must verify that each member's composition is perfect according to the criteria set by the teacher. One of their scores for the composition will be the total number of errors made by the pair (the number of errors in their composition plus the number of errors in their partner's composition). An individual score on the quality of the composition may also be given.

Procedure:

1. The teacher assigns students to pairs with at least one good reader in each pair. The task of writing individual compositions is given.

2. Student A describes to Student B what he or she is planning to write. Student B listens carefully, probes with a set of questions, and outlines Student A's composition. The written outline is given to Student A.

3. This procedure is reversed with Student B describing what he or she is going to write and Student A listening and completing an outline of Student B's composition, which is then given to Student B.

4. The students research individualistically the material they need to write their compositions, keeping an eye out for material useful to their partner.

5. The two students work together to write the first paragraph of each composition to ensure that they both have a clear start on their compositions.

6. The students write their compositions individualistically.

7. When completed, the students proofread each other's compositions, making corrections in capitalization, punctuation, spelling, language usage, topic sentence usage, and other aspects of writing specified by the teacher. Suggestions for revision are also encouraged.

8. The students revise their compositions, making all of the suggested revisions.

9. The two students then reread each other's compositions and sign their names (indicating that they guarantee that no errors exist in the composition).

While the students work, the teacher monitors the pairs, intervening where appropriate to help students master the needed writing and cooperative skills. When the composition is completed, the students discuss how effectively they worked together (listing the specific actions they engaged in to help each other), plan what behaviors they are going to emphasize in the next writing pair, and thank each other for the help and assistance received.

Criteria For Success: A well-written composition by each student. Depending on the instructional objectives, the compositions may be evaluated for grammar, punctuation, organization, content, or other criteria set by the teacher.

Individual Accountability: Each student writes his or her own composition.

Expected Behaviors: Explaining and listening.

Intergroup Cooperation: Whenever it is helpful to do so, check procedures with another group.

DRILL-REVIEW PAIRS

This procedure was developed for math classes. Any class in which drill-review is required, however, may use this procedure.

Task: Correctly solve the assigned problems.

Cooperative: The mutual goal is to ensure that both pair members understand the strategies and procedures required to solve the problems correctly. Two roles are assigned: **explainer** (explains step-by-step how to solve the problem) and **accuracy checker** (verifies that the explanation is accurate, encourages, and provides coaching if needed). The two roles are rotated after each problem.

Procedure: Assign students to pairs. Assign each pair to a foursome. Implement the following procedure:

1. Person A reads the problem and explains step-by-step the procedures and strategies required to solve it. Person B checks the accuracy of the solution and provides encouragement and coaching if it is needed.

2. Person B solves the second problem, describing step-by-step the procedures and strategies required to solve it. Person A checks the accuracy of the solution and provides encouragement and coaching if it is needed.

3. When two problems are completed, the pair checks their answers with another pair. If they do not agree, they resolve the problem until there is consensus about the answer. If they do agree, they thank each other and continue work in their pairs.

4. The procedure continues until all problems are completed.

Individual Accountability: One member will be picked randomly to explain how to solve a randomly selected problem.

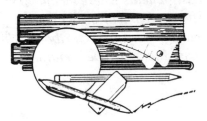

Checking Homework

One repetitive activity within math classes is checking students' homework. Such responsibilities may be turned over to cooperative learning groups through the use of the following procedure. Once planned, the procedure should be used daily until the students automatically perform the procedure in a quick and orderly way.

Subject Area: Any

Grade Level: Any

Instructional Objectives: The **academic** objective is to ensure that all class members have completed the homework and understand how to do it. The **social skills** objective is to increase students' ability to check the accuracy of the groupmate's explanation of how to solve the math problems.

Lesson Summary: Go through the answers one-by-one and ensure that everyone agrees. If there is disagreement, discuss until consensus is reached and all members understand how to answer the question correctly. The group should concentrate on parts of the assignments where members were confused and did not understand. Ensure that all members understand how to do each problem assigned. For any problem on which the group members do not agree on the answer, the page number and paragraph of the textbook where the procedure for solving the problem is explained must be identified.

Procedure: Quickly discuss each problem. One member (the explainer) explains how to solve the problem and the other members (accuracy checkers) check the explanation for accuracy. The roles are rotated so that each member does an equal amount of explaining.

If there is disagreement as to how part of the assignment is completed correctly, discuss until consensus is reached. The group should concentrate on parts of the assignments where members were confused and did not understand. For any part of the assignment on which the group members do not agree, the page number and paragraph of the textbook where the procedure for completing the assignment is explained must be identified.

When the homework has been verified, the group places members' homework in the group folder and places it on the teacher's desk.

Materials: A group folder, current homework from each student, and textbook (one per student).

Time Required: 10 minutes when students learn and master the procedure.

Preinstructional Decisions

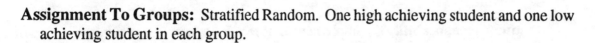

Group Size: Four

Assignment To Groups: Stratified Random. One high achieving student and one low achieving student in each group.

Roles:

Runner: Goes to the teacher's desk, picks up the group's folder, and hands out any materials in the folder to the appropriate members. The runner also records how much of the assignment each member completed.

Explainer: Explains step-by-step how to solve the problem. The role of explainer is rotated around the group. The other three members are accuracy checkers while one explains.

Accuracy checker: Verifies that the explanation is accurate.

Encourager of participation: Recognizes the hard work and the quality of the explanations of each group member.

Explaining Task and Cooperation

Students enter the classroom and meet in their cooperative learning groups. The groups should be heterogeneous in terms of math and reading ability. One member (the **runner**) goes to the teacher's desk, picks up the group's folder, and hands out any materials in the folder to the appropriate members. Once the homework is all checked, the runner puts the members' homework in the group folder and replaces it on the teacher's desk.

The **tasks** are to (a) check to see that each member has completed the homework and (b) go through the answers one-by-one and ensure that everyone agrees (if there is disagreement, discuss until consensus is reached and all members understand how to answer the question correctly). The group should concentrate on parts of the assignments where members were confused and did not understand. Ensure that all members understand how to do each problem assigned. For any problem on which the group members do not agree on the answer, the page number and paragraph of the textbook where the procedure for solving the problem is explained must be identified.

The **cooperative goal** is for all members to have completed the homework correctly and understand how to do the assignment. The runner records how much of the assignment each member completed. Then each problem is quickly discussed. One member explains how to solve the problem and the other members check the explanation for accuracy. The roles are rotated so that each member does an equal amount of explaining.

Individual accountability is implemented through regular examinations and daily randomly selecting group members to explain how to solve randomly selected problems from the homework.

The **criteria for success** are for all group members to complete correctly the homework and understand how to solve each assigned problem.
The **expected behaviors** are the participation of all members, encouragement of each other's participation, and checking to ensure that all members understand the homework.

Intergroup cooperation is encouraged. When your group finishes, find another group to help until all class members understand how to do the homework.

Monitoring and Intervening

Monitoring: While the students are working, watch to see how easily they are solving the problems and how well they are working together. Occasionally, ask a student to explain one of the answers already agreed on and recorded to emphasize the fact that all group members need to be able to explain the answers. Often, turn students' questions back to the group to solve, or ask students to check with a neighboring group.

Intervening: When a group is obviously struggling, watch for a moment, then intervene. Point out the problem and ask the group what can be done about it. This establishes the teacher's role as one of consultant rather than answer giver.

Evaluating and Processing

Evaluating: Randomly pick homework papers from each group and evaluate to ensure that the work has been done correctly.

Processing: Have students turn to their partner and list three things they did to help each other learn and one thing they could do to be even better tomorrow.

Closure: Inform students that the time is up. The runner should return the group's folder to the teacher's desk. The teacher then begins today's lesson.

Preparing for a Test

Whenever a test is given, cooperative learning groups can serve as bookends by preparing members to take the test and providing a setting in which students review the test. Two of the purposes of testing are to evaluate how much each student knows and assess what he or she needs to review. Using the following procedure will result in achieving both purposes **and** students learning the material they did not understand before the test. It also prevents post-test arguments with students over which answer is correct.

Instructors give students (a) study questions on which the examination will be based and (b) class time to prepare for the examination. Students meet in a cooperative group of four and work to understand how to answer correctly each study question.

Subject Area: Any

Grade Level: Any

Instructional Objectives: Prepare students to take a test.

Time Required: 10 - 20 minutes

Lesson Summary: Students meet in their cooperative groups. Teacher gives each group (a) study questions on which the examination will be based and (b) class time to prepare for the examination. Students discuss each study question and come to consensus about its answer. They ensure that all group members understand how to answer the question correctly. For any question for which there is disagreement among group members about how to derive the answer, the page number and paragraph on which the procedures required to attain the answer must be found. After the review time is over, the teacher gives the exam. Each student takes it individually.

Pre-Instructional Decisions

Group Size: Three

Assignment to Groups: Random to ensure heterogeneity in terms of math and reading ability.

Roles: Explainer and accuracy checker. While one group member explains how to answer a question, the other two listen carefully and check for accuracy. The roles are rotated after each question.

Materials: Copy of study questions for each group.

Explaining Task And Cooperation

Instructional Task: Understand how to answer correctly each study question.

Positive Interdependence: One answer from the group, everyone must agree, and everyone must be able to explain how to answer each question correctly. All group members must know and understand the material on which they will be tested.

If all group members score over 90 percent correct on the test, each will receive five bonus points.

Criteria For Success: Each group member understands the material on which they are to be tested.

Expected Behaviors: Roles of explainer and accuracy checker. The roles are rotated after each question.

Monitoring And Processing

Monitoring: While the students are working, watch to see how easily they are solving the problems and how well they are working together. Occasionally, ask a student to explain one of the answers already agreed on and recorded to emphasize the fact that all group members need to be able to explain the answers. Often, turn students' questions back to the group to solve, or ask students to check with a neighboring group.

Intervening: When a group is obviously struggling, watch for a moment, then intervene. Point out the problem and ask the group what can be done about it. This establishes the teacher's role as one of consultant rather than answer giver.

Processing: At the end of the lesson, have groups list three things they did to help each other learn and one thing they could do to be even better tomorrow.

Individual Test Followed By Group Test

Subject Area: Any

Grade Level: Any

Materials: Two answer sheets and one copy of the test for each student.

Instructional Objectives: To evaluate how much each student knows and to assess what students need to review.

Time Required: 50 minutes

Lesson Summary: Cooperative groups work together to complete their assignments all week. On Friday, an examination is given. The test is given first individually for a grade. Students make two copies of their answers. One answer sheet they hand in to the teacher (who then scores the answers). One answer sheet they keep. After all members have finished the test, the group meets to take the test again. The test is then regiven to a cooperative group for understanding.

Preinstructional Decisions

Group Size: Four

Assignment To Groups: Random to ensure heterogeneity in terms of reading and math ability.

Explaining Task And Goal Structures

Individual Test: An examination is given individually for a grade. The **individual goal** is to answer each question correctly. Students make two copies of their answers. One answer sheet they hand in to the teacher (who then scores the answers). One answer sheet they keep. After all members have finished the test, it is given again in cooperative groups.

Group Test: The test is regiven in cooperative groups to ensure that all students understand how to answer each question correctly.

The next class period, the teacher randomly assigns students to groups of four. Each group is divided into two pairs. Each pair takes the test, conferring on the answer to each question. The **task** *is to correctly answer each question. The* **cooperative goal** *is to have one answer for each question that both agree upon and both can explain. Group members cannot proceed until they agree on the answer.*

The groups of four meet. Their **task** *is to answer each question correctly. Their* **cooperative goal** *is for all group members to understand the material covered by the test. Group members confer on each question. On any question to which the two pairs have different answers, they find the page number and paragraph in the textbook where the procedures required to solve the problem are explained. Each group is responsible for ensuring that all members understand the material they missed on the test. If necessary, group members assign review homework to each other.*

Individual Accountability: Teacher observes the groups to ensure that they are following the procedure.

Criteria for Success: All students understand the material covered by the test. If all members of a group score 90 percent or better on the individual test, each receives 5 bonus points. These bonus points are added to their individual scores to determine their individual grade for the test.

Expected Behaviors: The expected behaviors include active participation by all members, helping, and explaining. A variety of roles may be used, including problem restater, strategy suggester, approximator, checker, and accuracy coach.

Intergroup Cooperation: If there is any question that the group cannot answer and cannot find the page and paragraph in the text where the answer is explained, the group should ask other groups for help.

Monitoring And Processing

Monitoring: While the students are working, watch to see how easily they are solving the problems and how well they are working together. Occasionally, ask a student to explain one of the answers already agreed on and recorded to emphasize the fact that all group members need to be able to explain the answers. Often, turn students' questions back to the group to solve, or ask students to check with a neighboring group.

Intervening: When a group is obviously struggling, watch for a moment, then intervene. Point out the problem and ask the group what can be done about it. This establishes the teacher's role as one of consultant rather than answer giver.

Processing: At the end of the lesson, have groups list three things they did to help each other learn and one thing they could do to be even better tomorrow.

Classroom Presentations

When students are required to give class presentations assign them to cooperative groups and require each group to prepare and conduct a group presentation.

Task: Prepare and present an informative and interesting presentation.

Cooperation: The **cooperative goal** is for all members to learn the material being presented and gain experience in making presentations. The **reward interdependence** may be either a group grade for the presentation **or** each student may be graded on their part of the presentation and bonus points given if all members participate in an integrated (rather than sequential) way.

Procedure:

1. Assign students to groups of four, give each group a topic, require them to prepare one presentation that all will participate in. The presentation should be given within a certain time frame and should be supported with visuals and/or active participation by students.

2. Give students time to prepare and to rehearse. All group members should be able to give the presentation.

3. Divide the class into four groups and place them in separate corners of the classroom. Have each group member make the presentation to one-fourth of the class simultaneously. In this way, all group members demonstrate their mastery of the topic and are individually accountable for learning the assigned material.

4. Systematically observe all presentations. Evaluate the presentations on the basis of whether or not it was (a) scholarly and informative, (b) interesting, concise, easy to follow, (c) involving (audience active, not passive), and (d) intriguing (audience interested in finding out more on their own). In addition, add points if all members contributed, and if their contributions were integrated not sequential.

5. Have presentation groups process how well they worked together as a group.

Individual Accountability: All members must make a presentation to a subgroup of the class.

Criteria for Success: All students make a presentation that meets the criteria listed above.

Expected Behaviors: The expected behaviors include presenting and explaining.

Intergroup Cooperation: If there are any questions about the assignment or procedures ask other groups for help.

Laboratory Groups

One of the most common ways to involve students actively in the learning situation is the use of laboratory or experimental groups where students use the scientific method to conduct an inquiry. Teachers direct and supervise students working in pairs, triads, or fours to investigate, prove, and formulate hypotheses. In the **old paradigm**, labs were demonstrations of a theory or concept that followed lectures. The rule was, "Teach them the basic science, teach them the applied science, then give a practicum." Students were often told what to do and what their findings should be.

In the **new paradigm**, labs are introductory activities that build direct experiences in which to understand the procedures, concepts, and theories being studied. The rule is, "Give them a problem, coach their problem solving, have them present their solutions, and give the relevant theory."

Task: To conduct an inquiry using the scientific method.

Cooperation: The **cooperative goal** is for each group to complete the project. Members sign the project to indicate that they have contributed their share of the work, agree with its content, and can present/explain it. When a variety of materials are used (such as microscopes, slides, samples), each group member may be given the responsibility for one of the materials. If appropriate, assign each student a specific role.

Procedure:

1. Students are assigned an initial problem to solve and are placed in cooperative learning groups to do so. The required materials such as microscopes are given to each group.

2. The group solves the problem and prepares a preliminary written report.

3. The teacher presents the relevant algorithm, procedure, concept, or theory required to solve the problem.

4. Students are given a more complex problem that requires them to apply the algorithm, procedure, theory, or concept they have just learned. The teacher systematically observes the groups and provides coaching where it is needed.

5. Students are given an even more complex problem in which they have to go beyond the algorithm, procedure, concept, or theory in order to solve it. The teacher systematically observes the groups and provides coaching where it is needed.

6. Each group writes a report on their solution and hands the report in to the teacher.

7. The teacher pairs each group member with a member of another group. Each presents their group's solution to the other.

8. The groups process how well they worked together.

Individual Accountability:

1. Have each group member present his or her group's report to a member of another group.

2. Observe the groups to verify that all members are actively participating.

3. Give an individual test on the content covered by the problems.

Criteria for Success: Defensible solution to each problem that all members can explain.

Expected Behaviors: All students participate actively in solving the problems and explain their group's solutions to a member of another group.

Intergroup Cooperation: If there are any questions about the assignment or procedures ask other groups for help.

INFORMAL COOPERATIVE LEARNING:

THE COOPERATIVE LECTURE

The Lure Of Lecturing

Our survey of teaching methods suggests that...if we want students to become more effective in meaningful learning and thinking, they need to spend more time in active, meaningful learning and thinking--not just sitting and passively receiving information.

McKeachie (1986)

No logic or wisdom or will-power could prevail to stop the sailors. Buffeted by the hardships of life at sea, the voices came out of the mist to the ancient Greek sailors like a mystical, ethereal love song with tempting and seductive promises of ecstasy and delight. The voices and the song were irresistible. The mariners helplessly turned their ships to follow the Sirens' call with scarcely a second thought. Lured to their destruction, the sailors crashed their ships on the waiting rocks and drowned in the tossing waves, struggling with their last breath to reach the source of that beckoning song.

Centuries later, the Sirens still call. Teachers seem drawn to lecturing, crashing their teaching on the rocks due to the seductive and tempting attractions of explicating knowledge to an adoring audience and teaching as they were taught. The old paradigm has an irresistible call to many faculty. The new paradigm may seem idealistic but undoable. Cooperative learning provides an alternative to the "empty vessel" model of the teaching and learning process and encourages the development of student talent by proving a very carefully structured approach to getting students actively involved in constructing their own knowledge. Getting students cognitively, physically, emotionally, and psychologically involved in learning is an important step in turning around the passive and impersonal character of many classrooms.

What Is Lecturing?

Introduction

The obstacles to learning from a lecture were (again) made painfully aware to us recently. This was during a workshop for students and faculty in Norway. While conducting a workshop on cooperative learning for faculty and students at the Norwegian Institute of Technology, Karl was convinced that a short lecture (given in the informal cooperative learning format) on the latest research on learning would be very useful and effective. He asked a focus question at the start, lectured for about 12 minutes, and asked the participants to prepare a summary of the main points and to formulate at least one question. When he finished the short lecture, and asked for a summary, people didn't know what to write. One student jokingly said, "Karl, what did you say between 'Here's the research' and 'Your task is to create a summary?'" He got a big laugh, but when we took a break, several of the faculty came to him and said, "I didn't know what you were talking about. The concepts were somewhat new to me, you were enthusiastic and spoke slowly and clearly, but I really didn't understand what you were talking about."

After the break, Karl apologized to the workshop participants for wasting their time. It was painful since he thought he had given an excellent lecture. A couple of faculty came to his defense. They said, "Well, you know, it was a pretty good lecture. It was just kind of new to us." But then a student in the back said, "I understood a little at the beginning, but a lot of lectures are like this for me." And a student in the front said (with emphasis), "This is what it's like for me every day."

The look on the faces of those faculty! If only a photograph could have been taken. For the first time in a long time, we think they understood what it's like to be a student out there, trying to make sense out of these lectures, and not understanding, and being frustrated with not understanding. Perhaps Karl should have followed Wilbert McKeachie's advice on lecturing: "I lecture only when I'm convinced it will do more good than harm."

In this chapter we shall discuss the lure of lecturing and define what it is. The problems and enemies of lecturing will be detailed. The use of informal cooperative learning groups to make students cognitively active during lectures will then be described.

Definition

A **lecture** is an extended presentation in which the teacher presents factual information in an organized and logically sequenced way. It typically results in long periods of uninterrupted teacher-centered, expository discourse that relegates students to the role of passive "spectators" in the classroom. Normally, lecturing includes the use of reference notes, an occasional use of visuals to enhance the information being presented, and responding to students' questions as the lecture progresses or at its end. Occasionally, students are provided with handouts to help them follow the lecture. The lecturer presents the material to be learned in more or less final form, gives answers, presents principles, and elaborates the entire content of what is to be learned.

Lecturing is currently the most common teacher behavior in schools and colleges. Lecturing is particularly popular in secondary schools and in the teaching of large introductory sections of college courses in a wide variety of disciplines (e.g., psychology, chemistry, mathematics). Even in training programs within business and industry, lecturing dominates. Some of the reasons why lecturing is so popular are that it can be adapted to different audiences and time frames and it keeps the teacher at the center of all communication and attention in the classroom.

The rationale for and the pedagogy of lecturing are based on (a) theories of the structure and organization of knowledge, (b) the psychology of meaningful verbal learning, and (c) ideas from cognitive psychology associated with the representation and acquisition of knowledge. Jerome Bruner (1960) emphasized that knowledge structures exist and become a means for organizing information about topics, dividing information into various categories, and showing relationships among various categories of information. David Ausubel (1963) emphasized that meaning emerges from new information only if it is tied into existing cognitive structures and, therefore, teachers should organize information for students, present it in clear and precise ways, and anchor it into cognitive structures formed from prior learning. Ellen Gagne (1985) emphasized that (a) declarative knowledge is represented in interrelated propositions or unifying ideas, (b) existing cognitive structures must be cued so that students bring them from long-term memory into working memory, and (c) students must process new knowledge by coding it and then storing it in their long-term memory.

Appropriate Use

The correct question is not, "Is lecturing better or worse than other alternative teaching methods?" but "For what purposes is the lecture method appropriate?" There has been considerable research on lecturing. From the research directly evaluating lecturing (see reviews by Bligh, 1972; Costin, 1972; Eble, 1983; McKeachie, 1967; Verner & Dickinson, 1967) it may be concluded that lecturing is appropriate when the purpose is to:

1. **Disseminate information:** Lecturing is appropriate when faculty wish to communicate a large amount of material to many students in a short period of time, when faculty may wish to supplement curriculum materials that need updating or elaborating, the material has to be organized and presented in a particular way, or when faculty want to provide an introduction to an area.

2. **Present material that is not available elsewhere:** Lecturing is appropriate when information is not available in a readily accessible source, the information is original, or the information might be too complex and difficult for students to learn on their own

3. **Expose students to content in a brief time that might take them much longer to locate on their own.** Lecturing is appropriate when faculty need to teach information that must be integrated from many sources and students do not have the time, resources, or skills to do so.

4. **Arouse students' interest in the subject.** When a lecture is presented by a highly authoritative person and/or in a skillful way with lots of humor and examples, students may be intrigued and want to find out more about the subject. Skillful delivery of a lecture includes maintaining eye contact, avoiding distracting behaviors, modulating voice pitch and volume, and using appropriate gestures. Achievement is higher when presentations are clear (Good & Grouws, 1977; Smith & Land, 1981), delivered with enthusiasm (Armento, 1977), and delivered with appropriate gestures and movements (Rosenshine, 1968).

5. **Teach students who are primarily auditory learners.**

Parts Of A Lecture

A lecture has three parts: the introduction, the body, and the conclusion. Proponents of lecturing advise teachers, "Tell them what you are going to tell them; then tell them; then tell them what you told them." First you describe the learning objectives in a way that alerts students to what is to be covered in the lecture. You then present the material to be learned in small steps organized logically and sequenced in ways that are easy to follow. You end with an integrative review of the main points. More specifically, during the **introduction** you will want to:

1. Arouse students' interest by indicating the relevance of the lecture to their goals.

2. Provide motivational cues, such as telling students that the material to be covered is important, useful, difficult, and will be included on a test.

3. Make the objectives of the lecture clear and explicit and set expectations as to what will be included.

4. Use advance organizers by telling students in advance how the lecture is organized. **Advance organizers** are concepts given to the student prior to the material actually to be learned that provide a stable cognitive structure in which the new knowledge can be subsumed (Ausubel, 1963). The use of advance organizers may be helpful when (1) the students have no relevant information to which they can relate the new learning and (2) when relevant cognitive structures are present but are not likely to be recognized as relevant by the learner. Advance organizers provide students with general learning sets that help cue them to key ideas and organize these ideas in relationship to one another. Announce the topic as a title, summarize the major points to be made in the lecture, and define the terms they might not know. Give them a cognitive structure to fit the material being presented into. This will improve their comprehension of the material, make it meaningful to them, and improve their ability to recall and apply what they hear.

5. Prompt awareness of students' relevant knowledge by asking questions about knowledge or experience related to the topic. Give and ask for examples. Ask questions to show how the students' prior knowledge relates to the material covered in the lecture. Explicitly relate students' prior knowledge to the topic of the lecture.

During the **body** of the lecture, you will want to cover the content while providing a logical organization for the material being presented. There are a variety of ways of organizing the body of a lecture (see Bligh, 1972 for examples). What is important is that the body have a logical organization that is explicitly communicated to students.

Conclude by summarizing the major points, asking students to recall ideas or give examples, and answering any questions.

Despite the popularity of lecturing, there are (a) obstacles to and (b) problems associated with its use.

Problems With Lecturing

Much of the research on lecturing has compared lecturing with group discussion. While the conditions under which lecturing is more successful than group discussion have **not** been identified, a number of problems with lecturing have been found.

The first problem with lectures is that students' attention to what the teacher is saying decreases as the lecture proceeds. Research in the 1960s by D. H. Lloyd, at the University of Reading in Berkshire, England found that student attending during lectures followed the pattern of five minutes of settling in, five minutes of readily assimilating material, confusion and boredom with assimilation falling off rapidly and remaining low for the bulk of the lecture, and some revival of attention at the end of the lecture (Penner, 1984). The concentration during lectures of medical students, who presumably are highly moti-vated, rose sharply and peaked 10 to 15 minutes after the lecture began, and then fell steadily thereafter (Stuart & Rutherford, 1978). J. McLeish in a research study in the 1960s analyzed the percentage of content contained in student notes at different time intervals through the lecture (reported in Penner, 1984). He found that students wrote notes on 41 percent of the content presented during the first fifteen minutes, 25 percent presented in a thirty-minute time period, and only 20 percent of what had been presented during forty-five minutes.

The second problem with lecturing is that it takes an educated, intelligent person oriented toward auditory learning to benefit from listening to lectures. Verner and Cooley (1967) found that in general, very little of a lecture can be recalled except in the case of listeners with above average education and intelligence. Even under optimal conditions, when intelligent, motivated people listen to a brilliant scholar talk about an interesting topic there can be serious problems with a lecture. Verner and Dickinson (1967, p. 90) give this example:

...ten percent of the audience displayed signs of inattention within fifteen minutes. After eighteen minutes one-third of the audience and ten percent of the platform guests were fidgeting. At thirty-five minutes everyone was inattentive; at forty-five minutes, trance was more noticeable than fidgeting; and at forty-seven minutes some were asleep and at least one was reading. A causal check twenty-four hours later revealed that the audience recalled only insignificant details, and these were generally wrong.

The third problem with lecturing is that it tends to promote only lower-level learning of factual information. Bligh (1972), after an extensive series of studies, concluded that while lecturing was as (but not more) effective as reading or other methods in transmitting information, lecturing was clearly less effective in promoting thinking or in changing attitudes. A survey of 58 studies conducted between the years of 1928 and 1967 comparing various characteristics of lectures versus discussions, found that lectures and discussions did not differ significantly on lower-level learning (such as learning facts and principles), but discussion appeared superior in developing higher-level problem- solving capabilities and positive attitudes toward the course (Costin, 1972). McKeachie and Kulik (1975) separated studies on lecturing according to whether they focused on factual learning, higher-level reasoning, attitudes, or motivation. They found lecture to be superior to discussion for promoting factual learning, but discussion was found to be superior to lecture for promoting higher-level reasoning, positive attitudes, and motivation to learn. Lecturing at best tends to focus on the lower-level of cognition and learning. When the material is complex, detailed, or abstract; when students need to analyze, synthesize, or integrate the knowledge being studied; or when long-term retention is desired, lecturing is not such a good idea. Formal cooperative learning groups should be used to accomplish goals such as these.

Fourth, there are problems with lecturing as it is based on the assumptions that all students need the same information, presented orally, presented at the same pace, without dialogue with the presenter, and in an impersonal way. While students have different levels of knowledge about the subject being presented, the same information is presented to all. The material covered in a lecture may often be communicated just as well in a text assignment or a handout. Lectures can waste student time by telling them things that they could read for themselves. While students learn and comprehend at different paces, a lecture proceeds at the lecturer's pace. While students who listen carefully and cognitively process the information presented will have questions that need to be answered, lectures typically are one-way communication situations and the large number of classmates inhibit questioning asking. If students cannot ask questions, misconceptions, incorrect under-standing, and gaps in understanding cannot be identified and corrected. Stones (1970), for example, surveyed over 1,000 college students and found that 60 percent stated that the presence of a large number of classmates would deter them from asking questions, even if the teacher encouraged them to do so. Lecturing by its very nature impersonalizes learning. There is research indicating that personalized learning experiences have more impact on achievement and motivation.

The fifth problem with lecturing is that students tend not to like it. Costin's (1972) review of literature indicates that students like the course and subject area better when they learn in discussion groups than when they learn by listening to lectures. This is important in introductory courses where disciplines often attempt to attract majors.

Finally, there are problems with lecturing as it is based on a series of assumptions about the cognitive capabilities and strategies of students. When you lecture you assume that all students learn auditorially, have high working memory capacity, have all the required prior knowledge, have good notetaking strategies and skills, and are not susceptible to information processing overload.

Besides the identified problems of lecturing, there are obstacles to making lectures effective.

Enemies Of The Lecture

There are a number of obstacles that interfere with the effectiveness of a lecture. We call these obstacles the enemies of the lecture. They are as follows.

1. **Preoccupation with what happened during the previous hour or with what happened on the way to class.** In order for lectures to succeed faculty must take students' attention away from events in the hallway or campus and focus student attention on the subject area and topic being dealt with in class.

2. **Emotional moods that block learning and cognitive processing of information.** Students who are angry or frustrated about something are **not** open to new learning. In order for lectures to work, faculty must set a constructive learning mood. Humor helps.

3. **Disinterest by students who go to sleep or who turn on a tape recorder while they write letters or read comic books.** In order for lectures to work, faculty must focus student attention on the material being presented and ensure that they cognitively process the information and integrate it into what they already know.

4. **Failure to understand the material being presented in the lecture**. Students can learn material incorrectly and incompletely because of lack of understanding. In order to make lectures work there has to be some means of checking the accuracy and completeness of students' understanding of the material being presented.

5. **Feelings of isolation and alienation and beliefs that no one cares about them as persons or about their academic progress**. In order to make lectures work students have to believe that there are other people in the class who will provide help and assistance because they care about the students as people and about the quality of their learning.

6. **Entertaining and clear lectures that misrepresent the complexity of the material being presented**. While entertaining and impressing students is nice, it often does not help students understand and think critically about complex material. To make lectures work students must think critically and use higher-level reasoning in cognitively processing course content. One of our colleagues is a magnificent lecturer. His explanation of the simplex algorithm for solving linear programming problems is so clear and straightforward that the students go away with the view that it is very simple. Later when they try to solve a problem on their own, they find that they don't have a clue as to how to begin. Our colleague used to blame himself for not explaining well enough. Sometimes he blamed the students. Now he puts small cooperative groups to work on a simple linear programming problem, circulates and checks the progress of each student, provides help where he feels it is appropriate, and only gives his brilliant lectures when the students understand the problem and are ready to hear his proposed solution. Both he and the students are much happier with their increased understanding.

After considering these problems and barriers, it may be concluded that alternative teaching strategies have to be interwoven with lecturing if the lecture method is to be effective. While lecturing and direct teaching have traditionally been conducted within competitive and individualistic structures, lectures can be made cooperative. Perhaps the major procedure to interweave with lecturing is informal cooperative learning groups.

Informal Cooperative Learning Groups

In order for lecturing to be successful, and to overcome the obstacles to effective lecturing, students must become active cognitively. In what traditionally has been a passive learning environment for students created by lecturing, teachers must activate the learner through cooperative interaction with peers.

Informal cooperative learning groups are temporary, ad hoc groups that last for only one discussion or one class period. Their **purposes** are to focus student attention on the material to be learned, set a mood conducive to learning, help organize in advance the material to be covered in a class session, ensure that students cognitively process the material being taught, and provide closure to an instructional session. Informal cooperative learning groups also ensure that misconceptions, incorrect understanding, and gaps in understanding are identified and corrected, and learning experiences are personalized. They may be used at any time, but are especially useful during a lecture or direct teaching.

During lecturing and direct teaching the instructional challenge for the teacher is to ensure that students do the intellectual work of organizing material, explaining it, summarizing it, and integrating it into existing conceptual networks. This may be achieved by having students do the advance organizing, cognitively process what they are learning, and provide closure to the lesson. Breaking up lectures with short cooperative processing times will give you slightly less lecture time, but will help counter what is proclaimed as the main problem of lectures: "The information passes from the notes of the teacher to the notes of the student without passing through the mind of either one."

Lecturing With Informal Cooperative Learning Groups

The following procedure will help you plan a lecture that keeps students more actively engaged intellectually. It entails having **focused discussions** before and after the lecture (i.e., bookends) and interspersing **pair discussions** throughout the lecture. Two important aspects of using informal cooperative learning groups are to (a) make the task and the instructions explicit and precise and (b) require the groups to produce a specific product (such as a written answer). The procedure is as follows.

1. **Introductory Focused Discussion**: Assign students to pairs. The person nearest them will do. You may wish to require different seating arrangements each class period so that students will meet and interact with a number of other students in the class. Then give the pairs the cooperative assignment of completing the initial (advance organizer) task. Give them only four or five minutes to do so. The discussion task is aimed at promoting **advance organizing** of what the students know about the topic to be presented and **establishing expectations** about what the lecture will cover.

2. **Lecture Segment One:** Deliver the first segment of the lecture. This segment should last from 10 to 15 minutes. This is about the length of time an adult can concentrate on a lecture.

3. **Pair Discussion 1**: Give the students a discussion task focused on the material you have just presented that may be completed within three or four minutes. Its purpose is to ensure that students are actively thinking about the material being presented. The discussion task may be to (a) give an answer to a question posed by the teacher, (b) give a reaction to the theory, concepts, or information being presented, or (c) elaborate (relate material to past learning so that it gets integrated into existing conceptual frameworks) the material being presented. Discussion pairs respond to the task in the following way:

   a. Each student **formulates** his or her answer.

   b. Students **share** their answer with their partner.

   c. Students **listen** carefully to partner's answer.

   d. Pairs **create** a new answer that is superior to each member's initial formulation through the process of association, building on each other's thoughts, and synthesizing.

   Randomly choose two or three students to give 30 second summaries of their discussions. **It is important that students are randomly called on to share their answers after each discussion task.** *Such* **individual accountability** *ensures that the pairs take the tasks seriously and check each other to ensure that both are prepared to answer.*

4. **Lecture Segment 2:** Deliver the second segment of the lecture.

5. **Pair Discussion 2:** Give a discussion task focused on the second part of the lecture.

6. Repeat this sequence of lecture segment and pair discussion until the lecture is completed.

7. **Closure Focused Discussion:** Give an ending discussion task to summarize what students have learned from the lecture. Students should have four or five minutes to summarize and discuss the material covered in the lecture. The discussion should result in students integrating what they have just learned into existing conceptual frameworks. The task may also point students toward what the homework will cover or what will be presented in the next class session. This provides closure to the lecture.

Process the procedure with students regularly to help them increase their skill and speed in completing short discussion tasks. Processing questions may include (a) how well prepared were you to complete the discussion tasks and (b) how could you come even better prepared tomorrow?

The informal cooperative learning group is not only effective for getting students actively involved in understanding what they are learning, it also provides time for you to gather your wits, reorganize your notes, take a deep breath, and move around the class listening to what students are saying. Listening to student discussions can give you direction and insight into how well the concepts you are teaching are being grasped by your students (who, unfortunately, may not have graduate degrees in the topic you are presenting).

In the following sections more specific procedures for the initial focused discussion, the intermittent pair discussions, and the closure focused discussion will be given.

Introductory Focused Discussion

At the beginning of a class session students may be required to meet in a permanent base group or in ad-hoc informal cooperative discussion pairs or triads to (a) review their homework and (b) establish expectations about what the class session will focus on. Three ways of structuring such informal cooperative learning groups are discussion pairs, peer critiques of advanced preparation papers and question-and-answer pairs.

Introductory
Focussed Discussion Pairs

To prepare for the class session students may be required to complete a short initial focused discussion task. Plan your lecture around a series of questions that the lecture answers. Prepare the questions on an overhead transparency or write them on the board so that students can see them.

Task: Answer the questions.

Cooperative: Create a joint answer to each question within a pair through the following sequence:

1. Each student **formulates** his or her answer.

2. Students **share** their answer with their partner.

3. Students **listen** carefully to partner's answer.

4. Pairs **create** a new answer that is superior to each member's initial formulation through the process of association, building on each other's thoughts, and synthesizing.

The discussion is aimed at promoting advance organizing of what the students know about the topic to be presented and to set expectations as to what the lecture will cover.

Expected Criteria For Success: Each student must be able to explain the answer.

Individual Accountability: One member from the pair will be randomly chosen to explain the answer. Periodically use the simultaneous explaining procedure of having each group member explain the group's answers to a member of another group.

Expected Behaviors: Explaining, listening, synthesizing by all members.

Intergroup Cooperation: Whenever it is helpful, check procedures, answers, and strategies with another group.

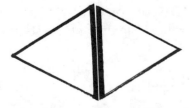

Advanced Preparation Paper

To prepare for each class session students may be required to complete a short writing assignment. Even if it is not graded it compels them to organize their thoughts and take some responsibility for how the class goes.

Task: Write a short paper on an aspect of the assigned readings to prepare for class. Before each class session students:

1. Choose a major theory, concept, research study, or theorist/researcher discussed in the assigned reading.

2. Students write a two-page analysis of it:

   a. Summarizing the relevant assigned reading.

   b. Adding material from another source (research article or book) to enrich their analysis of the theory, concept, research study, or theorist/researcher.

Cooperative: Students bring four copies of the paper to the class. The members of their base group or discussion pair will read, edit, and criticize the paper. The criteria they will use to do so include the following. Does each paper have a(n):

1. Introductory paragraph that outlines the content of the paper.

2. Clear conceptual definition of concepts and terms.

3. Summary of and judgment about what is known empirically. (R = Substantial Research Support, r = some research support).

4. Description of and judgment about theoretical significance. (T = Substantial Theoretical Significant, t = some theoretical significance)

5. Description of and judgment about practical significance. (P = Substantial Practical Significance, p = some practical significance)

6. Brief description of relevant research study that should be conducted.

3:14

7. New information beyond what is contained in the assigned readings.

Expected Criteria For Success: Each student writes a paper and edits groupmates' papers.

Individual Accountability: Each student writes a paper and signs each paper he or she edits. If each group member uses a different color ink pen the quality of their editing is easily apparent. Periodically use the simultaneous explaining procedure of having each group member explain their papers to a member of another group.

Expected Behaviors: Critically evaluating the papers of groupmates.

Intergroup Cooperation: Whenever it is helpful, check editing procedures and strategies with another group.

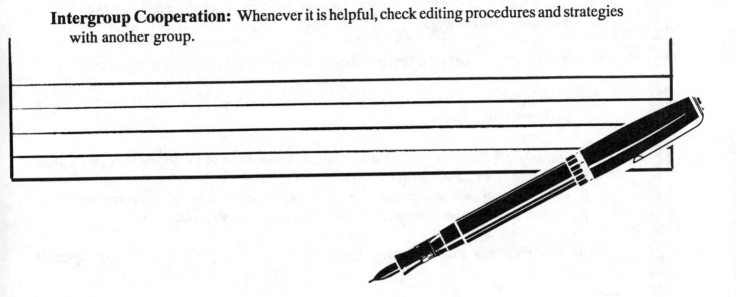

Question-and-Answer Pairs

Task: Answer questions on the homework.

Cooperative: Question-and-answer pairs alternate asking and answering questions on the assigned reading:

1. To prepare for the discussion, students read an assignment and write questions dealing with the major points raised in the assigned reading or other related materials.

2. At the beginning of each class, students are randomly assigned to pairs, and one person (Student A) is chosen randomly to ask their first question.

3. Their partner (Student B) gives an answer. Student A can correct B's answer or give additional information.

4. Student B now asks the first member a question and the process is repeated.

5. During this time, the instructor goes from dyad to dyad, giving feedback and asking and answering questions.

A similar procedure was promoted by Marcel Goldschmid of the Swiss Federal Institute of Technology in Lausanne (Goldschmid, 1971). A variation on this procedure is the **jigsaw**, in which each student reads or prepares different materials. Each member of the group then teaches the material to the other member and vice versa.

Expected Criteria For Success: Each student writes a paper and edits groupmates papers.

Individual Accountability: Each student writes out a set of questions on the assignment and must answer his or her partner's questions. The instructor observes to ensure that each student arrived with a set of questions and gives reasonable answers to his or her partner's questions.

Expected Behaviors: Ask and answer questions, giving good explanations.

Intergroup Cooperation: Whenever it is helpful, check answers, procedures, and strategies with another group.

Progress Checks

Students can be given a progress check (similar to a quiz but not graded). A **progress check** consists of questions (multiple choice, short answer, essay) testing students' knowledge of the assigned reading. Similar to the test procedures described in Chapter 4, students (a) individually complete the progress check (b) retake the progress check and compare answers with a partner from their base group and, if time permits, (c) retake the progress check in the whole base group to broaden the discussion of each question. On any question that the students do not agree on, students should identify the page number and paragraph in the text where the correct answer may be found.

Intermittent Discussion Pairs

Whole-class discussions rarely involve many students. Barnes (1980) found in an observational study of teacher-student interaction that when teachers attempted to solicit student participation through whole-class questioning, students responded only 50 percent of the time. When faculty do manage to obtain student participation, a very small minority of students tends to dominate. Karp and Yoels (1987) documented that in classes of less than 40 students, four to five students accounted for 75 percent of all interactions and, in classes with more than 40 students, two to three students accounted for over half of the exchanges. In his survey of over 1,000 students, Stones (1970) found that 60 percent stated that the presence of a large number of classmates would deter them from asking questions, even if the teacher encouraged them to do so.

Students often say, "I understood it at the time, but I do not remember it now." Experimental research on human memory (Kappel & Underwood, 1962; Waugh & Norman, 1965) indicates that two types of memory interference build up to cause forgetting during long periods of uninterrupted information processing such as an hour-long lecture. The two types are **retroactive interference** which occurs when the information processed toward the end of the lecture interferes with the retention of the information processed at the beginning of the lecture and **proactive interference** when the information processed at the beginning of the lecture interferes with retention of information processes at the end of the lecture. The rehearsal of information soon after it has been received or processed results in greater retention of that information (Atkinson & Shiffrin, 1971; Broadbent, 1970). This is due to the fact that the rate of human forgetting is sharpest immediately after the information is received. If the information is rehearsed orally soon after its reception, however, the brain has an opportunity to consolidate or lock in the memory trace and offset the rapid rate of forgetting that normally follows just- processed information. By interspersing pair discussions throughout the lecture such long periods of uninterrupted listening and information-processing can be avoided thus minimizing retroactive and proactive interference. Students' retention of lecture information would thereby be enhanced. In addition, pair discussions provide the opportunity for students to receive from classmates frequent and immediate feedback regarding their performance. Such frequent and immediate feedback serves to increase students' motivation to learn (Mackworth, 1970).

There is evidence that students do their best in courses that include frequent checkpoints of what they know, especially when the checkpoints occur in small cooperative groups. Ruhl, Hughes, and Schloss (1987) conducted a study on the use of cooperative discussion pairs in combination with lecturing. The study was conducted in separate courses over two semesters. In the two experimental classes the teacher paused for two minutes three times during each of five lectures. The intervals of lecturing between the two-minute pauses ranged from 12 to 18 minutes. During the pauses there was no teacher-student interaction. The students worked in pairs to discuss and rework the notes they took during the lecture. Two types of tests were given--immediate free-recall tests given at the end of each lecture (students were given three minutes to write down everything they could remember from the lecture) and a sixty-five item multiple-choice test measuring long-term retention (administered twelve days after the final lecture). A control group received the same lectures without the pauses and were tested in the same manner. In both courses, students who engaged in the pair discussions achieved significantly higher on the free-recall quizzes and the comprehensive retention test than did the students who did not engage in the pair discussions. The eight-point difference in the means between the experimental and control groups was large enough to make a difference of up to two letter grades, depending on the cutoff points.

During the lecture the teacher stops every ten to fifteen minutes and gives students a short discussion task that students can complete in three or four minutes. Such a use of informal cooperative learning groups ensures that students are actively thinking about the material being presented. The discussion task may be to (a) give an answer to a question posed by the teacher, (b) give a reaction to the theory, concepts, or information being presented, or (c) elaborate (relate material to past learning so that it gets integrated into existing conceptual frameworks) on the material being presented. This can be done through a variety of types of pairing.

Requesting Active Responses

There are a number of other active-response strategies that may be used as part of lectures. They include asking students to indicate their answer or opinion by "raise your hand," "thumbs up or thumbs down" or "clap once if you agree."

Simultaneous Explanation Pairs

When a teacher asks a class "Who knows the answer?" and one student is chosen to respond, that student has an opportunity to clarify and extend what he or she knows through explaining. In this situation only one student is involved and active. The rest of the class is passive. A teacher may ensure that all students are active by using a procedure that requires all students to explain their answers simultaneously. When each student has to explain his or her answer and reasoning to a classmate, all students are active and involved. No one is allowed to be passive. There are two basic ways of structuring simultaneous explaining: (a) the individual student formulates an answer and then explains to a classmate or (b) a small group formulates an answer and each member explains their group's answer and reasoning to a member of another group.

Task: Each student is to explain his or her answers and reasoning to a classmate.

Cooperative: Create a joint answer within a pair through the following sequence:
1. Each student **formulates** his or her answer.
2. Students **share** their answer with their partner.
3. Students **listen** carefully to partner's answer.
4. Pairs **create** a new answer that is superior to each member's initial formulation through the process of association, building on each other's thoughts, and synthesizing.

Expected Criteria For Success: Each student must be able to explain the answer.

Individual Accountability: One member from the pair will be randomly chosen to explain the answer. Periodically use the simultaneous explaining procedure of having each group member explain the group's answers to a member of another group.

Expected Behaviors: Explaining, listening, synthesizing by all members.

Intergroup Cooperation: Whenever it is helpful, check procedures, answers, and strategies with another group.

There needs to be a quick turnaround of what is being learned. Knowledge must be communicated to another person as soon as possible after it is learned.

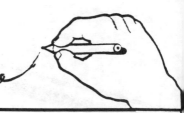

Cooperative Note-Taking Pairs

The notes students take during a lecture are of great importance in understanding what a student learns. In fact, most of the research on lecturing has focused on the value of notetaking, distinguishing between the encoding function of notes and the storage function of notes (Anderson & Armbruster, 1986). There is support for both the encoding (i.e., notetaking assists learning from lectures) and storage (i.e., review of notes is helpful) functions of notetaking. Taking notes during lectures has been shown to be more effective than listening (Kiewra, 1989), but using the notes for review is more important than the mere fact of taking notes (Kiewra, 1985b).

Students often take notes very incompletely (Hartley & Marshall, 1974; Kiewra, 1985a). There are several reasons why notes may be incomplete:

1. Students with low working memory capacity have difficulty taking notes during lectures, possibly because of difficulties in keeping information available in memory while writing it down (Kiewra & Benton, 1988).

2. The information processing load of a student in a lecture is increased when the student has little prior knowledge of the information (White & Tisher, 1986). When the lecturer uses visual aids frequently a student may become overloaded from the pressure to take notes from visual presentations in addition to the verbal statements.

3. Students who are unskilled in notetaking may take incomplete notes.

4. Students may have a false sense of familiarity with the material presented and, therefore, not bother taking notes.

To improve learning from lectures, students may focus on increasing the quantity and quality of the notes they take and/or improving their methods of reviewing the notes they have taken. Research on improving the quantity and quality of notes taken by students during lectures has often focused on the stimulus characteristics of the lecture itself (e.g, pace of the lecture, use of advance organizers) or on the characteristics of the lecturer (White & Tisher, 1986).

Task: For students to focus on increasing the quantity and quality of the notes they take and/or improving their methods of reviewing the notes they have taken.

Cooperative: Two students work together with the common goal of mastering the information being presented.

Procedure: After exposure to a lecture segment, one partner summarizes his or her notes to the other, who in turn adds and corrects. Students may ask each other, "What have you got in your notes so far?" "What are the three key points made by the instructor?" "What was the most surprising thing the instructor said?" The **rule** is that each member must take something from the other's notes to improve his or her own.

Individual Accountability: The notes of a student may be randomly chosen to be examined by the instructor.

Criteria For Success: Complete and accurate notes that have been orally reviewed by each student.

Expected Behaviors: Explaining, listening, synthesizing by all group members.

Intergroup Cooperation: Whenever it is helpful, check procedures, answers, and strategies with another group.

Cooperative notetaking pairs are a tool for structuring active cognitive processing by students during lectures and reducing the information processing load of students. Among other things, it allows for a quick turnaround of what is being learned. Knowledge must be communicated to another person as soon as possible after it is learned if it is to be retained and fully understood. The cooperative note-taking pair procedure results in:

1. The students immediately rehearsing and more deeply processing the information. Appropriate encoding of information in long-term memory requires rehearsal, reorganization, or elaboration of the information. A typical student rarely has the opportunity to rehearse the information from a lecture while that information is still fresh in his or her mind.

2. Students making multiple passes through the material, cognitively processing the information they are learning, and explicitly using metacognitive strategies.

When students are provided with the instructor's lecture notes for review, performance is improved (e.g., Masqud, 1980).

Read-and-Explain Pairs

Whenever reading material is given to students, it may be read in cooperative pairs more effectively than by individuals.

Task: Establish the meaning of each paragraph and then integrate the meaning of the paragraphs into the meaning of the assigned material as a whole.

Cooperative: Both members become experts on the assigned material. Students are to agree on the meaning of each paragraph, formulate one summary, and be able to explain the meaning of their answer. Two roles are assigned: **summarizer** (summarizes in their own words the meaning of a paragraph) and **accuracy checker** (corrects inaccuracies, adds anything left out, encourages and coaches, and relates the meaning of the paragraph to previous learning). The roles are rotated after each paragraph.

Procedure:
1. Both persons silently read the first paragraph. Person A summarizes the content to Person B.
2. Person B checks the accuracy of the summary, corrects anything misstated, adds anything left out, encourages and coaches Person A, and relates the content to previous learning).
3. They move on to the next paragraph, the roles are rotated and the procedure is repeated.

Expected Criteria For Success: Everyone must be able to explain the meaning of the assigned material correctly.

Individual Accountability: One group member will be randomly chosen to explain the meaning of a paragraph.

Expected Behaviors: Active participating, checking, encouraging, and elaborating by all members.

Intergroup Cooperation: Whenever it is helpful, check procedures, answers, and strategies with another group. When you are finished, compare your answers with those of another group and discuss.

Concept Induction

Concepts may be taught inductively as well as deductively. Concept formation may be done inductively by instructing students to figure out why the examples have been placed in the different boxes.

Tasks: Analyze the examples the teacher places in each box. Identify the concept represented by each box. Then create new examples that may be placed in the boxes.

Cooperative: Students turn to the person next to them and create an answer they can agree on.

Procedure:
1. Draw two (or three) boxes on the chalkboard. Label them Box 1, Box 2, or Box 3.
2. Place one item in each box.
3. Instruct students to use the **formulate, explain, listen, create** procedure to discuss how the items are different.
4. Place another item in each box and repeat. Tell students not to say outloud to another group or the class how the items are different. Each pair must discover it.
5. Once a pair "has it," the members are to make a definition for each box. They then create new examples that may be placed in the boxes.

The procedure for students is:
1. **Formulate** an individual answer.
2. **Share** their answer with their partner.
3. **Listen** carefully to their partner's answer.
4. **Create** a new answer that is superior to their initial formulations through the processes of association, building on each other's thoughts, and synthesizing.

Expected Criteria For Success: Each student must be able to identify the concept represented by each box.

Individual Accountability: One member from the pair will be randomly chosen to explain the answer.

Expected Behaviors: Explaining, listening, synthesizing by all members.

Closure Focussed Discussion

After the lecture has ended, students should work in small discussion groups to reconstruct the lecture conceptually. Menges (1988) states that a number of research studies conducted in the 1920's document students' forgetting curve for lecture material. The average student had immediate recall of 62 percent of the material presented in the lecture, but that recall declined to 45 percent after three to four days, and fell to 24 percent after 8 weeks. If students were asked to take an examination immediately after the lecture (systematically reviewing what they had just learned), however, they retained almost twice as much information after 8 weeks, both in terms of factual information and conceptual material. There is every reason to believe that other types of systematic reviews, such as focused discussions and writing assignments, will have similar effects on the retention of the material being lectured on. At the end of the lecture have students discuss the content presented.

Task: Summarize what has been learned from the lecture and answer questions posed by the instructor that point towards the homework and future class topics.

Cooperative: One set of answers from the pair, both members have to agree, and both members have to be able to explain their answers.

Procedure: The instructor gives an ending discussion task to summarize what students have learned from the lecture. Students should have four or five minutes to summarize and discuss the material covered in the lecture. The discussion should result in students integrating what they have just learned into existing conceptual frameworks. The task may also point students toward what the homework will cover or what will be presented in the next class session. This provides closure to the lecture. The pairs of students may be asked to list:

1. What are the five most important things you learned?

2. What are two questions you wish to ask?

The instructor collects the answers and records them to support the importance of the procedure and to see what students have learned. Handing the papers back periodically with brief comments from the instructor on them helps reinforce this procedure for students.

Individual Accountability: One group member will be randomly selected to explain the group's answers.

Expected Behaviors: Explaining, listening, synthesizing by all members.

Intergroup Cooperation: Whenever it is helpful, check procedures, answers, and strategies with another group. When you are finished, compare your answers with those of another group and discuss.

Closure Cooperative Writing Pairs

Faculty benefit from asking students to write a "one-minute paper" at the end of each teaching session describing the "major point you learned today" and "the main unanswered question you still have" (Light, 1990). This helps students to focus on the central themes of the course. In writing their papers, students should first write an introductory paragraph that outlines the content of the lecture, clear conceptual definitions of concepts and terms presented, a summary of and judgment about the information presented, a description of and judgment about theoretical significance of the information presented, a description of and judgment about practical significance, and anything the student knows beyond what was covered in the lecture.

Closure Note-Taking Pairs

Closure note-taking pairs are similar to the cooperative note-taking pairs used intermittently during the lecture. Students review and complete their lecture notes, reflecting on the lecture, and writing the major concepts and pertinent information presented. More specifically, two students work together with the common goal of mastering the information being presented. After the lecture, one partner summarizes his or her notes to the other, who in turn adds and corrects. Students may ask each other, "What have you got in your notes?" "What are the three key points made by the instructor?" "What was the most surprising thing the instructor said today?"

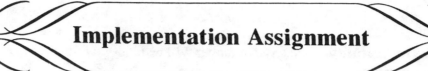

Implementation Assignment

Task: For students to make a specific contract with their base group as to how they will apply what they have learned.

Cooperative: Each group member must commit him- or herself to the group to apply what they have learned. The group becomes the keeper of the contract.

Procedure: At the end of the class session each member plans how to apply what they have learned. This implementation assignment functions as a learning contract with the base group. Each member discusses with the group and then writes down three specific answers to the questions:

1. What have I learned?

2. How will I use it?

In planning how to implement what they have learned, it is important for students to be as specific as possible about implementation plans and to keep a careful record of their implementation efforts.

Individual Accountability: Each group member may be randomly selected by the instructor to explain his or her implementation plans and results.

Expected Behaviors: Explaining, listening, summarizing by all members.

Book-Ends for Films or Demonstrations

A **demonstration** is the modeling of skills or procedures. Use informal cooperative learning groups whenever you are giving a demonstration, showing a film, or having a guest speaker. Informal cooperative learning groups are very useful in setting an anticipatory set for the demonstration before it begins and processing what was learned from the demonstration afterwards.

Peer Feedback Groups

Students like courses that offer frequent opportunities to revise and improve their work as they go along. They learn best when they have a chance to submit an early version of their work, get detailed feedback and criticism, and then hand in a final version for a grade. While this can most easily be done with writing assignments, quizzes, tests, brief papers, and oral examinations will also work.

Cooperative Study Groups

The Harvard Assessment Seminars (Light, 1990) compared the grades of students who studied alone with those of students who studied in groups of four to six. Invariably, the students who studied in small groups did better than students who studied alone. The students in small study groups spoke more often, asked more questions, and were generally more engaged than those in the larger groups. Some class time may be allocated to form and organize study groups.

Conclusions

Do you want to be a sage on the stage or a guide on the side? The sage talks without interruption. The guide has students do the talking. When direct teaching procedures such as lecturing are being used, **informal cooperative learning groups** can be used to focus student attention on the material to be learned, set a mood conducive to learning, help set expectations as to what will be covered in a class session, ensure that students cognitively process the material being taught, keep students' attention focused on the content, ensure that misconceptions, incorrect understanding, and gaps in understanding are corrected, provide an opportunity for discussion and elaboration which promote retention and transfer, make learning experiences personal and immediate, and provide closure to an instructional session. Students can summarize in three-to-five minute discussions what they know about a topic before and after a lecture. Short five minute discussions in cooperative pairs can be interspersed throughout a lecture. In this way the main problem of lectures can be countered: "The information passes from the notes of the teacher to the notes of the student without passing through the mind of either one."

Besides the use of formal and informal cooperative learning groups, there is a need for a permanent base group that provides relatively long-term relationships among students. It is to this use of cooperative learning that we now turn.

EXERCISE

MATERIALS

Informal Cooperative Learning Planning Form

Description of the Lecture

1. **Lecture Topic:**_____

2. **Objectives** (Major Understandings Students Need To Have At The End Of The Lecture):

   a._____

   b._____

3. **Time Needed:**_____

4. **Method For Assigning Students To Pairs Or Triads:**_____

5. **Method Of Changing Partners Quickly:**_____

6. **Materials** (such as transparencies listing the questions to be discussed and describing the **formulate, share, listen, create** procedure):_____
   _____

Advanced Organizer Question(s)

Questions should be aimed at promoting **advance organizing** of what the students about the topic to be presented and **establishing expectations** as to what the lecture will cover.

   1.

   2.

   3.

   4.

Cognitive Rehearsal Questions

List the specific questions to be asked every 10 or 15 minutes to ensure that participants understand and process the information being presented. Instruct students to use the **formulate, share, listen, and create** procedure.

1.

2.

3.

4.

Monitor by systmatically observing each pair. Intervene when it is necessary. Collect data for whole class processing. Students' explanations to each other provide a window into their minds that allows you to see what they do and do not understand. Monitoring also provides an opportunity for you to get the know your students better.

Summary Question(s)

Give an ending discussion task and require students to come to consensus, write down the pair or triad's answer(s), sign the paper, and hand it in. Signatures indicate that students agree with the answer, can explain it, and guarantee that their partner(s) can explain it. The questions could ask for a summary of the lecture, an elaboration or extension of the material presented, or precue a lab assignment or the next lecture.

1.

2.

Celebrate Students' Hard Work

1.

2.

COOPERATIVE

BASE GROUPS

Introduction

> *The biggest disease today is not leprosy or tuberculosis, but rather the feeling of being unwanted, uncared for, and deserted by everybody.*
>
> Mother Teresa, Nobel Peace Prize 1979

Author William Manchester wrote several years ago in Life Magazine about revisiting Sugar Loaf Hill in Okinawa, where 34 years before he had fought as a Marine. He describes how he had been wounded, sent to a hospital and, in violation of orders, escaped from the hospital to rejoin his Army unit at the front. Doing so meant almost certain death. "Why did I do it?" he wondered. The answer lies in long-term relationships in which group members depend upon and support each other.

The more social support a student has, the higher the student's achievement will tend to be, the more the student will persist on challenging tasks, the more likely students will be graduated, the healthier psychologically and physically the students will tend to be, the better able students will be to manage stress, and the more likely students will be to challenge their competencies to grow and develop (Johnson & Johnson, 1989a). The success of a school depends largely on the social support students have while they are in attendance.

Cooperative Learning And Social Support

> *To state quite simply what we learn in time of pestilence:...There are more things to admire in men than to despise.*
>
> Albert Camus (1947)

Like anyone else, students can feel isolated, lonely, and depressed. Their achievements can be seen as meaningless when parents get divorced, their peers reject them, or they are victims of crime. Anyone, no matter how intelligent or creative, can have such feelings.

Recently in a Minnesota school district, a popular star athlete committed suicide. Even though he was widely liked, the note he left indicated feelings of loneliness, depression, and isolation. He is not unusual. A recent national survey reported that growing feelings of worthlessness and isolation led 30 percent of America's brightest teenagers to consider suicide, and 4 percent have tried it.

We are in an epidemic of depression and anxiety among our adolescents and young adults (Seligman, 1988). And it seems to be spreading downward as more and more elementary school students are becoming depressed. The stark emptiness of the self and the vacuousness of "me" is revealed when students are faced with a personal crisis. What is denied is that personal well-being cannot exist without commitment to and responsibility for joint well-being.

A number of years ago, a speeding car carrying five teenagers slammed into a tree, killing three of them. It was not long before small, spontaneous memorials appeared at the tree. A yellow ribbon encircled its trunk. Flowers were placed nearby on the ground. There were a few goodbye signs. Such quiet testimonies send an important message: When it really matters, we are part of a community, not isolated individuals. We define ourselves in such moments as something larger than our individual selves--as friends, classmates, teammates, and neighbors.

Many students have the delusion that each person is separate and apart from all other individuals. It is easy to be concerned only with yourself. But when classmates commit suicide and when cars slam into trees killing classmates, the shock waves force us out of the shallowness of self into the comforting depth of community. An important advantage of placing students in cooperative learning groups and having them work together with a wide variety of peers to complete assignments is the sense of belonging, acceptance, and caring that results. In times of crisis, such community may mean the difference between isolated misery and deep personal talks with caring friends.

Being part of a community does not "just happen" when a student enters school. Being known, being liked and respected, and being involved in relationships that provide help and support do not magically happen when the freshman year begins. School life can be lonely. Many students start school without a clear support group. Students can attend class without ever talking to other students. While many students are able to develop the relationships with classmates and fellow students to provide themselves with support systems, other students are unable to do so. Schools have to carefully structure student experiences to build a learning community. A **learning community** is characterized by two types of social support. The **first** is an academic support group that provides any needed assistance and

needed assistance and helps students succeed academically in college. The **second** is a personal support group made up of people who care about and are personally committed to the student. Working in formal and informal cooperative groups provides an opportunity to begin long-term relationships, but for some students it is not enough. Base groups may be needed. Two years ago, for example, a student in the Social Psychology of Education gave David the following feedback. "This is my last quarter of course work for my doctorate. I have taken 120 quarter hours of courses. This is the first class in which I really got to know other students on a personal level. I got to know the members of my base group. Why didn't this happen in all my classes?"

It is important that some of the relationships built within cooperative learning groups are permanent. College has to be more than a series of temporary encounters that last for only a semester. College students should be assigned to permanent base groups to create permanent caring and committed relationships with classmates who will provide the support, help, encouragement, and assistance students need to make academic progress and develop cognitively and socially in healthy ways. In this chapter we will first define base groups and then detail how they may be used to provide a permanent support system for each student.

Base Groups: What Are They?

United we stand, divided we fall.

Watchword of the American Revolution

Aesop tells a story of a man who had four sons. The father loved them very much, but they troubled him greatly, for they were always fighting with each other. Nothing the father said stopped their quarreling. "What can I do to show my sons how wrong it is to act this way?" the father thought. One day he called his sons to him and showed them a bundle of sticks. "Which of you, my sons, can break this bundle of sticks?" he asked them. All the boys tried in turn, but not one of them could do it. Then the father untied the bundle and gave each son a single stick. "See if you can break that," he said. Of course, they could easily do it. "My sons," the father said, "each of you alone is weak. He is as easy to injure as one of these sticks. But if you will be friends and stick together, you will be as strong as the bundle of sticks."

Base groups:

1. Are heterogeneous in membership so that they represent a cross-section of the school population in terms of gender, ability, ethnic and cultural backgrounds.

2. Last for the duration of the class (a semester or year) and preferably from the freshman through the senior year. When students know that the cooperative base group will stay together until each member is graduated, they become committed to find ways to motivate and encourage their groupmates. Problems in working with each other cannot be ignored or waited out.

3. Meet regularly.

4. Personalize the work required and the learning experiences.

The two purposes of the base groups are for members to:

1. Provide each other with the support, encouragement, and assistance needed to complete assignments and make good academic progress. This includes letting absent group members know what went on in class and interacting informally every day within and between classes, discussing assignments and helping each other with homework.

2. Hold each other accountable for striving to make academic progress.

In other words, **base groups** are long-term, heterogeneous cooperative learning groups with stable membership whose primary responsibilities are to provide support, encouragement, and assistance in completing assignments and hold each other accountable for striving to learn.

There are several key ingredients in using base groups effectively. **First**, frequently use formal cooperative learning groups for instructional purposes until the five essential elements (see Chapter 2) are understood and some expertise in using cooperative learning groups is gained. **Second**, make base groups slightly larger than formal cooperative learning groups (base groups may have four or five members rather than two or three). **Third**, do not assign students to base groups the first day of class. Wait for a few days until you get to know the students somewhat and the class membership stabilizes. **Fourth**, schedule frequent meetings of base groups. **Fifth**, plan an important agenda for each meeting. The agendas for base groups can include:

1. **Academic support tasks,** such as checking to see what assignments each member has and what help they need to complete them. Members can give each other advice on how to take tests and "survive" in school. Members can prepare each other to take tests and go over the questions missed afterwards. Members can share their areas of expertise (such as art or computers) with each other. Above all, members monitor each other's academic progress and make sure all members are achieving.

2. **Routine tasks** such as taking roll or collecting homework.

3. **Personal support tasks,** such as listening sympathetically when a member has problems with parents or friends, having general discussions about life, giving each other advice about relationships, and helping each other solve nonacademic problems. Teachers may increase the likelihood of personal support by conducting trust-building exercises with the base groups, such as sharing their favorite movie, a childhood experience, a memory from high school, and so forth.

Finally, expect some base groups to have relationship problems. Not all base groups cohere right away. Be ready to help unskillful members integrate themselves into their groups. You may wish to periodically structure a base group meeting to process the relationships among members or give the group hypothetical problems to solve (such as, "What if one member of your group did 90 percent of the talking? What are three strategies to help them listen as well as contribute?"). Persistence and patience are good teacher qualities with poorly functioning base groups.

Base Group Procedures

Elementary Base Groups

At the beginning of the academic year, students should be assigned to base groups. Some attention should be paid to building a group identity and some group cohesion. The first week the base groups meet, for example, base groups can pick a name, design a flag, or choose a motto. If a teacher in the school has the proper expertise, the groups will benefit from participating in an age-appropriate "challenge course" involving ropes and obstacles. This type of physical challenge that the groups complete together builds cohesion quickly.

During the year, elementary base groups meet twice each day, first thing in the morning and last thing in the afternoon. **At the beginning of each day members meet in their base groups to:**

1. Congratulate each other for coming to school on time with all their books and materials and check to see that none of their group is under undue stress. The two questions to discuss are: "Are we all prepared for the day?" and "How are you today?"

2. Check to see if members have completed their homework or need help and assistance in doing so. The questions to discuss are: "Did you do your homework?" "Is there anything you did not understand?" If there is not time to help each other during the base group meeting, an appointment is made to meet again during free time or lunch. Periodically, the base groups may be given a checklist of academic skills and assess which ones each member needs to practice more.

3. Review what members have read and done since the evening before. Members should be able to give a brief, terse, succinct summary of what they have read, thought about, and done. They may come to class with resources they have found and want to share, or copies of work they have completed and wish to distribute to their base group members.

4. Get to know each other better and provide positive feedback by discussing such questions as: "What do you like about each other?" "What do you like about yourself?" and "What is the best thing that has happened to you this week?"

At the end of the day members meet in their base groups to see that everyone is taking their homework home, understands the assignments to be completed, and has the help and assistance they need to do their work (during the evening students can confer on the telephone or even study together at one house). In addition, base groups may wish to discuss what members have learned during the day and check to see if all members have plans to do something fun and interesting that evening.

In elementary schools, base groups should stay together for at least a year and ideally, for six years. If each year base groups are promoted to the same classroom, the base group that begins in the first grade could thus stay together for six years.

Secondary Base Groups

If all members of the same elementary school base groups attend the same junior high school, the group can be continued. If not, base groups should be formed at the beginning of the academic year. An initial emphasis should be placed on building group identity and cohesion. If a teacher in the school has the proper expertise, the groups will benefit from participating in an age- appropriate "challenge course" involving ropes and obstacles. This type of physical challenge that the groups complete together builds cohesion quickly.

In junior high and high schools, class schedules should be arranged so that members of base groups are assigned to as many of the same classes as possible. Members will then spend much of the day together. In essence, the computer is programmed to assign base groups to classes (whenever possible) rather than individuals.

Each week base groups formally meet at least twice (perhaps first thing on Monday and last thing on Friday) to discuss the academic progress of each member, provide help and assistance to each other, and hold each member accountable for completing assignments and progressing satisfactorily through the academic program. The **meeting on Monday morning** refocuses the students on school, provides any emotional support required after the weekend, reestablishes personal contact among base group members, and helps students set their academic goals for the week (what is still to be done on assignments that are due, and so forth). The **meeting on Friday afternoon** helps students review the week, set academic goals for the weekend (what schoolwork has to be done before Monday), and share weekend plans and hopes. Tasks similar to the elementary school base group meetings could be given. Members should carefully review each other's assignments and ensure that members have the help and assistance needed. In addition, they should hold each other accountable for committing serious effort to succeed in school.

Base Groups At The College Level

There are two ways base groups may be used in the college level. The **first** is to have a base group in each college course. Class base groups stay together only for the duration of the course. The **second** is to organize all students within the college into base groups and have the groups function as an essential component of college life. Base groups stay together for at least a year and preferably for four years or until all members are graduated.

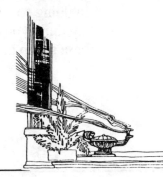

Class Base Groups

The larger or more impersonal the class, and the more complex the subject matter, the more important it is to have base groups. The members of base groups should exchange phone numbers and information about schedules as they may wish to meet outside of class. **The class base group functions as a support group for members that:**

1. Gives assistance, support, and encouragement for mastering the course content and skills and provides feedback on how well the content and skills are being learned.

2. Gives assistance, support, and encouragement for thinking critically about the course content, explaining precisely what one learns, engaging in intellectual controversy, getting the work done on time, and applying what is learned to one's own life.

3. Provides a set of interpersonal relationships to personalize the course and an arena for trying out the cooperative learning procedures and skills emphasized within the course.

4. Provides a structure for managing course procedures, such as homework, attendance, and evaluation.

Members of class base groups are responsible for mastering and implementing the theories, concepts, and skills emphasized in the course, to ensure that all members of their base group do likewise and, finally, to ensure that all members of the class master and appropriately implement the theories, concepts, and skills emphasized in the course. In other words, if the group is successful, members should find another group to help until all members of the class are successful. There is intergroup cooperation, not intergroup competition.

At the beginning of each session class members meet in their base groups to:

1. Congratulate each other for living through the time since the last class session and check to see that none of their group is under undue stress. The two questions to discuss are: "Are we all prepared for this class period?" and "How are you today?"

2. Check to see if members have completed their homework or need help and assistance in doing so. The questions to discuss are: "Did you do your homework?" "Is there anything you did not understand?" If there is not time to help each other during the base group meeting, an appointment is made to meet again during free time or lunch.

Periodically, the base groups may be given a checklist of academic skills and assess which ones each member needs to practice more.

3. Review what members have read and done since the last class session. Members should be able to give a brief, terse, succinct summary of what they have read, thought about, and done. They may come to class with resources they have found and want to share, or copies of work they have completed and wish to distribute to their base group members.

4. Get to know each other better and provide positive feedback by discussing such questions as: "What do you like about each other?" "What do you like about yourself?" and "What is the best thing that has happened to you this week?"

Class base groups are available to support individual group members. If a group member arrives late, or must leave early on an occasion, the group can provide information about what that student missed. Additionally, group members may assist one another in writing required papers. Assignments may be discussed in the base groups, papers may be planned, reviewed, and edited in base groups, and any questions regarding the course assignments and class sessions may be first addressed in the base group. If the group is not able to resolve the issue, it should be brought to the attention of the teacher.

All members are expected to contribute actively to the class discussion, work to maintain effective working relationships with other participants, complete all assignments, assist classmates in completing their assignments, express their ideas, not change their minds unless they are persuaded by logic or information to do so, and indicate agreement with base group's work by signing the weekly contract.

There is no way to overemphasize how important class base groups can be. In the early 1970's, for example, a graduate student in the Social Psychology of Education course suffered a psychological breakdown and was hospitalized for most of the quarter in a locked psychiatric ward of a local hospital. Two years later, she came to visit David and thank him for the course. She stated that it was the only course she had completed that very difficult year. The other members of her base group had obtained permission from her psychiatrist to visit her weekly in the hospital. They spent two hours a week with her, going over her assignments, helping her write her papers, giving her the tests, and ensuring that she completed the course. She got a "B."

College Base Groups

At the beginning of the academic year, students should be assigned to base groups. Class schedules should be arranged so that members of base groups are assigned to as many of the same classes as possible. Members will then spend much of the day together. In essence, the computer is programmed to assign base groups to classes (whenever possible) rather than individuals. Base groups should stay together for at least a year and ideally, for four years.

Some attention should be paid to building a group identity and group cohesion. The first week the base groups meet, for example, base groups can pick a name, design a flag, or choose a motto. If an teacher in the school has the proper expertise, the groups will benefit from participating in a "challenge course" involving ropes and obstacles. This type of physical challenge that the groups complete together builds cohesion quickly.

During the year, base groups meet either (a) twice each day or (b) twice a week, or some variation in between. When base groups meet twice each day, they meet first thing in the morning and last thing in the afternoon. **At the beginning of each day students meet in their base groups to:**

1. Congratulate each other for showing up with all their books and materials and check to see that none of their group is under undue stress. The two questions to discuss are: "Are we all prepared for the day?" and "How are you today?"

2. Check to see if members are keeping up with their work in their classes or need help and assistance in doing so. The questions to discuss are: "Tell us how you are doing in each of your classes?" "Is there anything you did not understand?" If there is not enough time to help each other during the base group meeting, an appointment is made to meet again during free time or lunch. Periodically, the base groups may be given a checklist of academic skills and assess which ones each member needs to practice more.

3. Review what members have read and done since the evening before. Members should be able to give a brief, terse, succinct summary of what they have read, thought about, and done. They may come to class with resources they have found and want to share, or copies of work they have completed and wish to distribute to their base group members.

4. Get to know each other better and provide positive feedback by discussing such questions as: "What do you like about each other?" "What do you like about yourself?" and "What is the best thing that has happened to you this week?"

At the end of the day members meet in their base groups to see that everyone is taking their homework home, understands the assignments to be completed, and has the help and assistance they need to do their work (during the evening students can confer on the telephone or even study together at one house). In addition, base groups may wish to discuss what members have learned during the day and check to see if all members have plans to do something fun and interesting that evening.

When base groups meet twice each week (perhaps first thing on Monday and last thing on Friday), they meet to discuss the academic progress of each member, provide help and assistance to each other, and hold each member accountable for completing assignments and progressing satisfactorily through the academic program. The **meeting on Monday morning** refocuses the students on school, provides any emotional support required after the weekend, reestablishes personal contact among base group members, and helps students set their academic goals for the week (what is still to be done on assignments that are due, and so forth). Members should carefully review each other's assignments and ensure that members have the help and assistance needed. In addition, they should hold each other accountable for committing serious effort to succeed in school. The **meeting on Friday afternoon** helps students review the week, set academic goals for the weekend (what homework has to be done before Monday), and share weekend plans and hopes.

The Seven-Minute Advisee/Base Group

In many secondary schools it will seem difficult to implement base groups. Two opportunities are homerooms and advisor/advisee groups. Teachers may take their homeroom and divide students into base groups and then plan an important agenda for them to follow each day.

In a school we work with all students are assigned an advisor. The teacher then meets once a week with all of his or her advisees. The meeting lasts for seven minutes. While at first this seemed like an impossible time limitation, here is the procedure one teacher derived. First, the teacher divided the nine advisees into three base groups of three members each. The rule was set that all students are expected to be in their base group when the bell rings so that no time is lost in getting started. The base groups are then given four tasks:

1. A quick **self-disclosure task** such as, *What is the most exciting thing you doing over Christmas break? What is the worst thing that happened to you last weekend? What is your biggest fear? What is your favorite ice cream?*

2. Any **administrative task** (such as lunch count) is conducted.

3. A quick **academic task** such as, *You have midterms coming up. As a group, write out three pieces of advice for taking tests. I will type up the suggestions from each group and hand them out next week.*

4. Members wish each other good luck for the day.

Turnover Of Membership

When considering using base groups, teachers may wonder about how to manage turnover. In many schools there is considerable student turnover during the year. While teachers cannot prevent the parent(s) of students from moving, they can ease the students' transitions from school to school by having a structured "hello" and a structured "goodbye."

When a new student arrives, he or she should have immediate support. Instead of wandering the halls for two or three weeks to find someone to relate to, a new student could be immediately assigned to a base group. The base group should have some skill in welcoming a new member. One teacher has her base groups practice welcoming a new member. Each member role plays arriving as a new student (to give some insight into how it feels) and the other three members role play welcoming the new member. The teacher then brainstorms ideas from the whole class as to how the welcoming can be best done.

When students move away, the worse thing that can happen is for the students to believe that in the old school no one knew them, no one cared, and no one will miss them now they are gone. A structured goodbye in a base group will prevent such feelings. One teacher reported the following procedure. Members of a base group gave a student who was leaving four self-addressed, stamped envelopes. *We want to hear from you after you get to your new school,* they said. *We especially want to know how you are doing in math. We have worked hard on math with you. We want to know how well you do in your new school.*

Why Use Cooperative Base Groups

Hold onto what is good
  Even if it is a handful of earth
Hold onto what you believe in
  Even if it is a tree which stands by itself
Hold onto what you must do
  Even if it is a long way from here
Hold onto life
  Even if it is easier to let go
Hold onto my hand
  Even when I have gone away from you

Pueblo Indian Poem

There are many reasons why cooperative base groups should be used in schools. One of the major outcomes of cooperative learning is that students who "work together to get the job done" develop positive relationships with each other. The longer the group is together, the more positive and personal the relationships among members become. The caring and committed relationships built within base groups are essential for motivating long-term efforts to achieve, and for healthy social, cognitive, and physical development. The development of academically-oriented values depends on long-term caring relationships.

Need For Long-Term Permanent Relationships

Most relationships in schools are, at best, ship-board romances. When most teachers face their classes, and when most classmates look at each other, they implicitly say, "I will know you for the duration of this course." Students know that next semester or year, they will have a different teacher and different classmates. Relationships are temporary because in most schools it is assumed that "any classmate will do" and "any teacher will do." Classmates and teachers are perceived to be replaceable parts in the education machine. It is assumed that a student's teachers and classmates are basically irrelevant to the educational process.

It is important that some of the relationships built within schools are permanent. School has to be more than a series of ship-board romances. **Receiving social support and being held accountable for appropriate behavior by peers who care about you and have a long-term commitment to your success and well-being is an important aspect of**

progressing through school. It increases achievement and promotes psychological health. In permanent relationships there is increased opportunity to transmit achievement-oriented values. Learning for your caring and committed groupmates is a powerful motivator. Thus, permanent cooperative base groups may be formed to create the caring and committed relationships that improve attendance, personalize the school experience, increase achievement, and improve the quality of life within the classroom.

Meaning, Purpose, And Psychological Health

The feelings and commitment that drove William Manchester to risk his life to help protect his comrades do not automatically appear when students are placed in learning groups. There are barriers to positive interdependence. Among many current high school and college students, their own pleasures and pains, successes and failures, occupy center stage in their lives (Conger, 1988; Seligman, 1988). Each person tends to focus on gratifying his or her own ends without concern for others. Physical, psychological, and material self-indulgence has become a primary concern (Conger, 1988; National Association of Secondary School Principals, 1984). Over the past 20 years, self-interest has become more important than commitment to community, country, or God. Young adults have turned away from careers of public service to careers of self-service. Many young adults have a **delusion of individualism**, believing that (a) they are separate and apart from all other individuals and, therefore, (b) others' frustration, unhappiness, hunger, despair, and misery have no significant bearing on their own well-being. With the increase in the past two decades in adolescents' and youth's concern for personal well-being, there has been a corresponding diminished concern for the welfare of others (particularly the less advantaged) and of society itself (Astin, Green, & Korn, 1987; Astin, Green, Korn, & Schalit, 1986). Self-orientation interferes with consideration of others' needs in that it actively prevents concern for others as equally deserving persons.

The self is a very poor site for finding meaning. Hope does not spring from competition. Meaning does not surface in individualistic efforts aimed at benefiting no one but yourself. Empowerment does not come from isolation. Purpose does not grow from egocentric focus on own material gain. Without involvement in interdependent efforts and the resulting concern for others, it is not possible to realize oneself except in the most superficial sense (Conger, 1981; Slater, 1971). Without a balance between concern for self and concern for others, concern for self leads to a banality of life and, even worse, to self- destructiveness, rootlessness, loneliness, and alienation (Conger, 1988). Individuals are empowered, are given hope and purpose, and experience meaning when they contribute to the well- being of others within an interdependent effort. Almost all people, when asked what makes their life meaningful, respond "friends, parents, siblings, spouses, lovers, children, and feeling loved and wanted by others (Klinger, 1977).

Accountability And Motivation

Education is not successful unless each student is working hard to do the best he or she can. Not everyone has a 130 IQ or complex talents. But every student can work hard to maximize his or her achievements, conceptual understanding of the material being studied, level of reasoning, and creativity. Numerous students, however, spend very little time studying, even those students who get good grades. Students often avoid hard subjects like math, science, and foreign languages and simply coast along, doing far less than they are capable of doing.

In order to increase the effort students commit to learning and achievement, they must be involved in caring and committed relationships within which they are (a) held accountable for exerting considerable effort to learn and (b) given the help, assistance, encouragement, and recognition they need to sustain their efforts to achieve. **Long-term, hard, persistent efforts to achieve come from the heart, not from the head.** When faced with the choice to watch television or do their homework, the decision may be based more on emotional than intellectual grounds. There may be no more powerful motivator than students realizing that they have to turn off the television and do their schoolwork because "their group is counting on them." Many a student who could care less what an teacher thinks will say, "I did my homework because I couldn't face my group and tell them I didn't do it. I couldn't let my group down."

Changing Students' Attitudes About Academic Work

There are many students who do not value schoolwork, do not aspire to do well in school, do not plan to take the more difficult courses, and plan to just get by. One of the responsibilities of the faculty is to change the attitudes of these students so that they value school, education, and hard work to learn. In doing so, there are several general principles, supported by research (see Johnson & F. Johnson, 1991), to guide your efforts:

1. Attitudes are changed in groups, not individual by individual. Focus your efforts on having students within small groups persuade each other to value education.

2. Attitudes are changed as a result of small group discussions that lead to public commitment to work harder in school and take education more seriously. Attitudes are rarely modified by information or preaching.

3. Messages from individuals who care about, and are committed to, the student are taken more seriously than messages from indifferent others. Build committed and caring relationships between academically-oriented and nonacademically- oriented students.

4. Personally tailor appeals to value education to the student. General messages are not nearly as effective as personal messages. The individuals best able to construct an effective personal appeal are peers who know the student well.

5. Plan for the long term, not sudden conversions. Internalization of academic values will take years of persuasion by caring and committed peers.

6. Support from caring and committed peers is essential to modifying attitudes and behaviors and maintaining the new attitudes and behaviors. Remember, "You can't do it alone. You need help from your friends."

Students may be best encouraged to value education, work hard in school, take the valuable but difficult courses (such as math, science, and foreign languages), and aspire to go to graduate school, by placing them in permanent base groups that provide members with help and encouragement and hold members accountable for working hard in school. The base group provides a setting in which academic values may be encouraged and the necessary caring and committed relationships may be developed.

Base Groups And Dropping Out Of School

In many schools large numbers of students drop out. Base groups provide a means of both preventing and combating dropping out of school. Any student who believes that "in this school, no one knows me, no one cares about me, no one would miss me when I'm gone," is at risk of dropping out. Base groups provide a set of personal and supportive relationships that may prevent many students from dropping out of school. Dropping out often results from being alienated from the school and the other students. **Base groups also provide a means of fighting a student's inclination to drop out.** A faculty member may approach a base group and say, "Roger thinks he is dropping out of college. Go find and talk to him. We're not going to lose Roger without a fight."

The Necessities Of Life

There are certain basics in life that all students need to develop in healthy ways. One set of necessities involves good nutrition, adequate sleep, and appropriate clothing and shelter. Another set involves caring and committed relationships. All students need to know that there are people in the world who are committed to them and will provide them with help and assistance when it is needed. Colleges need to ensure that every student is involved in caring and committed relationships with peers. One way to do so is through cooperative base groups.

Staying In Love

Love is loyalty. Love is teamwork. Love respects the dignity of the individual. Heart-power is the strength of your corporation.

Vice Lombardi

In revisiting Sugar Loaf Hill in Okinawa William Manchester gained an important insight. "I understand at last, why I jumped hospital that long-ago Sunday and, in violation of orders, returned to the front and almost certain death. It was an act of love. Those men on the line were my family, my home. They were closer to me than I can say, closer than any friends had been or ever would be. They were comrades; three of them had saved my life. They had never let me down, and I couldn't do it to them. I had to be with them, rather than let them die and me live with the knowledge that I might have saved them. Men, I now knew, do not fight for flag or country, for the Marine Corps or glory or any other abstraction. They fight for their friends."

Long-term committed efforts to achieve come from the heart, not the head. It takes courage and hope to continue the quest. Striving for increased expertise is an arduous and long-term enterprise. Students can become exhausted, frustrated, and disenchanted. They can be tempted to exert minimal effort and just get by. They can be tempted to give up.

In the process of working to achieve shared goals students come to care about one another on more than just a professional level. Extraordinary accomplishments are not achieved without everyone getting personally involved with the task and each other. Genuine personal relationships are formed among members of cooperative groups, especially if the groups have stable membership for considerable period of time.

Base groups are long-term heterogeneous cooperative learning groups with stable membership whose primary responsibilities are to provide support, encouragement, and assistance in completing assignments and hold each other accountable for striving to learn. There are two ways base groups may be used. The first is to have a base group in each college course. The second is to organize all students within the college into base groups and have the groups function as an essential component of college life. College base groups stay together for at least a year and preferably for four years or until all members are graduated. Base groups focus the power of long-term relationships on supporting academic progress, motivating academic effort, creating positive attitudes toward learning, increase retention and graduation rates, and provide the caring and commitment necessary for a full and complete college experience.

The coordinated use of cooperative formal, informal, and base groups provides the basis for educating college students. As students spend more and more time in cooperative learning groups, however, the competitive/individualistic relationships among faculty become more apparent and less defensible. What is good for students is even better for faculty. Cooperation among faculty is discussed in Chapter Nine.

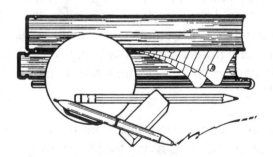

Base Group Meeting Worksheet

When: Base groups meet at the beginning and end of each class session.

Opening Tasks: Ask and answer two or more of the following questions:

1. How are you today? What is the best thing that has happened to you since the last class session?

2. Are you prepared for this class session?

3. Did you do your homework? Is there anything you do not understand?

4. What have you read, thought about, or done relevant to this course since the last class session?

5. May I read and edit your advanced preparation paper? Will you read and edit mine?

Closing Task: Answer the following questions.

1. Do you understand the assignment? What help do you need to complete it?

2. What are three things you learned in today's class session?

3. How will you use/apply what you have learned?

Celebrate the hard work and learning of group members.

Cooperative: One set of answers from the group, everyone must agree, and everyone must be able to explain.

Individual Accountability: One member of your group will be selected randomly to present your group's answers. The next class session group members will ask you if you have followed through on your assignments and plans.

Expected Behaviors: Active participating, encouraging, summarizing, and synthesizing.

Base Group Meeting Worksheet

Intergroup Cooperation: Whenever it is helpful, check procedures, answers, and strategies with another group. When you are finished, compare your answers with those of another group and discuss.

Plan

1. _____

2. _____

3. _____

Signatures

1. _____

2. _____

3. _____

Introduction

*Have you learned lessons only of
those who admired you, and were tender
with you, and stood aside for you?*

*Have you not learned great lessons
from those who braced themselves
against you, and disputed the passage
with you?*

Walt Whitman, 1860

In an English class students are considering the issue of civil disobedience. They learn that in the civil rights movement, individuals broke the law to gain equal rights for minorities. In numerous literary works, such as **Huckleberry Finn**, individuals wrestle with the issue of breaking the law to redress a social injustice. Huck wrestles with the issue of breaking the law in order to help Jim, the run-away slave. In the 1970s and 1980s, however, prominent public figures from Wall Street to the White House have felt justified in breaking laws for personal or political gain. In order to study the role of civil disobedience in a democracy, students are placed in a cooperative learning group of four members. The group is divided into two pairs. One pair is given the assignment of making the best case possible for the constructiveness of civil disobedience in a democracy. The other pair is given the assignment of making the best case possible for the destructiveness of civil disobedience in a democracy. In the resulting conflict students draw from such sources as the **Declaration of Independence** by Thomas Jefferson, **Civil Disobedience** by Henry David Thoreau, **Speech at Cooper Union, New York** by Abraham Lincoln, and **Letter from Birmingham Jail** by Martin Luther King, Jr. to challenge each other's reasoning and analyses concerning when civil disobedience is, and is not, constructive.

Such intellectual "disputed passages" create a high level of reasoning, thinking, and meta-cognition when they occur within cooperative learning groups and when they are carefully structured to ensure students manage them constructively. Cooperation, controversy, cognition, and metacognition are all intimately related. Cooperative learning provides the context within which cognition and metacognition best take place. The interpersonal exchange within cooperative learning groups, and especially the intellectual challenge resulting from conflict among ideas and conclusions (i.e., controversy), promotes critical thinking, higher-level reasoning, and metacognitive thought. Within this chapter cooperative learning is defined and its impact on cognition and metacognition is discussed. The nature of controversy and its effects on higher-level reasoning and critical thinking is then addressed.

Nature Of Controversy

The best way ever devised for seeking the truth in any given situation is advocacy: presenting the pros and cons from different, informed points of view and digging down deep into the facts.

Harold S. Geneen, Former CEO, ITT

A social studies teacher asks students to think about what problems the people described in a curriculum unit on the major problems facing hunting and gathering societies had to solve. Immediately, Jim jumps up and states that the major problem was how to hunt better so they could have more food. Jane disagrees. She says the major problem was how to store food so it would last longer. Jeremy stands up and tells both Jim and Jane that they are wrong; the major problem was how to domesticate the wild grains that grew in the area so that the people would be less dependent on hunting. Jim, Jane, and Jeremy begin to argue forcefully, bringing out the facts supporting why each thinks he or she is right.

Using academic conflicts for instructional purposes is one of the most dynamic and involving, yet **least-used** teaching strategies. Although creating a conflict is an accepted writer's tool for capturing an audience, teachers often suppress students' academic disagreements and consequently miss out on valuable opportunities to capture their own audiences and enhance learning.

Controversy exists when one student's ideas, information, conclusions, theories, and opinions are incompatible with those of another, and the two seek to reach an agreement. Structured academic controversies are most often contrasted with concurrence seeking, debate, and individualistic learning. For instance, students can inhibit discussion to avoid any disagreement and compromise quickly to reach a consensus while they discuss the issue (concurrence-seeking). Or students can appoint a judge and then debate the different positions with the expectation that the judge will determine who presented the better position (debate). Finally, students can work independently with their own set of materials at their own pace (individualistic learning).

Over the past 10 years, we have developed and tested a theory about how controversy promotes positive outcomes (Johnson, 1979, 1980; Johnson & Johnson, 1979, 1985, 1987). Based on our findings, we have developed a series of curriculum units on energy and environmental issues structured for academic controversies. We have also worked with schools and colleges through the United States and Canada to field-test and implement the units in the classroom. We will review these efforts by discussing the process of controversy, how teachers can organize and use it, and the advantages of using controversy to enhance learning and thinking.

How Students Benefit

Conflict is the gadfly of thought. It stirs us to observation and memory. It instigates invention. It shocks us out of sheep-like passivity, and sets us at noting and contriving...conflict is a 'sine qua non' of reflection and ingenuity.

John Dewey

When students interact, conflicts among their ideas, conclusions, theories, information, perspectives, opinions, and preferences are inevitable. Teachers who capitalize on these differences find that academic conflicts can yield highly constructive dividends. Over the past 15 years, we have conducted a systematic series of research studies to discover the consequences of structured controversy (Johnson & Johnson, 1979, 1985, 1987, 1989; Johnson, Johnson & Smith, 1986). Compared with concurrence-seeking, debate, and individualistic efforts, controversy tends to result in:

1. Greater student mastery and retention of the subject matter being studied as well as greater ability to generalize the principles learned to a wider variety of situations. In a meta- analysis of the available research, Johnson and Johnson (1989a) found that

Table 7.1 Meta-Analysis Of Controversy Studies

	Voting			Effect-Size			Z-Score		
	Negative	NoDif	Positive	Mean	sd	n	Z	n	fsn
Controversy/Concurrence	13	54	94	0.42	0.57	49	8.55	55	1,421
Controversy/Debate	4	27	87	0.77	0.41	20	8.04	23	523
Controversy/Individualistic	1	34	89	0.65	0.32	20	8.89	24	672
Debate/Individualistic	0	8	0	0.36	1.03	3	1.76	6	1

controversy produced higher achievement that did debate (effect-size = 0.77), individualistic learning (effect- size = 0.65), and concurrence seeking (effect- size = 0.42).

2. Higher-quality decisions and solutions to complex problems for which different viewpoints can plausibly be developed. If students are to become citizens capable of making reasoned judgments about the complex problems facing society, they must learn to use the higher-level reasoning and critical thinking processes involved in effective problem solving, especially problems for which different viewpoints can plausibly be developed. Educating students to solve problems for which different points of view can plausibly be developed is an important aspect of schooling. To do so, students must enter empathically into the arguments of both sides of the issue and ensure that the strongest possible case is made for each side, and arrive at a synthesis based on rational, probabilistic thought. Participating in structured controversy teaches students of all ages how to find high-quality solutions to complex problems.

3. More frequent creative (a) insights into the issues being discussed and (b) synthesis combining both perspectives. Controversy increased the number of ideas, quality of ideas, creation of original ideas, the use of a wider range of ideas, originality of expression in problem solving, more creative solutions, more imaginative solutions, more novel solutions, and use of more varied strategies.

4. Greater exchange of expertise. Students often know different information and theories, make different assumptions, and have different opinions. Within any cooperative learning group, students with a wide variety of expertise and perspectives are told to work together to maximize each member's learning. Many times students study different parts of an assignment and are expected to share their expertise with the other members of their group. Conflict among their ideas, information, opinions, preferences, theories, conclusions, and perspectives is inevitable. Yet such controversies are typically avoided or managed destructively. Having the skills to manage the controversies constructively and knowing the procedures for exchanging information

and perspective among individuals with differing expertise are essential for maximal learning and growth.

5. Greater perspective-taking accuracy.

6. Greater task involvement reflected in greater emotional commitment to solving the problem, greater enjoyment of the process, more feelings of stimulation and enjoyment.

7. More positive relationships among participants and greater perceived peer academic support.

8. Higher academic self-esteem.

In addition to these outcomes, **there are a number of critical thinking skills required by the controversy structure.** Students must develop at least four sets of conceptual skills to prepare a "best case" presentation, based on evidence, of an assigned position (Johnson & Johnson, 1987). **First,** students must collect, analyze, and present evidence to support a position. This involves (a) researching, gathering, and collecting all facts, information, and experiences available and relevant to the issue being studied, (b) analyzing and organizing the information into a position statement or claim, a listing of all supporting evidence, and a coherent, reasoned, valid, and logical rationale (this requires conceptual analysis and the use of inductive and deductive reasoning), and (c) presenting that position with vigor, sincerity, and persuasiveness while keeping an open mind. Students must present and advocate that position in a way that takes into account who the audience is and how they may be persuaded. **Second,** students must evaluate and criticize the opposing positions. Students critically analyze the opposing position and challenge and attempt to refute it based on the rules of logic and evidence. At the same time, students rebut attacks on their position. This requires a continual reconceptualizing of both positions and determining when the opposing pair presents faulty information or uses faulty reasoning. **Third,** students are required to see the issue from both perspectives. **Fourth,** students make tentative conclusions based on a synthesis and/or integration of the best evidence from both sides. This requires probabilistic rather than dualistic or relativistic thinking. It also requires considerable divergent as well as convergent thinking. Such cognitive skills are valuable contributors to creative problem solving.

Process Through Which Controversy Affects Academic Outcomes

Since the general or prevailing opinion on any subject is rarely or never the whole truth, it is only by the collision of adverse opinion that the remainder of the truth has any chance of being supplied.

John Stuart Mill

Roger regularly conducts an academic controversy on whether or not the wolf should be a protected species. He gives students the cooperative assignment of writing a report on the wolf in which they summarize what they have learned about the wolf and recommend the procedures they think are best for regulating wolf populations and preserving wolves within the continental United States. Students are randomly assigned to groups of four, ensuring that both male and female and high-, medium-, and low- achieving students are all in the same group. The group is divided into two pairs; one pair is assigned the position of an environmental organization that believes wolves should be a protected species and the other pair is assigned the position of farmers and ranchers who believe that wolves should not be a protected species.

Each side is given a packet of articles, stories, and information that supports their position. During the **first** class period each pair develops their position and plans how to present the best case possible to the other pair. Near the end of the period pairs are encouraged to compare notes with pairs from other groups who represent the same position. During the **second** class period each pair makes their presentation. Each member of the pair has to participate in the presentation. Members of the opposing pair are encouraged to take notes and listen carefully. During the **third** class period the group members discuss the issue following a set of rules to help them criticize ideas without criticizing people, differentiate the two positions, and assess the degree of evidence and logic supporting each position. During the first half of the **fourth** hour the pairs reverse perspectives and present each other's positions. Students drop their advocacy positions, clarify their understanding of each other's information and rationale and begin work on their group report. The first half of the **fifth** period is spent finalizing their report. The report is evaluated on the basis of the quality of the writing, the evaluation of opinion and evidence, and the oral presentation of the report to the class. The students then each take an individual test on the wolf and, if every member of the group achieves up to criterion, they all receive bonus points. Finally, during the **sixth** class period each group makes a 10-minute presentation to the entire class summarizing their report. All four members of the group are required to participate orally in the presentation.

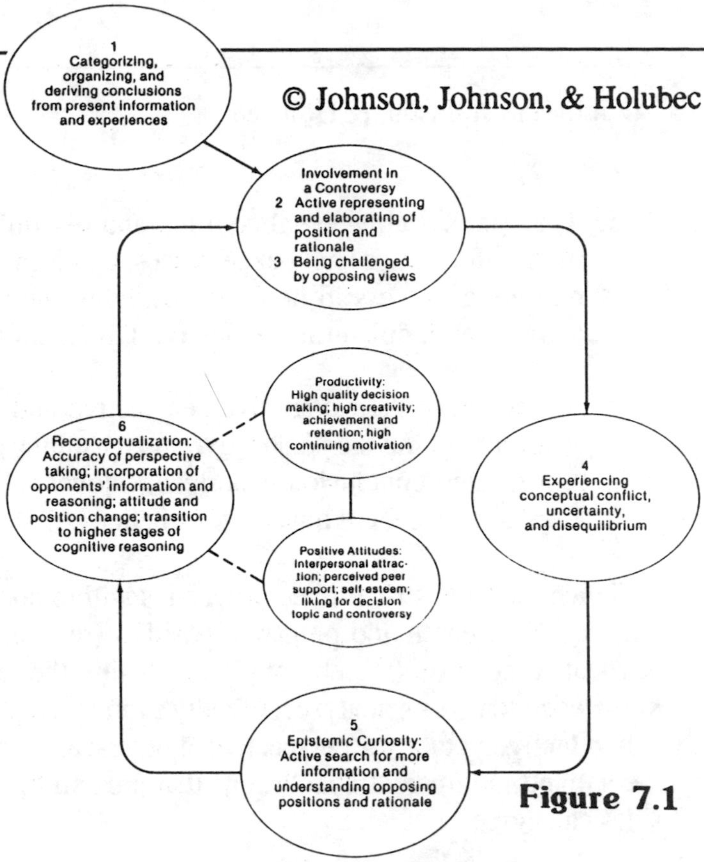

Figure 7.1

Process of Controversy

© Johnson, Johnson, & Holubec

Within this lesson **positive interdependence** is structured by having each group arrive at a consensus, submit one written report, and make one presentation; by jigsawing the materials to the pairs within the group; and by giving bonus points if all members learn the basic information contained in the two positions and score well on the test. **Individual accountability** is structured since each member of the pair orally participates in the presentation of the position and in the perspective reversal, each member of the group orally participates in the group presentation, and each member takes an individual test on the material. The **social skills** emphasized are those involved in systematically advocating an intellectual position and evaluating and criticizing the position advocated by others, as well as the skills involved in synthesis and consensual decision making.

The hypothesis that intellectual challenge promotes higher-level reasoning, critical thinking, and metacognitive thought is derived from a number of premises (see Figure 7.1):

1. When individuals are presented with a problem or decision, they have an initial conclusion based on categorizing and organizing incomplete information, their limited experiences, and their specific perspective.

2. When individuals present their conclusion and its rationale to others, they engage in cognitive rehearsal, deepen their understanding of their position, and discover higher-level reasoning strategies.

3. Individuals are confronted by other people with different conclusions based on other people's information, experiences, and perspectives.

4. Individuals become uncertain as to the correctness of their views. A state of conceptual conflict or disequilibrium is aroused.

5. Uncertainty, conceptual conflict, and disequilibrium motivate an active search for more information, new experiences, and a more adequate cognitive perspective and reasoning process in hopes of resolving the uncertainty. Berlyne (1965) calls this active search **epistemic curiosity**. Divergent attention and thought are stimulated.

6. By adapting their cognitive perspective and reasoning through understanding and accommodating the perspective and reasoning of others, a new, reconceptualized, and reorganized conclusion is derived. Novel solutions and decisions are detected that are, on balance, are qualitatively better.

When teachers structure controversies within cooperative learning groups, students are required to research and prepare a position (reasoning both deductively and inductively); advocate a position (thereby orally rehearsing the relevant information and teaching their knowledge to peers); analyze, critically evaluate, and rebut information; reason deductively and inductively; take the perspective of others; and synthesize and integrate information into factual and judgmental conclusions that are summarized into a joint position to which all sides can agree.

Controversies are resolved by engaging in the discussion of the advantages and disadvantages of proposed actions aimed at synthesizing novel solutions. In controversy there is advocacy and challenge of each other's positions in order to reach the highest possible quality decision based on the synthesis of both perspectives. There is a reliance on argumentative clash to develop, clarify, expand, and elaborate one's thinking about the issues being considered.

Structuring Academic Controversies

Difference of opinion leads to inquiry, and inquiry to truth.

Thomas Jefferson

Here is an example of a controversy on environmental education. The teacher assigns students to groups of four and asks them to prepare a report entitled, "The role of regulations in the management of hazardous waste." There is to be one report from the group representing the members' best analysis of the issue. The groups are divided into two-person advocacy teams with one team being given the position that "more regulations are needed" and the other team being given the "fewer regulations are needed" position. Both advocacy teams are given articles and technical materials supporting their assigned position. They are then given time to read and discuss the material with their partner and to plan how best to advocate their assigned position so that (a) they learn the information and perspective within the articles and technical reports, (b) the opposing team is convinced of the soundness of the team's position, and (c) the members of the opposing team learn the material contained within the articles and technical reports. To do so, students proceed through five steps.

First, students **research the issue, organize their information, and prepare their positions**. Learning begins with students gathering information. They then categorize and organize their present information and experiences so that a conclusion is derived. Second, the two advocacy teams actively **present and advocate their positions**. Each pair presents their position and reasoning to the opposition, thereby engaging in considerable cognitive rehearsal and elaboration of their position and its rationale. When the other team presents, students' reasoning and conclusions are **challenged by the opposing view** and they experience **conceptual conflict and uncertainty**. Third, students engage in a general discussion in which they advocate their position, rebut attacks on their position, refute the opposing position, and seek to learn both positions. The group discusses the issue, critically evaluates the opposing position and its rationale, defends positions, and compares the strengths and weaknesses of the two positions. When students are challenged by conclusions and information that are incompatible with and do not fit with their reasoning and conclusions, conceptual conflict, uncertainty, and disequilibrium result. As a result of their uncertainty, students experience **epistemic curiosity** and, therefore, students actively (a) search for more information and experiences to support their position and (b) seek to understand the opposing position and its supporting rationale. During this time students' uncertainty and information search are encouraged and promoted by the teacher. Fourth, students **reverse perspectives** and present the opposing position. Each advocacy pair presents the best case possible for the opposing position. Fifth, the group of four reach a consensus and prepare a group report. The emphasis during this instructional period is on students **reconceptualizing** their position and **synthesizing** the best information and reasoning from both sides. The group's report should reflect their best reasoned judgment. Each group member then individually takes an examination on the factual information contained in the reading materials.

For the past several years we have been training teachers and professors throughout North America in the use of structured academic controversies. Structured academic controversies are now being used at the University of Minnesota in engineering, psychology, and education courses. They are being used in elementary and secondary schools in the United States and Canada. The basic format for doing so follows. A more detailed description of conducting academic controversies may be found in Johnson and Johnson (1992).

Structure The Academic Task

The task must be structured (a) cooperatively and (b) so that there are at least two well-documented positions (e.g., pro and con). The choice of topic depends on the interests of the teacher and the purposes of the course. Topics on which we have developed curriculum units include the following and many others: "What caused the dinosaurs extinction? Should the wolf be a protected species? Should coal be used as an energy source? Should nuclear energy be used as an energy source? Should the regulation of hazardous wastes be increased? Should the Boundary Waters Canoe Area be a national park? How should acid precipitation be controlled?

Prepare Instructional Materials

Prepare the instructional materials so that group members know what position they have been assigned and where they can find supporting information. The following materials are needed for each position:

1. A clear description of the group's task.

2. A description of the phases of the controversy procedure and the interpersonal and small group skills to be used during each phase.

3. A definition of the position to be advocated with a summary of the key arguments supporting the position.

4. Resource materials (including a bibliography) to provide evidence for the elaboration of the arguments supporting the position to be advocated.

Structure The Controversy

The principal requirements for a successful structured controversy are a cooperative context, skillful group members, and heterogeneity of group membership. These are structured by:

1. Assigning students to groups of four. Divide each group into two pairs. A high reader and a low reader may be assigned to each pair. The responsibility of the pair is to get to know the information supporting its assigned position and prepare a presentation and a series of persuasive arguments to use in the discussion with the opposing pair.

2. Assigning pro and con positions to the pairs and giving students supporting materials to read and study. A bibliography of further sources of information may also be given. A section of resource materials may be set up in the library.

3. Highlighting the cooperative goals of (a) reaching a consensus on the issue, (b) mastering all the information relevant to both sides of the issue (measured by a test), and (c) writing a quality group report on which all members will be evaluated. Also highlight the group reward--each group member will receive five bonus points if all score 90 percent or better on the test.

Conduct The Controversy

1. **Assign each pair the tasks of** (a) learning its position and the supporting arguments and information, (b) researching all information relevant to its position, (c) giving the opposing pair any information found supporting the opposing position, (d) preparing a persuasive presentation to be given to the other pair, and (e) preparing a series of persuasive arguments to be used in the discussion with the opposing pair. They research and prepare their position, presentation, and arguments. Students are given the following instructions:

   Plan with your partner how to advocate your position. Read the materials supporting your position. Find more supporting information in the library reference books. Plan a persuasive presentation. Make sure you and your partner master the information supporting your assigned position and present it in a persuasive and complete way so that the other group members will comprehend and learn the information.

2. **Have each pair present its position to the other.** Presentations should involve more than one media and persuasively advocate the "best case" for the position. There is no arguing during this time. Students should listen carefully to the opposing position. Students are told:

   As a pair, present your position forcefully and persuasively. Listen carefully and learn the opposing position. Take notes, and clarify anything you do not understand."

3. **Have students openly discuss the issue by freely exchanging their information and ideas.** For higher-level reasoning and critical thinking to occur, it is necessary to probe and push each other's conclusions. Students ask for data to support each other's statements, clarify rationales, and show why their position is a rationale one. Students evaluate critically the opposing position and its rationale, defend their own positions, and compare the strengths and weaknesses of the two positions. Students refute the claims being made by the opposing pair, and rebut the attacks on their own position. Students are to follow the specific rules for constructive controversy. Students should also take careful notes on and thoroughly learn the opposing position. Sometimes a "time-out" period needs to be provided so that pairs can caucus and prepare new arguments. Teachers encourage more spirited arguing, take sides when a pair is in trouble, play devil's advocate, ask one group to observe another group engaging in a spirited argument, and generally stir up the discussions. Students are instructed to:

Argue forcefully and persuasively for your position, presenting as many facts as you can to support your point of view. Listen critically to the opposing pair's position, asking them for the facts that support their viewpoint, and then present counter-arguments. Remember this is a complex issue, and you need to know both sides to write a good report."

4. **Have the pairs reverse perspectives and positions by presenting the opposing position as sincerely and forcefully as they can.** It helps to have the pairs change chairs. They can use their own notes, but may not see the materials developed by the opposing pair. Students' instructions are:

Working as a pair, present the opposing pair's position as if you were they. Be as sincere and forceful as you can. Add any new facts you know. Elaborate their position by relating it to other information you have previously learned.

5. **Have the group members drop their advocacy and reach a decision by consensus.** Then they:

   a. Write a group report that includes their joint position and the supporting evidence and rationale. Often the resulting position is a third perspective or synthesis that is more rational than the two assigned. All group members sign the report indicating that they agree with it, can explain its content, and consider it ready to be evaluated.

   b. Take a test on both positions. If all members score above the preset criteria of excellence, each receives five bonus points.

© Johnson, Johnson, & Holubec

c. Process how well the group functioned and how members' performance may be improved during the next controversy. Teachers may wish to structure the group processing to highlight the specific conflict management skills students need to master.

Students are instructed to:

*Summarize and synthesize the best arguments for **both** points of view. Reach consensus on a position that is supported by the facts. Change your mind only when the facts and the rationale clearly indicate that you should do so. Write your report with the supporting evidence and rationale for your synthesis that your group has agreed on. When you are certain the report is as good as you can make it, sign it. Organize your report to present it to your entire class."*

Teach Students Conflict Skills

...the noise could be heard all over the city. Our fights over words were furious, blasphemous, and frequent, but even in their hottest moments we both knew that we were arguing academically and not personally.
                    Richard Rodgers (recalling his work with lyricist Larry Hart)

No matter how carefully teachers structure controversies, if students do not have the interpersonal and small group skills to manage conflicts constructively the controversy does not produce its potential effects. Students should be taught the following skills.

1. Emphasize the mutuality of the situation and avoid win-lose dynamics. Focus on coming to the best decision possible, not on winning.

2. Confirm others' competence while disagreeing with their positions and challenging their reasoning. Be critical of ideas, not people. Challenge and refute the ideas of the opposing pair, but do not reject the students personally.

3. Separate your personal worth from criticism of your ideas.

4. Listen to everyone's ideas, even if you do not agree with them.

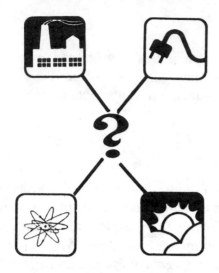

5. First bring out the all the ideas and facts supporting both sides and then try to put them together in a way that makes sense. Be able to differentiate the differences between positions before attempting to integrate ideas.

6. Be able to take the opposing perspective in order to understand the opposing position. Try to understand both sides of the issue.

7. Change your mind when the evidence clearly indicates that you should.

8. Paraphrase what someone has said if it is not clear.

9. Emphasize rationality in seeking the best possible answer, given the available data.

10. Follow the golden rule of conflict. The golden rule is, act towards your opponents as you would have them act toward you. If you want people to listen to you, then listen to them. If you want others to include your ideas in their thinking, then include their ideas in your thinking. If you want others to take your perspective, then take their perspective.

Controversy In Math

There are a number of ways to conduct controversies in mathematics courses. One **topic** is reaching a decision under risk while comparing the relative advantages of using expected value criterion and the minimax criterion. The **instructional task** is to determine the conditions under which each criterion is appropriate. Any problem may be given to students to solve. The students are organized into cooperative learning groups with four students in each group. Two students are assigned the position that the solution should be derived by using the expected-value criterion. The other two students are assigned the position that the solution should be derived by the minimax criterion. The controversy procedure is then conducted. Another topic is to compare the Newton-Raphson and Bisection ways of solving for roots of a polynominal.

Structured Controversies In Science

Within science classes any number of issues may be structured as academic controversies. A few of the topics we have used in our classes are **Acid Rain** (more research is needed vs. we know enough to act now), **Electrical Power Generation** (coal vs. nuclear vs. renewable), **Hazardous Waste** (more regulations needed vs. fewer regulations needed), **Land Use** (preservation vs. economic/business planned utilization), and **Endangered Species** (endangered vs. protected). Faculty interested in these controversies may want to write the Cooperative Learning Center at the University of Minnesota for more complete descriptions and supporting materials.

Summary

Our...advantage was that we had evolved unstated but fruitful methods of collaboration....If either of us suggested a new idea, the other, while taking it seriously, would attempt to demolish it in a candid but nonhostile manner.
Politeness is the poison of all good collaboration in science.
Francis Crick, Nobel Prize Winner (codiscoverer of the double helix)

To promote students' higher-level reasoning and critical thinking, as well as metacognition, requires the two steps of carefully structuring (a) cooperation among students and (b) academic controversy within the cooperative groups. Cooperation, controversy, cognition, and metacognition are all intimately related. Cooperative learning provides the context within which cognition and metacognition best take place. They are stimulated by the interpersonal exchange within cooperative learning groups. To ensure that higher-level reasoning, critical thinking, and meta-cognition take place, however, students need the intellectual challenge resulting from conflict among ideas and conclusions (i.e., controversy).

Cooperative learning needs to be carefully structured to include positive interdependence, face-to-face promotive interaction, individual accountability, the appropriate use of interpersonal and small group skills, and processing how effectively the group has functioned. Under these conditions, cooperative learning results in higher achievement, more frequent use of higher quality reasoning strategies, the generation of new ideas and solutions, and more frequent meta-cognitive thinking than do competitive or individualistic learning situations. Within cooperative learning groups there is a process of interpersonal exchange that involves expectations to teach what one learns to groupmates, explaining and elaborating what is being learned, exposure to diverse perspectives and ideas, taking others' perspectives, externalization of ideas and reasoning, and feedback. Perhaps most important of all, is that intellectual conflict occurs within cooperative groups.

Controversy exists when one student's ideas, information, conclusions, theories, and opinions are incompatible with those of another, and the two seek to reach an agreement. Controversy, compared with concurrence seeking, debate, and individualistic efforts, results in higher achievement, higher-quality decisions and problem-solving, more creative thinking, more higher-level reasoning and critical thinking, greater perspective-taking accuracy, greater task involvement, more positive relationships among group members, and higher academic self-esteem.

These outcomes occur as a result of the structured process of controversy. Students make an initial judgment, present their conclusions to other group members, are challenged with opposing views, become uncertain about the correctness of their views, actively search for new information and understanding, incorporate others' perspectives and reasoning into their thinking, and reach a new set of conclusions. While this process sometimes occurs naturally within cooperative learning groups, it may be considerably enhanced when teachers structure academic controversies. This involves dividing a cooperative group into two pairs and assigning them opposing positions. The pairs then develop their position, present it to the other pair, listen to the opposing position, engage in a discussion in which they attempt to refute the other side and rebut attacks on their position, reverse perspectives and present the other position, and then drop all advocacy and seek a synthesis that takes both perspectives and positions into account. Participation in such a process requires a set of social and cognitive skills. To promote higher-level reasoning, critical thinking, and metacognitive skills, teachers are well-advised to first establish cooperative learning and then structure academic controversies.

EXERCISE

MATERIALS

INK

The Teacher's Role
in Controversy

Make Decisions

Specifying Academic and Controversy Skills Objectives. What academic and/or controversy skills do you want students to learn or practice in their groups? Start with something easy.

Decide on Group Size. Unless there are three or four sides to the issue (avoid more than two sides to an issue unless your students are highly experienced and skilled), use groups of four.

Assign Students To Groups. Heterogeneous groups are the most powerful, so mix abilities, sexes, cultural backgrounds, and task orientations. Assign students to groups randomly or select groups yourself.

Plan Materials. Divide materials into pro and con so that each pair of students has the materials needed to complete the task. This includes the position to be advocated, supporting information to be organized, and a guide to further resources.

Assign Roles. In addition to assigning pro and con roles, there are roles that will help students work together, such as perspective-taker, checker, accuracy coacher, and elaborator.

Set The Lesson

Explain The Academic Task. Explain lesson objectives, define concepts, explain procedures, give examples, and ask questions to ensure that students understand what they are supposed to accomplish.

Structure Positive Interdependence. Students must believe that they need each other to complete the group's task, that they "sink or swim together." Use mutual goals, joint rewards, shared materials and information, and assigned roles to create a perception of mutuality.

Structure The Controversy. Students must understand the procedure and the time limits for preparing their position, presenting it, advocating it, reversing perspectives, and reaching a conclusion.

Structure Individual Accountability. Each student must believe he or she is responsible for learning the material and helping his or her groupmates. Frequent oral quizzing of group members picked at random and individual tests are two ways to ensure this.

Explain Criteria For Success. Student work should be evaluated on a criteria-referenced rather than on a norm- referenced basis. Make clear your criteria for evaluating the work of individual students and the entire group.

Specify Desired Behaviors. Clearly explain the constructive controversy rules.

Teach Controversy Skills. After students are familiar with the controversy procedures, pick one controversy skill, point out the need for it, define it by giving students specific phrases they can say to engage in the skill, observe for it, and give students feedback about their use of the skill. Encourage the use of the skill until students are performing it automatically.

Structure Intergroup Cooperation. Having students check with and help other groups and giving rewards or praise when all class members do well can extend the benefits of cooperation to the whole class.

Monitor And Intervene

Ensure All Students Present, Advocate, Criticize, And Synthesize. The beneficial educational outcomes of controversy are due to the oral interaction among students.

Monitor Students' Behavior. This is the fun part! While students are working, circulate to see whether they understand the assignment, the procedure, the material. Give immediate feedback and praise the appropriate use of controversy skills.

Provide Task Assistance. If students are having trouble with the academic material, you can clarify, reteach, or elaborate on what they need to know.

Intervene To Teach Controversy Skills. If students are having trouble with the controversy process, you can suggest more effective procedures for working together on more effective behaviors for them to engage in.

Provide Closure. To reinforce student learning, you may wish to have groups share answers or paper, summarize major points in the lesson, or review important facts.

Evaluate And Process

Evaluate Student Learning. Assess the quality of the group report and give students the individual test on the material being studied.

Process Group Functioning. In order to improve, students need time and procedures for reflecting on how well their group is functioning and how well they are using controversy skills. Processing can be done by individuals, small groups, or the whole class.

CONTROVERSY LESSON PLAN

Title _____

Your Name _____

School and District _____

Subject Area _____ **Grade Level** _____

Lesson Topic and Summary _____

_____

_____

Instructional Objectives _____

_____

Materials Needed

    Pro _____

    Con _____

Time Required _____ **Group Size** _____

Assignment to Groups _____

_____

Roles _____

  (Name and _____

  Explain) _____

_____

The Lesson

Task _____

_____

_____

_____

_____

Positive Goal/Reward Interdependence _____

_____

_____

Controversy Procedures

    Preparing Positions _____

_____

    Presenting Positions _____

_____

    Discussing the Issue _____

_____

    Reversing Perspectives _____

_____

    Reaching a Decision _____

_____

Individual Accountability _____

_____

_____

Criteria for Success _____

_____

_____

Expected Behaviors _____

_____

_____

Monitoring and Processing

Monitor for _____

_____

_____

Intervene if _____

_____

_____

Process by _____

_____

_____

End by _____

_____

(Attach any materials needed to run the lesson)

Structuring Academic Controversies

Within cooperative groups students often disagree as to what answers to assignments should be and how the group should function in order to maximize members' learning. Conflict is an inherent part of learning as old conclusions and conceptions are challenged and modified to take into account new information and broader perspectives. **Controversy** is a type of academic conflict that exists when one student's ideas, information, conclusions, theories, and opinions are incompatible with those of another, and the two seek to reach an agreement. When students become experienced in working cooperatively, and when teachers wish to increase students' emotional involvement in learning and motivation to achieve, teachers may structure controversy into cooperative learning groups. Numerous academic and social benefits are derived from participating in such structured controversies (Johnson & Johnson, 1989a; Johnson, Johnson, & Smith, 1986).

Task: To learn the assigned material and write a report detailing the student's analysis and conclusions about the issue being studied.

Cooperation: The **cooperative goal** is for group members to arrive at a consensus and submit one written report. Each group submits one report that summarizes their collective best judgment. Each group member signs the report indicating that they agree with the report and can explain the conclusions and rationale included in the report. **Resource interdependence** is structured by jigsawing the materials to the pairs within the group. **Reward interdependence** is structured by giving bonus points to members if all members learn the information contained in the two positions and score well on the test.

Procedure:

1. **Students are given the cooperative assignment** of discussing a designated topic and writing a group report in which they summarize what they have learned and recommend the procedures they think are best for solving the problem. Students are randomly assigned to groups of four, ensuring that both male and female and high-, medium-, and low-achieving students are all in the same group. The group is divided into two pairs and one pair is assigned the pro position and the other pair is assigned the con position on an issue being studied. Each pair prepares their position. Each side is given a packet of articles, stories, or information that supports their position. During the first class period each pair develops their position and plans how to present the best case possible to the other pair. Near the end of the period pairs are encouraged to compare notes with pairs from other groups who represent the same position.

2. **Each pair presents its position to the other pair.** Each member of the pair has to participate in the presentation equally. Members of the opposing pair are encouraged to take notes and listen carefully.

3. **The group discusses the issue following a set of rules** to help members criticize ideas without criticizing people, differentiate the two positions, and assess the degree of evidence and logic supporting each position.

4. **Pairs reverse perspectives** and argue the opposing position.

5. **Students drop their advocacy positions, clarify their understanding of each other's information and rationale, and begin work on their group report.** Groups of four reach a decision and come to a consensus on a position that is supported by facts and logic and can be defended by each group member. The report is evaluated on the basis of the quality of the writing, the evaluation of opinion and evidence, and the oral presentation of the report to the class. The students then take an individual test and, if every member of the group achieves up to criterion, they all receive the bonus points. Finally, during the sixth class period each group makes a 10-minute presentation to the entire class summarizing their report. All four members of the group are required to participate orally in the presentation.

Individual Accountability: Each member of the pair orally participates in the presentation of the position and in the perspective reversal, each member of the group orally participates in the group presentation, and each member takes an individual test on the material.

Expected Behaviors: The social skills emphasized are those involved in systematically advocating an intellectual position and evaluating and criticizing the position advocated by others, as well as the skills involved in synthesis and consensual decision making.

Controversy Exercise:
Schedule

1. **Preparing Positions:** Meet with your partner and plan how to argue effectively for your position. Make sure you and your partner have mastered as much of the position as possible.

2. **Presenting Positions:** Be forceful and persuasive in presenting your position. Take notes and clarify anything you do not understand when the opposing pair presents their position.

3. **Discussing the Issue:** Argue forcefully and persuasively for your position, presenting as many facts as you can to support your point of view. Critically listen to the opposing pair's position, asking them for the facts that support their point of view. Remember, this is a complex issue and you need to know both sides to write a good report. Work together as a total group to get all the facts out. Make sure you understand the facts that support both points of view.

4. **Reversing Perspectives:** Reverse the roles by arguing your opposing pair's position. In arguing for this position, be as forceful and persuasive as you can. See if you can think of any new facts that the opposing pair did not think to present. Elaborate their position.

5. **Reversing a Decision:** Come to a decision that all four of you can agree with. Summarize the best arguments for both points of view. Detail what you know (facts) about each side. When you have consensus in your group, organize your arguments to present to the entire room. Other groups may make the opposite decision and you need to defend the validity of your decision to everyone.

Rules for Constructive Controversy

1. I am critical of ideas, not people. I challenge and refute the ideas of the opposing pair, but I do not indicate that I personally reject them.

2. Remember, we are all in this together, sink or swim. I focus on coming to the best decision possible, not on **winning.**

3. I encourage everyone to participate and to master all the relevant information.

4. I listen to everyone's ideas, even if I don't agree.

5. I restate what someone has said if it is not clear.

6. I first bring out **all** ideas and facts supporting both sides, and then I try to put them together in a way that makes sense.

7. I try to understand both sides of the issue.

8. I change my mind when the evidence clearly indicates that I should do so.

Acid Precipitation:
Pro-Industry Position

You are members of an industrial policy group that believes the listed causes of acid precipitation are only hypotheses advanced by scientists to explain certain facts that puzzle them. Acid precipitation includes acid rain, acid snow, acid sleet, acid hail, acid frost, acid rime, acid fog, acid mist, acid dew, and "dry" deposits of acid particles, aerosols, and gases. It is a problem in the United States and elsewhere in the world. Scientists, however, have not conducted experiments tracing acid precipitation from the emission sources. Until cause-and-effect can conclusively be established, stringent controls on industry are presumptuous and costly.

Your position is that legislative action is not needed to increase the controls on emissions of utility plants burning coal and petroleum. You believe that no hard scientific evidence has been presented to justify new controls. In addition, environmentalists are vague about the level of control required and do not mention other remedial measures to control emissions from sources other than utilities. Whether or not you agree with this position, argue for it as strongly as you can. Use arguments that make sense and are rational. Be creative and invent new supporting arguments. Remember to learn the rationale for both your position and the industrial position. Challenge the industrial position, think of loopholes in their logic, and demand facts and information to back up their arguments.

1. Environmentalists are impling causality by association rather than by scientific proof of linkage. If the relationship between power plant emissions and acid precipitation is so overwhelming, then why have investigators been unable to trace acid precipitation back to the source emissions?

2. If both nitrate and sulfate in rain can be halved, the precipitation pH at most changes from 4.2 to 4.5. If sulfate alone is halved, the precipitation pH may change at most from 4.2 to 4.4. Emission controls, therefore, may be ineffective in changing precipitation pH values.

3. If interstate atmospheric deposition were regulated, at a minimum 2,980 mining jobs and 191 million dollars in annual economic input could be affective. The effect on these mines will be dependent on the control scheme adopted.

These points give you a start in preparing your position. Read the text materials, go to the library, and interview experts to gather additional material to support your position.

Acid Precipitation:
Pro-Environment Position

You are members of an environmental organization that believes a chemical leprosy is eating away at the face of the United States. It is popularly known as acid rain, but rain is not the only culprit. The true name for this phenomena is acid precipitation, which includes acid rain, acid snow, acid sleet, acid hail, acid frost, acid rime, acid fog, acid mist, acid dew, and "dry" deposits of acid particles, aerosols, and gases. While it is not only a United States problem, the United States needs to recognize the extreme dangers of acid precipitation and to take steps to remedy it before the damage becomes so pervasive that it is irreversible.

Your position is that legislative action is immediately needed to rectify the problem of acid precipitation by controlling emissions of utility plans burning coal and petroleum. You believe that industry policy groups have not accepted responsibility for the damage utility plants are causing. They seem unconcerned about the human and environmental costs of their current practices. Certainly they will not change voluntarily. Whether or not you agree with this position, argue for it as strongly as you can. Use arguments that make sense and are rational. Be creative and invent new supporting arguments. Remember to learn the rationale for both your position and the industrial position. Challenge the industrial position, think of loopholes in their logic, and demand facts and information to back up their arguments.

1. Acid precipitation occurs when sulfur dioxide and nitrogen oxides combine in the atmosphere and change chemically into acid, which falls to the earth mixed with some form of precipitation. The pollutants come primarily from burning coal and petroleum. About 90 percent of the sulfur in the atmosphere of the northeastern United States comes from human-made sources.

2. Acid precipitation can kill fish and other aquatic life outright. In Scandinavia, which is downwind of pollution pumped into the skies of Western Europe, acid precipitation has already destroyed fish life in 5,000 lakes in Southwestern Sweden, in several Atlantic salmon rivers, and in 1,500 lakes in southern Norway.

3. Acid precipitation can have damaging effects on human health through inhalation and through the leaching of toxic materials into drinking water.

These points give you a start in preparing your position. Read the text materials, go to the library, and interview experts to gather additional material to support your position.

INTEGRATED USE OF ALL TYPES OF COOPERATIVE LEARNING

Introduction

Pull together. In the mountains you must depend on each other for survival.
Willi Unsoeld, Renounded Mountain Climber

Within Yosemite National Park lies the famous Half Dome Mountain. The Half Dome is famous for its 2000 feet of soaring, sheer cliff wall. Unusually beautiful to the observer, and considered unclimbable for years, the Half Dome's northwest face was first scaled in 1957 by Royal Robbins and two companions. This incredibly dangerous climb took five days, with Robbins and his companions spending four nights on the cliff, sleeping in ropes with nothing below their bodies but air. Even today, the northwest face is a death trap to all but the finest and most skilled rock climbers. And far above the ground, moving slowly up the rock face, are two climbers.

The two climbers are motivated by a shared vision of successfully climbing the northwest face. As they move up the cliff they are attached to each other by a rope (**"the life line"**). As one member climbs (**the lead climber**), the other (**the belayer**) ensures that the two have a safe anchor and that he or she can catch the climber if the climber falls. The lead climber does not begin climbing until the belayer says "go." Then the lead climber advances, puts in a chock (removable anchor that does no damage to the rock), slips in the rope, and continues to advance. The chocks help the belayer catch the climber if the climber falls and they mark the path up the cliff. The life line (i.e., rope) goes from the belayer through the chocks up to the climber. When the lead climber has completed the first leg of the climb, he or she becomes the belayer and the other member of the team begins to climb. The chocks placed by the lead climber serve to guide and support the second member of the team up the rock face. The second member advances up the route marked out by the first member until the first leg is completed, and then leap-frogs and becomes the lead climber for the second leg of the climb. The roles of lead climber and belayer are alternated until the summit is reached.

All human life is like mountain climbing. The human species seems to have a **cooperation imperative:** We desire and seek out opportunities to operate jointly with others to achieve mutual goals. We are attached to others through a variety of "life lines" and we alternate supporting and leading others to ensure a better life for ourselves, our colleagues and neighbors, our children, and all generations to follow.

Cooperative efforts begin when group members commit themselves to a mutual purpose and coordinate and integrate their efforts to do so. What is true of the real life needs to be true of school life. In the classroom, the mutual purpose and coordinated actions spring from cooperative learning. By structuring cooperation among students faculty remind students that **"None of us is as smart as all of us!"**

Structuring cooperative learning in classrooms involves integrating the use of the four types of cooperative learning groups. Each course may have a mixture of cooperative formal, informal, and base groups with a periodic structured controversies to spice things up. Given below are two examples of how the different ways of using cooperative learning may be used. The examples are followed by a discussion of personalizing the learning environment of the class.

Fifty-Minute Class Session

A typical class session consists of base group meeting, a short lecture and/or a group project, and an ending base group meeting. The teacher formally starts the class by welcoming the students and instructing them to meet in their base groups. The introduction and warmup for the class is provided within base groups. The initial **base group** meeting includes one or more of the following tasks for members: greeting each other, checking to see if all members have completed their homework successfully or need help and assistance, and reviewing what members have read and done since the previous class session. Base group activities must be completed within about 5 minutes. Regularly structuring this time is essential for helping students get into a good learning mood, communicating high expectations about completing homework and helping others, and providing a transition between the student's (and teacher's) previous hour and the current class session.

In a 50-minute class session the teacher usually has four choices. The teacher can give a lecture utilizing informal cooperative learning groups, have students complete an assignment in formal cooperative learning groups, conduct a short controversy, or present a short lecture and assign a short group assignment. If a lecture is to be given, it begins and ends with a focused discussion in an informal cooperative learning group and has paired

6 : 2

discussions interspersed throughout the lecture (see Chapter 5). During both students would be asked to **formulate, share, listen, create**:

1. **Formulate** an answer to the question or solution to the problem individually (1 to 2 minutes).

2. **Share** your answer with your partner (1 minute each).

3. **Listen** carefully to your partner's answer.

4. **Create** an answer through discussion that is superior to your individual answers (1 to 2 minutes).

Students are slow and awkward at following this procedure initially but once they become familiar with it they work intensely. Again, this is an important time for the teacher to circulate among the students, listen in, and learn what they already know about the topic. In the long run it is important to vary the type of informal cooperative learning groups, using simultaneous explanation pairs one day and cooperative note-taking pairs another (see Chapter 3).

If a group assignment is given, it is carefully structured to be cooperative (see Chapter 2). The teacher notes the objectives of the lesson, makes a series of preinstructional decisions, communicates the task and the positive interdependence, monitors the groups as they work and intervenes when needed, and evaluates students' learning and has groups process how effectively members are working together. Formal cooperative learning groups are used when the teacher wishes to achieve an instructional objective that includes conceptual learning, problem solving, or the develop-ment of students' critical thinking skills. Formal co-operative learning groups are needed for simulations of first-hand experiences, role playing, or the sharing of expertise and resources among members.

If a controversy is to be structured, it may be a small issue that can be quickly discussed or it may be a complex issue that can last for several class sessions. Each step of the controversy process may be scheduled in consecutive class sessions.

Near the end of the class period summarizing and synthesizing needs to be structured in. In a shorter class period this may simply involve each student working with his or her partner to create a list of three or four major learnings and one or two questions. Periodically these can be collected by the teacher. Quickly reading and commenting on these student summaries provides the teacher with valuable information about what the students are learning and what questions they have, and sends a message to the students that the activity is important.

At the end of the class session students meet in their base groups to summarize and synthesize what they have learned. Base groups may hand in a written summary of the new concept learned today, or elaborate by relating the new learning to previously learned material, or apply what they have learned to a practical situation. Finally, members of the base groups should celebrate their hard work and success. At the end of the class session, after working cooperatively for 50 minutes, students (and the teacher) often have the joyful feeling "We did it." Students leave the class with an empowered sense of, "Since **we** did it, **I** can do it."

Ninety-Minute Class Session

The basic structure of a 90-minute period is essentially the same as for the 50-minute period except it is easier to both lecture and have cooperative learning groups complete an assignment within one class session. Class begins with a base group meeting, the teacher gives a lecture using informal cooperative learning groups to ensure that students are cognitively active while the teacher disseminates information, conducts a formal cooperative learning activity to promote problem-solving and higher-level learning, and closes the class with a second base group meeting.

The base group meetings can be longer (up to 15 minutes) and more varied activities such as "reviewing advance preparation papers" or "progress checks" can be used. Valuable information can be gleaned by eavesdropping on the base groups and noting which parts of the assignment caused difficulty.

A lecture may follow. In using a variety of informal cooperative learning group procedures, faculty need to structure carefully the five basic elements of cooperative learning within the learning situation.

Formal cooperative learning groups become the heart of longer class periods. Students take increasing responsibility for each other's learning, and the teacher takes increasing

responsibility for guiding this process. Faculty should structure positive interdependence in a variety of ways and give students the opportunity to promote each other's learning face-to-face. It is helpful to use a variety of formal cooperative learning procedures, such as jigsaw, problem- solving, joint projects, and peer composition (see Chapter 2). Occasional reporting by the students to the whole class (by randomly calling on individual students to report for their group, of course) can help the teacher guide the overall flow of the class. Carefully monitor the cooperative groups and use formal observation sheets to collect concrete data on group functioning to use during whole class and small group processing.

A 90-minute class period allows adequate time to conduct a quick controversy if it is well planned.

Class ends with a base group meeting. Often base group members sign a contract as to how they will apply what they have learned (see Chapter 4). Longer class periods, such as three-hour sessions, may be structured similarly to the 90-minute class period with the addition of using more than one formal cooperative learning activity during class time.

The Evolution of Cooperative Learning

In implementing cooperative learning teachers need a time-line to guide their efforts. Although a few teachers take cooperative learning strategies and change their classrooms overnight, most teachers engage in a slower, more evolutionary approach. Both the collaborative skills of the students and the instructional skills of the teachers take time to develop and build. Overloading students and teachers with new demands and new situations rarely results in productive change. Teachers are well advised to take what they already know about using learning groups, add a clear cooperative goal structure, and slowly expand the use of cooperative learning until it dominates the classroom. Generally, the stages teachers pass through in becoming proficient in structuring learning situations cooperatively are:

1. **Nonuse.** Teachers have not heard of cooperative learning or are under pressures that prevent consideration of new instructional strategies.

2. **Decision to use and initial preparation.** Teachers learn enough about cooperative learning to be interested in trying it. They plan their first lesson.

3. **Initial use.** Teachers are using cooperative learning less than 10 percent of the time. They are attempting to deal with the initial "start-up" issues of:

   a. Logistical issues of moving furniture and making transitions in and out of cooperative learning, getting students to sit together and engage in such "forming" (see Chapter 5) behaviors as "using quiet voices," and getting students to turn and look at the teacher when instructions are given.

   b. Communication issues of clearly defining the positive interdependence and individual accountability so that students understand what actions are appropriate and inappropriate.

4. **Beginning use.** Teachers use cooperative learning between 10 and 20 percent of the time. Issues they focus on typically are:

   a. Teacher monitoring issues of determining how effectively students collaborate and counting frequencies of positive behaviors to share with the whole class or individual groups.

   b. Student monitoring and processing issues of training students to observe the collaborative interaction of group members and process how effectively their group is functioning. This can be done with any age student. Teachers have had kindergarten and first-grade students observing their group for "who talks," "who takes turns," and "who asks someone else to speak."

   c. Teaching students the collaborative skills they need to function effectively in cooperative learning groups. Teachers will move from "forming" to "functioning" skills. They may wish to emphasize the "formulating and fermenting" skills after students have mastered the basics of working collaboratively. Some care has to be taken in translating the skills into phrases and actions that are appropriate for the age and the background of the students being taught.

5. **Mechanical use.** Teachers follow the general procedures for implementing cooperative learning in a step-by- step fashion, planning each lesson, and reviewing recommended procedures before each lesson. Teachers at this point are usually using cooperative learning from 20 to 50 percent of the time. Some of the issues teachers deal with are:

a. Using a variety of ways to structure positive interdependence and individual accountability, to monitor and process, and to evaluate.

b. Expanding the use of cooperative learning from one subject area or class to several subject areas or classes.

c. Thinking in terms of curriculum units (rather than single lessons) being cooperative, and in terms of alternating among cooperative, competitive, and individualistic learning rather than the isolated use of cooperative learning.

d. Teaching collaborative and academic skills simultaneously.

6. **Routine use.** Teachers automatically structure cooperative learning situations without conscious thought or planning. The concurrent focus on academic and collaborative skills happens spontaneously. Teachers are usually using cooperative learning more than 50 percent of the time and are dealing with the following issues:

a. Integrating cooperative, competitive, and individualistic lessons.

b. Varying how cooperative learning is structured according to tasks, students, and circumstances.

c. Integrating cooperative learning with other teaching strategies in their repertoire.

d. Applying collaborative skills and understanding of positive interdependence to faculty relationships and other settings.

It may take a year for teachers to develop into mechanical users of cooperative learning and it often takes up to two years for teachers to become firmly routine users (see Figure 3.1). In planning how you will progress from beginning to routine use of cooperative learning the following advice may be helpful:

1. **Do not try to move too fast.** Start with a single lesson. Move to conducting at least one cooperative lesson per week and then to modifying a curriculum unit to be primarily cooperative. Finally, think of integrating cooperative, competitive, and individualistic learning within a class or subject area.

2. **Persevere!** Do not stop growing in your use of cooperative learning even though some students are not very skillful and no one else in your school seems to care. Lay

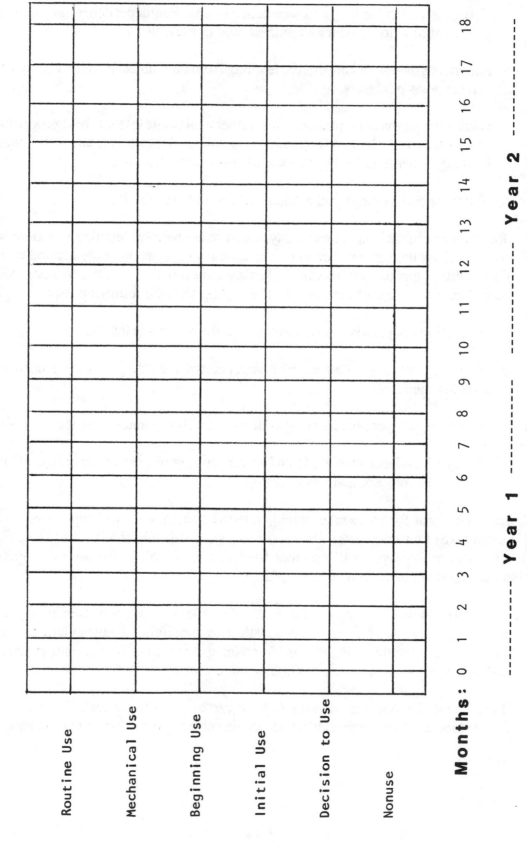

Figure 6.1 Evolutionary Implementation

out a long-range plan and stay with it. Especially persevere with students who have a hard time collaborating with peers.

3. **Seek support from one or more colleagues** and engage in joint sharing of successes, problems, new ideas, and curriculum modification.

4. **Make sure the teacher who has your students the following year understands what cooperative learning is and how good your students are in collaborating.**

5. **Plan carefully for the start of each school year so that cooperative learning is emphasized right away.**

Personalizing The Learning Environment

Learning is a personal experience. The more frequently cooperative learning is used, the more personalized the learning will be. Haines and McKeachie (1967) demonstrated that students in classes stressing competition for grades showed more tension, self-doubt, and anxiety than did students working in cooperative learning groups. There are a number of ways that the learning environment may be personalized.

First, monitor cooperative groups closely. Circulate among the groups, systematically observe, and often stop to (a) join in and interact with group members or (b) intervene within a group . The more attentive teachers are to individual students the more effective and personal the teaching. It is easier to make a direct comment to a student in a small group than in a whole- class setting.

Second, work to establish classroom norms that promote individuality, creativity, and sensitivity to students' needs. All students need to feel respected, free, and motivated to make the maximum contributions of what they are capable.

Third, demonstrate a willingness to learn from students. Every teacher- student interaction carries potential for learning for both the teacher and students. When faculty accept and learn from students' contributions, the learning experience becomes more personal for the students.

Fourth, present students with a realistic assessment of what they have learned and with high expectations as to what they can learn if they make the effort. Faculty offer students a tension between present and future, actuality and possibility. In a detailed and practical study of skills possessed by effective teachers of adults, Schneider, Klemp, and

Kastendiek (1981) concluded that effective teachers (a) believe that average students are competent, (b) identify and affirm students' capabilities, (c) express the view that students are capable of change, and (d) accept student suggestions for changes in learning plans when the changes are consistent with the students' learning objectives. Daloz (1987) found that effective teachers were described by students as "giving me confidence in myself," "kept pushing me and telling me I could do it," and "having faith in me even when I did not." Through their expectations of students, faculty can communicate where students are and what they can become without allowing either to eclipse the other.

Fifth, send them out of class feeling happy. John Wooden, the basketball coach at UCLA for many years, wrote out a detailed lesson plan for every one of his practices. At the end of each lesson plan he wrote "Send the players to the showers happy." Similarly, Durward Rushton (a principal in Hattisburg, Mississippi) states that each student should feel personally **secure**, have a sense of **belonging**, and experience some **success** each class session (SBS). Teachers should adopt similar attitudes toward creating a positive atmosphere for each class session. One step to doing so is eliminating put-downs. Being put-down by a teacher is the most common response given to the question "What is your most memorable experience from high school?" (Kohl, personal communication, 1989). Many students are afraid to contribute in class, some for lack of confidence, others because they fear their ideas are not worthy. The simple procedure of saying something positive about every student comment, question, or answer to a question has remarkable power for transforming a classroom.

A simple means for promoting a personalized learning environment is having students (and you) wear name tags to help students learn each other's names. Teachers often comment that for their students, the most important word in the English language is their name. Name tagging is a simple procedure that makes a profound difference in the atmosphere of the classroom. Students immediately "warm-up" to their colleagues and seem to appreciate the opportunity to meet and greet each other. The short time that this activity consumes is more than compensated by the improvement in the learning mood of the students.

On the first day have students complete a name tag. In the center the student (and teacher) places his or her name (actually the way he or she prefers to be addressed) in print large enough to be read 20 feet away. In the corners are placed other information about the student, such as, Birthplace, Favorite place, Hobbies, Favorite artist, Something they're looking forward to, and major or profession. Finally, surrounding their name they are asked to place two or three adjectives that describe them. The students are then given about 10 minutes to meet and learn something about as many other students in the class as possible.

Cooperate And Graduate

The message in many schools where cooperative learning is being implemented is "Succeeding in this class is hard work, difficult, and takes considerable effort. You do not have to do the work alone. Work together, help each other." Our motto is "Helping and sharing are not cheating during learning time." During testing time, of course, it's a different matter. At testing time we want to see what individuals can do. Students typically perform better on individual tests, however, after they have been prepared by their group. Succeeding academically results from group, not individual, efforts.

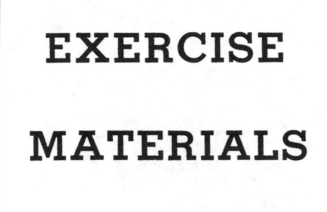

EXERCISE

MATERIALS

THE INTEGRATED USE OF ALL TYPES OF COOPERATIVE LEARNING

Task: Plan a day (week) with cooperative learning being used 100 percent of the time. The objective is to provide on overall gestalt as to how the four different types of cooperative learning and a wide variety of the lesson structures may be used in an integrated way.

Cooperation: Find a partner who teaches the same grade level and subject area as you do. Develop one plan for the two of you, both of you must agree that the plan will work, and both of you must be able to implement the plan.

Individual Accountability: Each person will have to present the plan to a member of another group.

Expected Behaviors: Explaining, listening, synthesizing by all members.

Intergroup Cooperation: Whenever it is helpful, check procedures and plans with other groups.

Note: Now that it has been established that cooperative learning may be used 100 percent of the day, the issue of the supplemental use of competitive and individualistic learning becomes relevant. The next chapter focuses on that issue.

Exercise on Solving Common Problems

1. Form a group of four members.

2. Your task is to read the problem situations and answer the question about each situation.

3. The goal structure is cooperative. This means that the group is to reach consensus on their answers and that all members participate.

᙭ Situation One ᙭

Anthony is a very bright student who resents the slowness of his group. He tends to take over the group's work, does it quickly, than gives it back to the other members to learn while he reads a book. While his group members are learning the material, they are not involved in developing the answers. The group acts negatively when it is time for cooperative groups, and Anthony complains that his group members are stupid.

1. What is the problem?

2. What things, if any, could you do differently to make the group function more effectively?

3. What social skills, if any, do the students need to work on?

4. What intervention would you make with this group?

SITUATION TWO

Refuting is attacking another person's position in an attempt to weaken or ɛ
It is an attempt to cast significant doubt on and/or show the inadequacies of the
so that the person (or interested other people) will be willing to change his or he

There are a number of ways to refute your opponent's position:

1. Challenge the quantity of the supporting evidence.

2. Challenge the quality of the supporting evidence.

3. Challenge the logic of the argument.

4. Challenge the assumptions underlying the position.

5. Challenge the perspective (do they see the whole picture).

Write out a phrase for each approach to refutation. For example, the quantity of evidence may be expressed in the statement, "You have only two facts; that is not enough to be convincing."

Form a pair. For each statement, share your phrase, listen carefully to your partner's phrase, then jointly create a new one that is better than either original one.

SITUATION THREE

Your cooperative groups are working on long-term projects which will end with presentations to the class. You have given them class time to plan and organize. One group is upset because Stella, one of their members, is a chronic absentee. She is continuing to attend school only two or three days a week, and she has not done any of the work the group has asked her to do. Since part of their grade will be based on how well everyone in the group participates, the group is afraid that Stella will bring down their grade. They want Stella out of their group.

1. What is the problem?

2. What things, if any, could you do differently to make this group function more effectively?

3. What social skills, if any, do the students need to work on?

4. What interventions would you make with this group?

INTEGRATED USE OF
COOPERATIVE, COMPETITIVE AND INDIVIDUALISTIC LEARNING

To Choose Or Not To Choose

Teachers have no choice but to choose a goal structure for each lesson they teach. If no overt choice is made, students will choose the goal structure they believe is most appropriate. When students are familiar with, and have had experience learning within, each type of goal structure, they will probably be very good judges as to which goal structure is most desirable for accomplishing specified learning goals. When students do not have past experience in each type of instructional situation, an informed and free choice cannot take place. Students' conception of the alternatives in a situation depend on their past experiences and their perceptions of the situational constraints. If students have rarely experienced a goal structure other than interpersonal competition in school, they will tend to assume competition when left to their own devices. If all organizational pressures within the school are based on the traditional interpersonal competitive goal structure, students will tend to behave competitively whenever they are left "free" to choose. Under such conditions, implementing no goal structure at all or giving students a superficial choice among the three goal structures is to ask students subtly (or not so subtly) to place the traditional interpersonal goal structure on themselves.

The **essential issues** are when each goal structure may be appropriately used, how to decide which goal structure to use, how frequently each goal structure should be used, the basic partnership between cooperative and individualistic learning, and how all three goal structures may be used in an integrated way.

Appropriately Using Interdependence

The three goal structures are not in competition with each other. Survival of the fittest does not apply when it comes to structuring learning situations appropriately. Each goal structure has its place. In the ideal classroom all three are used. This does not mean, however, that they will all be used equally. The basic foundation of instruction, the underlying context on which all instruction rests, is cooperation. Unless used within a context of cooperation, competitive and individualistic instruction lose much of their effectiveness.

Cooperation exists within the classroom on both a macro- and a micro-level. On a macro-level, cooperation pervades the social system of the classroom. Within instructional situations there are two complementary roles, teacher and student. Teachers and students engage in specified role-related behaviors and conform to organizational norms and values concerning appropriate behavior. The teacher is a person who teaches students; students are persons who learn with the aid of a teacher. The roles are interrelated; they reinforce each other, and are interdependent. One cannot function or exist without the other. The individuals within both the teacher and student roles must learn the role expectations of other members of the organization, accept them, and reliably fulfill them. Examples of teacher role requirements are putting students into contact with the subject matter, specifying learning goals, creating specific instructional conditions, disciplining students, and evaluating students. Examples of student role requirements are to be attentive, follow directions, exert effort to achieve assigned learning goals, arrive on time, and complete assignments. An example of a norm is that no physical violence takes place within the classroom, and an example of a value is that education is beneficial and worthwhile. Successful completion of the school's objectives depends on the fulfillment of the organizational role requirements and adherence to the norms and values of the school.

Certainly, aggressiveness exists in nature, but there is also a healthy nonruthless competition, and there exist very strong drives toward social and cooperative behavior. These forces do not operate independently but together, as a whole, and the evidence strongly indicates that, in the social and biological development of all living creatures, of all these drives, the drive to cooperation is the most dominant, and biologically the most important. . . . It is probable that man owes more to the operation of this principle than to any other in his own biological and social evolution.

When cooperation on this macro-level breaks down, competitive and individualistic learning activities become completely ineffectual. If students refuse to be "role-responsible," for example, no effective instruction can take place regardless of how interdependence among students is structured. It should also be noted that in order for competition to occur there must be cooperation on rules, procedures, time, place, and criteria for determining the winner. Without this underlying collaborative system, no competition can take place. Skills and information learned individualistically, furthermore, must at some time be contributed to a collaborative effort. No skill is learned without being enacted within a social system such as a family or business. Nothing is produced without being part of a larger economic system. What is learned alone today is enacted in collaborative relationships tomorrow or else it has no meaning or purpose.

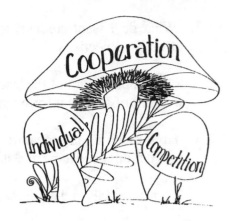

On the micro-level, cooperation is one of the three goal structures used to structure interdependence among students. Cooperative learning provides a context for the other two goal structures. Competition, as noted above, cannot exist if there is no underlying cooperation concerning rules and procedures. Most competitions have referees, umpires, judges, and teachers present to ensure that the basic cooperation overrules and procedures do not break down. Individualistic activities can be effectively used as part of division of labor in which students master certain knowledge and skills that will later be used in cooperative activities. Within instructional situations, cooperative learning must dominate. It has the most widespread and powerful effects on instructional outcomes, it is the most complex to implement effectively of the three goal structures, and it should be the one most frequently used. Competitive and individualistic learning should be used to supplement and enrich the basic cooperation among students. Finally, it is apparent that when the three goal structures are used appropriately and in an integrated way, the combination is far more powerful than any one of them employed separately.

The appropriate use of the three goal structures will improve your teaching effectiveness and make your life as a teacher considerably more productive, satisfying, and enjoyable. It is the inappropriate use of a goal structure that causes problems for students (and subsequently for the teacher). But when should you use each goal structure?

Deciding on a Goal Structure

A teacher may wish to teach certain lessons or units cooperatively and others competitively or individualistically. Matching the goal structure and the learning activity is one of the most important steps in structuring your classroom. It needs to be done carefully. When instruction is not going well, the first issue to address is whether the goal structure is appropriate. The following questions may help in determining the appropriateness of the goal structure you are using:

1. What do I want students to obtain from the lesson? What are the cognitive and affective objectives?

2. What is the nature of the instructional task? Is it conceptual learning, drill-review, or mastery of simple information or skills?

3. How much assistance and guidance do students need to complete the task? Will instructions need to be repeated several times or is the task simple and straightforward?

4. What materials and equipment are required by the lesson and how available are they?

5. What type of instructional climate and interaction among students is necessary to facilitate the accomplishment of the learning objectives?

Frequency of Use of Each Goal Structure

As a teacher, you will use all three goal structures over a period of time. However, the types of learning goals and the type of classroom climate you prefer will determine the frequency with which you use each one. Most teachers spend a large proportion of this time in promoting higher-level conceptual reasoning and problem-solving skills that give maximal thinking experience to the students, tasks that are best served by a cooperative goal structure. To a lesser extent, there are important and specific skills and knowledge that may be mastered by studying under an individualistic goal structure. Tasks calling for drill or review of facts may be learned under a competitive goal structure. Ideally, a cooperative goal structure may be used 60 to 70 percent of the time; an individualistic goal structure, 20 percent of the time; and a competitive goal structure, 10 to 20 percent of the time. With students now perceiving school as predominantly competitive, and with cooperation being used systematically in very few classrooms, your task in training students to function primarily within a cooperative goal structure and to shift quickly from one goal structure to another will not be an easy one at first.

Appropriate Use Of Competitive Learning

Interdependence

Competitive learning exists when students' goal attainments are negatively correlated; when one student obtains his or her goal, all other students with whom he or she are competitively linked fail to obtain their goals (Deutsch, 1949a). While competing students should view success as being relatively unimportant so that they can accept either winning or losing. The focus should be on learning rather than winning. It should always be more fun to win than to not win, but in school winning is not an end in itself. Students should focus first on learning, second on having fun, and lastly on winning.

Appropriate Tasks

Competitively structured learning activities can supplement cooperation through fun drill-reviews in which a change of pace and a release of energy is desirable. Competition should be used when well-learned material needs to be reviewed. The emphasis should be placed on having a fun drill-review rather than on winning. That the situation described at the begining of this chapter is appropriately structured is evidenced in the enjoyment of the students as they compete with one another in a review of something they have already practiced, in the students' awareness that winning is secondary to having fun, and in the fact that all students believe they have a good chance of winning.

Relation To Cooperative Learning

Competition is most appropriate when it is viewed not as a crucial test, but as an interlude, a fun change of pace, as students collaborate to complete an assignment or master a body of knowledge. Periodically, to have a low-key test of the success of cooperative learning groups in ensuring that all members have mastered the material being studied, a competition may be structured by the teacher. If students can compete for fun and enjoyment, win or lose, competitive drills are an effective change of pace in the classroom.

Teacher-Student Interaction

The teacher is perceived to be the major source of assistance, feedback, reinforcement, and support. The teacher needs to be available for questions and clarifications of the rules, to referee disputes, to judge the correctness of answers, and to reward the winners. Common teacher statements are, *Who has the most so far? What do you need to do to win next time?*

Student-Materials Interaction

In order to ensure that all students have appropriate access to the curriculum materials, a set of materials needs to be provided for each triad or for each student. Clear and specific rules, procedures, and answers are an absolute necessity. Ambiguity ruins competition, as too much time is spent worrying about what is fair and unfair, what the procedures actually are, and whether or not the answers are correct.

Student-Student Interaction

Interaction among students is strictly controlled through the rules of the competition. Although the students are encouraged to share their progress, they are not expected to share ideas or solutions. Students need to be able to observe each other's progress and some talking may be necessary. In general, however, there is little discussion allowed except where it deals with challenging the correctness of each other's answers. Within intergroup competition students are usually grouped in homogeneous triads to ensure that each student has an equal chance of winning.

All students need to be able to monitor the progress of their competitors during the competition, so that they know whether they are ahead or behind. In competition, the only way students can judge their progress is by comparing themselves with their competitors. In athletic events there is a scoreboard to keep players posted. Successful classroom competition requires the same sort of ongoing feedback.

Competition should be used only when it is relatively unimportant whether one wins or loses. Winning cannot be a life or death matter if competition is to be enjoyed. High levels of anxiety appear when winning becomes too important, along with all the destructive consequences of competition noted by the research. Healthy competition has a relatively low level of anxiousness and focuses on reviewing previously learned material in a fun way.

All students should perceive themselves as having a reasonable chance of winning. Motivation to achieve is based on the perceived likelihood of being able to achieve a challenging goal. If students believe they have little chance of winning, they will not be motivated to learn. By arranging a class into small clusters of evenly matched students, teachers can provide a challenging and realistic competiton among students and maximize the number of winners in the class at the same time.

Student Role Expectations

The basic role expectations for students within competitive learning situations are to expect to review previously learned material, to have an equal chance of winning, to enjoy the activity (win or lose), to monitor the progress of competitors, and to compare their abilities, skills, or knowledge with those of similar peers. In a competitive learning situation, students are to (1) interact in planned and informal ways to keep track of each other's progress, (2) look less to the teacher for judgment of progress and more to comparison with other students' progress, (3) have a set of materials either individually or in common with a triad of students, according to the demands of the situation, (4) follow the rules (i.e., play fair), (5) have fun, and (6) be good winners and losers. Fair play is embodied in modesty in victory, in graciousness in defeat, and in that generosity of outlook that creates warm and lasting human relationships.

Evaluation System

Within competitive learning situations a norm-referenced evaluation system is used, such as grading on the normal curve and having students ranked from best to worst.

Intergroup Vs. Interpersonal Competition

There are two ways in which competition may be used for instructional purposes. Individuals can compete against each other to see who has learned the assigned material the best or cooperative learning groups can compete to see which group has best mastered the assigned material. While interpersonal competition has many instructional drawbacks, intergroup competition can be used effectively under certain conditions.

Intergroup competition requires intragroup cooperation and competition between groups. It is important for the teacher to ensure that the intergroup competition does not become so

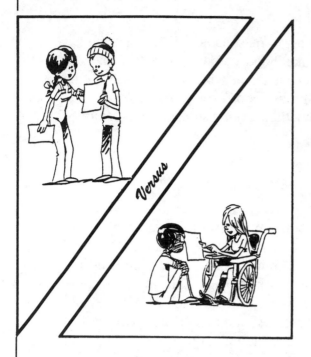

strong that it outweighs the intragroup cooperation. Once competition becomes too serious, all the destructive outcomes of competition will appear, and students resort to bickering, scapegoating, and negative interpersonal relationships. As the saying goes, "It's not whether you win or lose, it's how you play the game." The corollary in this situation would be, "It's not how fiercely you compete with the other groups, it's how comfortably you cooperate with your teammates."

What you are losing when you use intergroup competition is the flow of ideas and materials between groups and the overall class possbility of a division of labor. What you gain is a fun change of pace to provide some energy and variety within the classroom.

Establishing A Competitive Structure

The essence of a competitive goal structure is to give students individual goals and use a norm-referenced evaluation system in rewarding them. Assigning the individual goal of being the best speller in the class, giving a test, ranking students from best to worst on spelling, and distributing rewards accordingly would be an example. The teacher's role in using competition appropriately is, however, somewhat more complicated. A pioneering system for using intergroup competition for instructional purposes, **Teams-Games-Tournaments**, was developed by David DeVries and Keith Edwards (DeVries, Slavin, Fennessey, Edwards, & Lombardo, 1980). Their system is encorporated into the following definition of the teacher's role in establishing a competitive structure.

Objectives

Specifying instructional objectives. The academic objective needs to be specified at the correct level for each student and matched to the right level of instruction according to a conceptual or task analysis. Often the objective will be to review previously learned material.

Decisions

Assigning students to heterogeneous teams. Students are assigned to cooperative learning groups so that each group is a cross-section of the class in academic performance and various other individual characteristics such as sex and ethnic background. The teams should be balanced so that the average academic performance level of all the groups are about equal. The purpose of the team is to prepare its members to do well in the academic tournaments. The teams compete with each other to be the best group in the class. Teams are given time to study together so that peer tutoring and encouragement can take place, and team membership is held stable for a period of time so that group cohesion and commitment can be built up. In the tournament team grades are assigned on a competitive basis so that the teams are ranked from best to worst with the top one or two teams being declared the winners. A tournament takes place once or twice a week using teacher-designed games.

Planning the Tournament. The tournament is conducted as follows:

a. Students are assigned to three-person tournament tables so that each student is placed in competition with two other students, each of whom represents a different cooperative learning group. In order to create equitable competition each table consists of students of comparable academic achievement (as determined by prior performance).

b. During the tournament the students play an instructional game for 30 to 50 minutes. At the end of a tournament session the students at each table compare their scores to determine the top scorer, the middle scorer, and the low scorer. The game scores are converted into points, with a fixed number of points assigned to the top scorer (6 points), middle scorer (4 points), and the low scorer (2 points) at each table.

c. A team score is derived by adding the scores of all the individual members. Team scores are then ranked and listed. A newsletter can be used to announce the team standings. The newsletter can be distributed the day following the tournament. Included in the newletter would be the latest team standings for the grading period, the ranking of the teams on the previous day's tournament, and some commentary about the winners at each table and the performance of the members of the winning team.

Assigning students to competitive triads. A class tournament is structured around a game in which each student competes as a respresentative of his or her team with students of equal aptitude from other teams. When students compete, they should be placed in homogeneous groups based on ability or previous achievement. Groups of three maxmize the number of winners in the class (pairs tend to make the competition too personal). Rank the students in each cooperative learning group from highest to lowest on the basis of their previous achievement. Given that only one student from a group can be in a competitive triad, assign the three highest achieving students in the class to Table 1, the next three to Table 2, and so on until the three lowest achieving students in the class are in the bottom table. This creates equal competition within each triad and makes it possible for students of all achievement levels to contribute maximally to their team scores if they do their best. Figure 1 illustrates the relationship between the cooperative learning groups and the competitive triads.

Preparing instructional materials. Make a game sheet consisting of about 30 items, a game answer sheet, and a copy of the rules. Make a set of cards numbered from 1 to 30. On each card write one question from the game sheet. The questions can be either recognition or recall questions.

Arrange the classroom. The room should be arranged so that the triads are separated from each other and students within each triad sit close to each other.

Explaining The Task And Goal Structure

Explaining the Academic Task. The task may be from any subject area. It has to be explained so that the procedures, rules, criteria for winning, and the definition of what is and is not a correct answer are clearly understood by all students. Competition bogs down if there are disputes or misunderstandings over such matters.

Structuring Negative Goal Interdependence. Explain to students that their goal is to answer more questions correctly than the other two members of the triad in order to maximize the number of points they take back to their cooperative learning group so that their group can win by having more overall points than any other group in the class.

Explaining Criteria for Success. Within each triad, the student who answers the most questions correctly receives 6 points, the second place student receives 4 points, and the last place student receives 2 points to take back to his or her cooperative learning group. In a cooperative learning group of four members the group could have between 24 and 8 points total. The group that has the most points wins.

Specifying Desired Behaviors. Each student should try to win in their triad. They are to work alone answering each of their questions without consultation with other group members. If they need help or clarification they are to ask the teacher. They should keep track of where they stand in the competition and make adjustments in their strategy accordingly. In addition, they should:

a. Seek fun and enjoyment.

b. Win with humility and pleasure.

c. Lose with dignity.

d. Recognize and deal with inappropriate anxiety.

e. Monitor progress of competitors.

f. Form realistic perceptions of own skills.

Students need to know what behaviors are appropriate and desirable within a competitive learning situation.

Monitoring And Intervening

Monitoring Students' Behavior. After explaining the rules, procedures, and expected behaviors to students, teachers must observe to see that they are being followed. Much of the teacher's time should be spent in observing students in order to see what problems they are having in completing the assignment and in working competitively. The teacher should move throughout the room, checking triads for understanding, answering questions, settling disputes over answers, and checking for the expected student behaviors. Some systematic and anecdotal record keeping will enhance the processing at the end of the lesson and is easily done by tallying on an observation sheet the number of times teachers see targeted desired behaviors and jotting down specific instances of appropriate behavior.

Providing Task Assistance. In monitoring the triads, teachers will wish to clarify instructions, review important procedures and rules, and teach task skills as necessary. The teacher is the major resource for student learning, and is also the judge and jury in settling disputes over which answer is correct. The major focus of the competitive triads should be on reviewing the previously learned material and not arguing over answers. The teacher's task assistance should focus attention on the learning and minimize the importance of winning. Make sure that rules are followed, no one cheats, and disputes are settled quickly.

Intervening to Teach Competitive Skills. Students will have experience in competing but will often lack the skills to compete appropriately. Students may take the competition too seriously or feel so anxious that they do not enjoy it. Intervene to encourage the fun of competing or to deemphasize the importance of winning when it seems necessary. It is important that students learn to compete appropriately for fun and enjoyment. It strengthens cooperative learning when students can review previously learned material in a game-like situation.

Provide Closure to the Lesson. At the end of the lesson, students should have adequately reviewed previously learned material so that they are able to easily contribute their learnings to future collaborative efforts.

Evaluation and Reinforcement

Evaluating and Reinforcing the Quality and Quantity of Students' Learning. Students' learning needs to be evaluated by a norm-referenced procedure. Having a class newsletter to announce the winners of each triad and the group that wins will add further interest to the competition.

Processing the competition. It is important that competitions be discussed afterwards to allow students to evaluate their skills, discuss their feelings, and realize how to behave even more appropriately next time. Processing may be done individually with students completing a questionnaire on their reactions and behavior, may be done in their competitive triads or cooperative learning groups, or may be done as a whole class. A combination of individual and small group processing is usually effective. During their monitoring, teachers may observe students engaging in inappropriate actions and plan to provide personal feedback later. Most feedback, however, should be positive. An open and frank discussion of the competition can defuse hurt feelings and ensure increased constructiveness of future competitions.

● Teacher Role Checklist For Competitive Learning ●

1. What are the desired outcomes for the drill activity?

☐ a.

☐ b.

☐ c.

2. Is the classroom arranged so that students:

☐ *Are clustered together, working on their own, but able to monitor the progress of their competitors?*

☐ *Have access to each other only (a) if it is required by the nature of the competition or (2) to know whether they are ahead or behind the others?*

☐ *Have an individual set of self-contained materials?*

3. Have you effectively communicated to students that:

☐ *The instructional goal is an individual goal (to win as many points as possible for one's team)?*

☐ *Each student will be rewarded on the basis of how her work compares to the work of the other students in the triad?*

4. Have you effectively communicated the expected patterns of student-student interaction? Do students know that they should:

☐ *Interact only to check the progress of other students?*

☐ *Work on the assignment alone, trying to do the task better, faster, and more completely than the other students?*

☐ *Ignore comments from other students?*

☐ *Go to the teacher for all help and assistance needed?*

5. Have you effectively communicated the expected pattern of teacher-students interaction? Do students know that the teacher:

☐ *Wants each student to try to do better on the assignment than the other students and will evaluate students' work on the basis of how it compares with the work of other students?*

☐ *Will interact with each triad of students to clarify rules and the task without giving one student more help than another, and often making clarifications to the entire class?*

☐ *Will praise and support students working alone and trying to do better, faster, and more work than any other student in the triad or classroom?*

Competitive Skills

Competition, when it is appropriate, is fun and adds spice to classroom life. Because competition involves much less interaction among students and less coordination of behavior than collaboration, there are fewer skills essential to competing than to cooperating.

The first competitive skill is playing fair. This means students must understand and obey the rules. Rules should be clarified before the competition begins so that students know what is and is not fair. In some competitions, for example, students are allowed to enhance their chances of winning by obstructing their opponents' progress (e.g., "sending" another player's ball away from the wicket in croquet), while in other competitions such disruption of opponents' progress would be declared unfair (e.g., cutting in too soon in a track race). If the rules are clear in the beginning students' actions will usually be appropriate. If any student feels it is necessary to break the rules, the situation is probably inappropriate for competition (e.g., the student perceives that the goal is too important and the situation is too serious).

A second skill is being a good winner and a good loser. This means winning with humility, pleasure, and modesty, and being gracious when you lose. Any student should be able to win or lose gracefully and with dignity. **The third skill is enjoying the competition, win or lose.** The purpose of competition is to have an enjoyable experience drilling on previously learned material. **The fourth skill is monitoring the progress of competitors**

to know how one stands in the competition. Since winning is the goal of competition, the only way to know where one stands is to know where the others are. Teachers can promote the development and use of monitoring skills by:

1. Making clear that monitoring is part of the competition and that students can watch each other's progress.

2. Setting up several methods of monitoring including charting students' progress on the board, checking periodically to bring everyone up to date, and modifying the triads in which students compete.

Finally, **it is important for students to not overgeneralize the results of the competition.** Winning does not make a student a more worthwhile person and losing does not make a student less worthwhile. Being defeated in a spelling contest does not make a student a "loser." The results of any one competition provide very limited information about a student's personal worth. Clearly separating the results of competitions from one's view of oneself is an important competitive skill.

Summary Of Competition

The major concern with the instructional use of competition is that students bring more to the competition than is intended by the teacher. Students may begin a competition with the attitude that they would "prefer to die" rather than be defeated. The anxiety produced in such students and the students around them is counterproductive. Competitions need to be kept light and fun, emphasizing review or drill, probably in a game format. Students should be homogeneously grouped so that they perceive themselves as having a chance to win, probably in threesomes to maximize the number of winners. The instructions, rules, procedures, and materials need to be clear and specific. The teacher needs to be the major resource for all students and the arbitrator of disputes. The major teacher role is to keep students focussed on learning and not getting sidetracked by arguments or hurt feelings. Processing afterwards is a vital part of teaching students to handle competition appropriately and enjoy it. Students need to learn how to win with enjoyment and lose with dignity. Students can be defeated, but are never "losers."

The importance of spreading an umbrella of cooperation over the class before competition is initiated cannot be overemphasized. Having students work together, get to know each other, cheer for shared successes, and develop collaborative skills, is the best foundation for making competition appropriate. In one of our teacher-training sessions, a coach announced

that he was not excited about cooperation. He preferred competition, believed in it, and liked to stress it with his teams. After several cooperative experiences we structured a competition involving vocabulary words, and the coach lost badly. After quiet reflection, he concluded, "I learned something about myself today. I have always hated to lose, but I found that I do not mind losing nearly as much when I lose to people I like." Building a strong cooperative learning environment may be the best way to provide a setting in which students can learn how to compete appropriately.

Structuring Individualistic Learning

Love many, trust few.
Learn to paddle your own canoe.

Horatio Alger

You have just handed out a four-page programmed booklet on how to use a microscope. You explain, "For some of the things we are going to be doing, each student will need to know how to use a microscope. I will give each of you a microscope and the other things you will need to work through this booklet. Take your time and work carefully until you have mastered the tasks outlined in the booklet. Let me know if you need help with anything." You then see that each student has a microscope and set of materials and will begin to move from student to student to see how they are progressing. The goal structure described in the above learning situation is individualistic. In this chapter the conditions under which individualistic learning can be appropriately used are discussed and the teacher's role in structuring individualistic learning activities is detailed. Finally, the skills students need to function effectively within an individualistic learning situation are given.

Interdependence

Individualistic learning exists when the achievement of one student is unrelated to and independent from the achievement of other students; whether or not a student achieves his or her goal has no bearing on whether other students achieve their goals.

Appropriate Tasks

Individualistic learning is most appropriate when the instructional tasks include the learning of specific facts (such as important historical dates) or the acquisition of simple skills. The directions for completing the learning task need to be clear and specific so that students do not need further clarification on how to proceed and how to evaluate their work. It is important to avoid confusion as to how the students are to proceed and the need for extra help from the teacher. If several students need help or clarification at the same time, work grinds to a halt. Finally, the learning goal must be perceived as important and students should expect to be successful in achieving their learning goals.

Relation To Cooperative Learning

Individualistically structured learning activities can supplement cooperative learning through a division of labor in which each student learns material or skills to be subsequently used in cooperative activities. Learning facts and simple skills to be used in subsequent cooperative learning projects increases the perceived relevance and importance of individualistic tasks. Within individualistic learning situations it is crucial that students perceive the task as relevant and worthwhile. Self- motivation is a key aspect of individualistic efforts. The more important and relevant students perceive the learning goal to be, the more motivated they will be to learn.

Teacher-Student Interaction

Within individualistic learning situations the teacher is the major source of assistance, feedback, reinforcement, and support. Students should expect periodic visits from the teacher and a great deal of teacher time may be needed to monitor and assist the students.

Student-Materials Interaction

Each student needs a complete set of all necessary materials to complete the work individually. Each student has to be a separate, self-contained learner. Programmed materials, task cards, and demonstrations are among the techniques that can be used to facilitate the task. Students should sit at separate desks or carrels with as much space as possible between them..

Student-Student Interaction

No interaction should occur among students. Students should work on their own without paying attention to or interacting with classmates. Each student should have his or her own space and should be separated from other students. Since each student is working on his or her task at his or her own pace, student-student interaction is intrusive and not helpful.

Student Role Expectations

Students expect to be left alone by their classmates in order to complete the assigned task, to work at their own pace in their own space, to take responsibility for completing the task, to take a major part in evaluating their own progress and the quality of their efforts, to be successful in achieving the learning goal, and to perceive the learning goal to be important.

Evaluation System

Evaluation should be conducted on a criteria-referenced basis. Students should work on their own towards a criteria that is set so that every student could conceivably be successful. There is an "A" for everyone if each student earns it individually.

Establishing An Individualistic Structure

The essence of an individualistic goal structure is giving students individual goals and using a criteria-referenced evaluation system to assign rewards. In a ninth-grade English class, the students have been reading a cluster of novels centering on the building of the railroad in western United States. The teacher has taught a unit on character analysis covering the need to find out about the appearance, personality, and perspective of major characters in a story. The teacher now explains to the class that the names of several people from the novels are in a box and each student will draw a name. The assignment is for students to spend the next few days finding out as much as possible about their characters by reading appropriate passages in the novels and by using any other resources they can find. At the end of the week, there will be a number of discussions about the building of the railroad, and each student will be expected to introduce him- or herself and present the point-of-view of the character he or she drew from the box. Until the discussion each student is to work on his or her own, gathering the necessary information on his or her person; if the student needs help, the student is to come to the teacher so as not to intrude on the work

of classmates. The teacher will work with each student through the next few days to see that each has all the materials needed and has mastered the perspective of the character he or she has drawn, so that all can each contribute to the discussions. The specific procedures for teachers to structure such an individualistic learning situation are given below.

Objectives

Specifying instructional objectives. The academic objective needs to be specified at the correct level for each student and matched to the right level of instruction according to a conceptual or task analysis. Often the objective will be to learn specific information or a simple skill to be subsequently used in a cooperative learning situation. Learning the bones and muscles of the arm and shoulder in order to teach it to classmates who are studying other parts of the body, learning the meaning of vocabulary words in order to compose a group story with more understanding, and gathering information for a section of a group report, are examples.

Decisions

Arranging the Classroom. This means providing adequate space for each student so that he or she can work without being interrupted by others. Examples of isolating students from looking at and being disrupted by classmates include using the perimeter of the classroom by having students face the wall, having students sit back-to-back, and staggering rows of seats.

Planning the Instructional Materials to Promote Independence. Structuring the materials to be used in the lesson is especially important for individualistic learning. Each student needs a set of self-contained materials. And usually, the materials need to contain a procedure for students to evaluate their own work. The programmed instruction format is often useful. The materials are the primary resource for learning in the individualistic situation.

Explaining the Task and Goal Structure

Explaining the Academic Task. The academic task needs to be explained in a way that all students are clear about what they are supposed to do, realize that they have all the materials they need, feel comfortable that they can do the ask, and realize why they are doing the task. When assigning the academic task teachers will:

1. Set the task so that students are clear about the assignment. Instructions that are clear and specific are crucial in warding off student frustration.

2. Explain the objectives of the lesson and relate the concepts and information to be studied to students' past experiences and learning to maximize transfer and retention. Explaining the intended outcomes of the lesson increases the likelihood that students will focus on the relevant concepts and information throughout the lesson.

3. Define relevant concepts, explain procedures students should follow, and give examples to help students understand what they are to learn and to do in completing the assignment. To promote positive transfer of learning, point out the critical elements that separate this lesson from past learnings.

4. Ask the class specific questions to check the students' understanding of the assignment. Such questioning ensures that thorough two-way communication exists, that the assignment has been given effectively, and that the students are ready to begin completing it.

Students must perceive the task as relevant and have some idea of how the information and skills they are learning are going to be useful in future learning situations.

Structuring Goal Independence. Communicate to students that they have individual goals and must work individualistically. The basic individualistic goal is for students to work by themselves, at their own pace, to master the material specifically assigned to them, up to the preset critieria of excellence adjusted for their previous performances. Students

should work by themselves without interrupting and interfering with the work of classmates. Students are to ask for assistance from the teacher, not from other students. Students who finish quickly should go beyond the specific assignment and find ways to embellish it.

Structuring Individual Accountability. The purpose of the individualistic goal structure is for students to attend to a specific task and master it on their own. Individual accountability may be structured by the teacher circulating through the room and randomly asking individual students to explain their work.

Explaining Criteria for Success. A criterion for excellence is set to orient students toward the level of mastery required in the lesson. Students need to know specifically what is an acceptable performance on the task that signifies that they have completed the task successfully. Setting a criteria ensures that students are aware that everyone who achieves up to criteria gets an "A" and, therefore, students are not in competition with each other. How well one student does or does not learn the material does not affect the success of other students. Each student is rewarded separately on the basis of his or her own work.

Specifying Desired Behaviors. The word individualistic has different connotations and uses. Teachers need to define individualistic operationally by specifying the behaviors that are appropriate and desirable within the learning situation. These behaviors include:

1. Work alone without interacting with other students.

2. Focus on the task and tune out everything else.

3. Monitor your time and pace yourself accordingly.

4. Check with the teacher for help.

Students need to know what behaviors are appropriate and desirable within an individualistic learning situation.

Monitoring And Intervening

Monitoring Students' Behavior. Much of the teacher's time should be spent in observing students in order to see what problems they are having in completing the assignment and in working individualistically. The teacher should move throughout the room, checking students for understanding, answering questions, and checking for the expected student behaviors. The teacher needs to be active while students are working. While some teachers allow students to come to their desk for help, if that results in a line with students having to wait for assistance, it would be more efficient to have the teacher periodically circulate through the classroom to assess where all students are on their assigned tasks, what students do and do not understand, and what help each student needs to better complete their assignment. This allows teachers to work with students who are not requesting help as well as those who are. The teacher may wish to (a) observe the class as a whole to determine the number of students on task and exerting effort to achieve or (b) observe a few students intensely to obtain the data necessary for individual feedback and

© Johnson, Johnson, & Holubec

constructive suggestions on how to work more efficiently. Systematic observing provides feedback on how well the task is suited for individualistic work and how well students are working individualistically.

Providing Task Assistance. In monitoring individual students as they work, teachers will wish to clarify instructions, review important procedures and strategies for completing the assignment, answer questions, and teach task skills as necessary. After the materials are provided, the teacher is the major resource for student learning. In discussing the concepts and information to be learned, teachers should use the language or terms relevant to the learning. Instead of saying, "Yes, that is right," teachers may wish to say something more specific to the assignment, such as, "Yes, that is the suggested way to solve for the unknown in an equation." The use of specific statements reinforces the desired learning and promotes positive transfer. Typically, considerable task assistance is required within individualistic learning situations.

Intervening to Teach Individualistic Skills. Although it is likely that students have experience in working alone, many students lack some of the basic skills necessary to work well individualistically. While monitoring the class, teachers sometimes find students without the necessary individualistic skills to work effectively on their own. These skills will need to be taught. Some of the basic skills needed for individualistic learning are:

1. Clarifying the need to learn the material and making a personal commitment to learning it.

2. Tuning out extraneous noise and visual distractions and focusing on academic tasks.

3. Monitoring own progress and pacing self through the material. Charts and records are often helpful in evaluating one's progress.

4. Evaluating one's readiness to apply the material or skills being learned.

In an individualistic situation teachers should intervene as quickly as possible. The amount of time in which students are struggling to work more efficiently should be minimized. It is important that students learn to work autonomously on their own in the school setting. It strengthens cooperative learning when students can learn needed simple skills and factual information individualistically or participate successfully in a division of labor.

Providing Closure to the Lesson. At the end of the lesson, students should be able to summarize what they have learned and to understand where they will use it in future lessons. To reinforce student learning, teachers may wish to summarize the major points in the lesson, ask students to recall ideas or give examples, and answer any final questions they may have.

Evaluation and Reinforcement

Evaluating and Reinforcing the Quality and Quantity of Students' Learning. Student learning needs to be evaluated by a criteria-referenced system. Each student will be evaluated independently of other students. The teacher sets a standard as to how many points a student will receive for mastering the assigned material at different levels of proficiency and gives each student the appropriate grade. Having students mark their progress on a chart is often helpful. Personal reinforcement needs to be given to each student. It is the teacher, not classmates, who gives praise for good work.

● Teacher Role Checklist for Individualistic Instruction ●

1. What are the desired outcomes for the activity of learning specific knowledge and noncomplex skills?

   ☐ *a.*

   ☐ *b.*

   ☐ *c.*

2. Is the classroom arranged so that students:

   ☐ *Are isolated at separate desks or by a seating arrangement that separates them as much as possible?*

   ☐ *Are arranged to do their own work without approaching or talking with each other?*

   ☐ *Have individual sets of self-contained materials?*

3. Have you effectively communicated to students that:

☐ *The instructional goal is an individual goal (each student masters the material on his or her own)?*

☐ *Each student will be rewarded on the basis of how his or her work meets a fixed set of standards for quality and quantity?*

4. Have you effectively communicated the expected patterns of student-student interaction? Do students know that they:

☐ *Should not interact with each other?*

☐ *Should work on the assignment alone, trying to ignore completely the other students?*

☐ *Should perceive teacher praise, support, or criticism of other students as irrelevant to their own mastery of the assigned materials?*

☐ *Should go to the teacher for all help and assistance needed?*

5. Have you effectively communicated the expected patterns of teacher-student interaction? Do students know that the teacher:

☐ *Wants them to work by themselves and to master the assigned material without paying attention to other students, and will evaluate them on the basis of how their efforts match a fixed set of standards?*

☐ *Will interact with each student individually, setting up learning contracts, viewing student progress, providing assistance, giving emotional support for effort, and answering questions individually?*

☐ *Will praise and support students for working alone and ignoring other students?*

Individualistic Skills

Since there is no interaction with other students in an individualistic situation, learning under such a goal structure requires the fewest skills. Students need their own materials, enough space to be isolated from others, and a clear understanding of what they are supposed to do. The primary skill necessary is to be able to work on one's own, ignoring other students, and not being distracted or interrupted by what other students are doing.

Besides being able to "tune out" noises, movement, and distractions, students need to clarify why they need to learn the information or skill, make a personal commitment to do so, and assume responsibility for task completion. Each student must be motivated to complete the task and learn the assigned material on his or her own. Completing a task on one's own depends on the amount of importance one assigns to mastering the material. The importance will probably be greatest when the results of the individualistic efforts are to be contributed to a group project in which students collaborate with each other. Having one's classmates depend on one for certain skills or facts increases one's motivation to learn them.

Third, students must be able to monitor their own progress, pace themselves through the material, and evaluate their own progress. Charts and records are often used to help students evaluate themselves. Self-tests also are commonly used. Students must also be able to evaluate their readiness to apply the material or skills being learned.

Finally, students must take a personal pride and satisfaction from successfully completing individualistic assignments. While teachers can provide students with some recognition, support, and reinforcement for individualistic success, the students must learn to give themselves needed "pats on the back" for a job well done.

Summary Of Individualistic Learning

The basic elements of an individualistic goal structure include each student working on their own toward a set criteria, having their own materials and space, perceiving the task as relevant and important, tuning out other students and distractions, and using the teacher as their resource. It is most appropriate to use the individualistic goal structure when the material to be learned is simple and straight-forward and needed for use in the near future. The jigsaw of materials in a cooperative group where each group member is to research a different part of the topic and then help the group synthesize the different aspects of the subject into one group report is an example of where students see a need to learn material

on their own. The primary skill necessary is to be able to work on one's own, ignoring other students (that is, not being distracted or interrupted by what other students are doing).

The teacher's role in an individualistic learning situation is to arrange the room so that students will not be distracted by each other, give students their individual set of materials, explain that students are to work alone and check only with the teacher when they need help, set a clear criteria for success that everyone could conceivably reach, ask students to work on their own (clarifying the relevance of the assignment for themselves, turning out distractions, and monitoring their own progress and pacing), circulating among the students and monitoring their work, intervening to teach skills or help students to refocus on their task, and giving students time to evaluate how well they have learned.

The individualistic goal structure has the following basic components:

1. A critieria-referenced evaluation system is used. Each student works on his or her own towards a criteria that is set so that every student could conceivably be successful. There is an "A" for everyone if each student earns it individually.

2. Each student is given his or her own set of materials.

3. Each student is given his or her own space in which to work.

4. Resources consist primarily of the materials provided and the teacher.

5. Interaction with other students is not appropriate.

Partnership: Cooperative / Individualistic Learning

Probably the most frequent combination of goal structures used in classrooms is the combination of cooperative and individualistic learning situations. Individualistic and cooperative goal structures may be combined in three major ways. The first is task interdependence, in which a division of labor is created. While working on a cooperative task, a group may arrive at a division of labor in which it is necessary for different students to master different skills or different information in order to provide the resources the group needs to achieve its goal successfully. An ideal teaching situation is to assign a cooperative project and provide individual tasks for various aspects of the problems so that different group members can master different skills and information for later integration into the group's product. An example of this approach is to assign the individual tasks of learning how to make a microscope slide, how to gather pondwater, and how to use a microscope; and then to assign the cooperative task of writing a group report on the microscopic life within swampwater.

A second possible combination is through resource interdependence. This procedure is commonly referred to as a "jigsaw." A list of vocabulary words may be given to a cooperative learning group and then subdivided so that each member is responsible for (1) learning their subset of words, and (2) teaching their words to the other group members.

Finally, individualistic and cooperative goal structures may be combined through reward interdependence. Students can study material within a cooperative learning group, take an achievement test individually, and be rewarded on the basis of a performance ratio such as:

1. Students receive 67 percent credit for every problem they solve correctly and 33 percent of the average performance of group members.

2. Students receive their individual score and then are given bonus points on the basis of whether all members of their group achieve above a preset criterion for excellence.

Conversely, students could be assigned to a cooperative group and then study material individually, be tested individually, receive their own score, and receive bonus points on the basis of how well the members of their group do when their scores are compared to a preset criterion for excellence. Because such a procedure does not include the interaction among group members that contributes to learning, this procedure should be used infrequently.

Integrated Use of All Three Goal Structures

All three methods of structuring interdependence among students may be used in an integrated way within classrooms. A typical schedule for doing so is as follows:

1. Assign students to heterogeneous cooperative learning groups.

2. Give each member an individual assignment of learning a subsection of the material the group needs to complete its assignment.

3. Give each group a cooperative assignment of learning all of the material, with each member presenting their subsection to the entire group.

4. Conduct a competitive tournament to drill students on the material they have just learned.

5. Give a cooperative assignment to use the material learned to complete a group project.

6. Give an achievement test which each student takes individually and determine a group score on the basis of the performance of all group members.

An example of such an integrated unit is as follows:

1. Students are assigned to three-person heterogeneous cooperative learning groups.

2. Each group is given the cooperative assignment of ensuring that all group members learn a set of vocabulary words.

3. A list of 18 vocabulary words is given to each group. Each group member is given the individual assignment of mastering 6 of the vocabulary words and planning how to teach the 6 words to the other group members.

4. The group then meets with the cooperative goal of ensuring that all three members master all 18 vocabulary words. Each group member teaches his or her subset of 6 words to the other members.

5. A competitive class tournament is conducted to drill students on the 18 words and to see which group has been the most successful in mastering the vocabulary words.

6. Each group is given the cooperative assignment of writing a story in which 90 percent of the assigned vocabulary words are used appropriately and correctly. The group is to produce one story that contains contributions from all group members.

7. The students are tested individually on the 18 vocabulary words. All members of groups on which each member scored 90 percent or above receive an A on the unit.

When conducting an integrated unit, the important issues to keep in mind are:

1. Emphasize the underlying cooperation. The individualistic and competitive aspects of the unit are supplements to the overall cooperation among students. Individualistic and competitive learning activities should enhance but not detract from cooperative learning.

2. Begin and end with a group meeting. At the initial group meeting the division of labor or "jigsaw" may be agreed on and the goal of success of the group is emphasized. During the final meeting students should discuss how well the group functioned.

3. Remember that students will bring more to the competition than you want them to. They will want to make more of winning the competition than is appropriate. Remember to keep the reward for winning minor. In the students' past, winning has too often been a "life-or-death" matter. You will have to teach students to compete appropriately for fun. You may wish to have a class discussion about how enjoyable the competition was.

4. Vary the number of instructional periods according to the unit. The individualistic assignments could be done as homework. Cooperative tasks could take more than one instructional period.

Table 7.1 Goal Structures

	APPROPRIATE COOPERATION	APPROPRIATE COMPETITION	APPROPRIATE INDIVIDUALIZATION
Interdependence	Positive	Negative	None
Type of Instructional Activity	Any instructional task. The more conceptual and complex the task, the greater the cooperation.	Skill practice, knowledge recall and review, assignment is clear with rules for competing specified.	Simple skill or knowledge acquisition; assignment is clear and behavior specified to avoid confusion and need for extra help.
Perception of Goal Importance	Goal is perceived to be important.	Goal is not perceived to be of large importance to the students, and they can accept either winning or losing.	Goal is perceived as important for each student; students see tasks as worthwhile and relevant, and each student expects eventually to achieve his or her goal.
Teacher-Student Interaction	Teacher monitors and intervenes in learning groups to teach collaborative skills.	Teacher is perceived to be the major source of assistance, feedback, reinforcement, and support. Teacher available for questions and clarification of the rules; teacher referees disputes and judges correctness of answers; rewards the winners.	Teacher is perceived to be the major source of assistance, feedback, reinforcement, and support.
Teacher Statements	"David, can you explain the group's answer to #3?" "Be sure to ask me for help only when you've consulted all group members for help."	"Who has the most so far?" "What do you need to do to win next time?"	"Do not bother David while he is working." "Raise your hand if you need help." "Let me know when you are finished."
Student-Materials Interaction	Materials are arranged according to purpose of lesson.	Set of materials for each triad or for each student.	Complete set of materials and instructions for each student. Rules, procedures, answers are clear. Adequate space for each student.
Student-Student Interaction	Prolonged and intense interaction among students, helping and sharing, oral rehearsal of material being studied, peer tutoring, and general support and encouragement.	Observing other students in one's triad. Some talking among students. Students grouped in homogeneous triads to ensure equal chance of winning.	None; students work on their own with little or no interaction with classmates.
Student Expectations	Group to be successful. All members to contribute to success. Positive interaction among group members. All members master the assigned material.	Review previously learned material. Have an equal chance of winning. Enjoy the activity, win or lose. Monitor the progress of competitors. Follow the rules. Be a good winner and loser.	Each student expects to be left alone by other students; to work at one's own pace; to take a major part of the responsibility for completing the task; to take a major part in evaluating own progress and quality of efforts toward learning.
Room Arrangement	Small groups.	Students placed in triads or small clusters.	Separate desks or carrels with as much space between students as can be provided.
Evaluation Procedures	Criterion-referenced.	Norm-referenced.	Criterion-referenced.

7:30

Taken from: Learning Together and Alone: Cooperative, Competitive and Individualistic Learning (3rd ed.) by D. W. Johnson and R. T. Johnson. Englewood Cliffs, NJ: Prentice-Hall, 1991.

EXERCISE

MATERIALS

© Johnson, Johnson, & Holubec

INK

∽ Integrated Lesson: Writing A Story Cooperatively ∽

Purposes:

1. Present model of the integrated use of all three goal structures.

2. Demonstrate the appropriate use of each goal structure.

3. Experience the integrated use of all three goal structures.

4. Highlight student skills needed in each goal structure.

Part 1: Learning Words

Tasks: Learn assigned words to a recall level and plan how to teach the words to the other members of your group so they will never forget them for as long as they live.

Individualistic: Learn words by oneself at one's own pace and in one's own place.

Evaluation: 100 percent mastery is considered excellent.

Expectations: Do not talk to classmates. Ignore distractions.

Part 2: Teaching Words

Tasks: Teach your words to the other group members and learn their words so you will never forget them as long as you live.

Cooperative: Master all words to a recall level and ensure that other group members do likewise.

Evaluation: 95 percent mastery to recall level by all members is considered excellent.

Individual Accountability: All group members have to score 95 percent correct on vocabulary test.

Expecations: All members will clarify definitions, encourage others to learn, and praise others' teaching.

Part 3: Competitive Tournament

Tasks: Review words in game format, have fun, increase readiness to use words properly in story.

Competitive: Accurately define more words than anyone else in your triad.

Evaluation: Story-writing group with the most points wins.

> First Place = 6 points
> Second Place = 4 points
> Third Place = 2 points
> Two-way tie for first place = 5 points each
> Three-way tie for first place = 4 points each
> Two-way tie for second place = 3 points each

Expected Behaviors: Obey rules, challenge appropriately.

Part 4: Writing The Story

Task: Write a story using 95 percent of the assigned vocabulary words and at least three new words created from the prefixes, suffixes, and root words assigned.

Cooperative: One story from the group; members sign to indicate they have contributed and are proud of the story.

Individual Accountability: One member will be randomly selected to read the group's story and explain it.

Evaluation: To be excellent the story has to include 95 percent of the assigned words used, 3 new words created, has planned plot and reasonable story-line flow (beginning / plot development / ending), entertaining to listen to, and no basic grammatical or punctuation errors.

Expectations: Everyone participates, contributes, invents at least one new word, encourages and supports each other's participates and efforts to contribute.

Part 5: Reviewing Theory By Jigsawing Chapter

1. **Teach And Learn Traids**: Form heterogeneous groups of three. Number off from 1 to 3. Identify another triad near you to form pairs with. Each member is assigned one-third of the chapter to (a) become an expert on and (b) prepare to teach to the other two members of the group. The sections are:

   a. Section 1: 7:1 - 7:4, 7:26 - 7:29

   b. Section 2: 7:5 - 7:16

   c. Section 3: 7:16 - 7:26

2. **Preparation Pairs**: Join with the person who has the same section as you do from a nearby triad to form a preparation pair. Read and learn the material in your section. Plan how to teach it to the other triad members.

3. **Practice Pairs**: Meet with another person who has the same section you do. Practice presenting your section. Share ideas about how to best teach the section. Take the best ideas from both. Encorporate the good ideas of the other person into your presentation.

4. **Teach And Learn Triads**: Each member teaches his or her section to the other two members and learns the sections taught by the other triad members.

Part 6: Whole Class Discussion

The instructor will lead a discussion on the integrated use of all three goal structures.

Part 7: Planning An Integrated Lesson

Based on what you have learned from this chapter, plan a lesson that integrates all the three goal structures to teach in your classroom.

Integrated Lesson Plan

Instructional unit:

1. Cooperative tasks:

   a.

   b.

   c.

2. Individualistic task:

3. Competitive task:

Learning Objectives

   1.

   2.

   3.

Sequence

1. **Cooperative:** Students affirm joint goals and how they will achieve them.

2. **Individualistic:** Students work alone to prepare their part of the group's work.

3. **Cooperative:** Students share their work and ensure that all members have mastered the assigned material.

4. **Competitive:** Students compete with members of other groups to determine which group learned the material the best.

5. **Cooperative:** Students complete culminating assignment together.

Cooperative Lesson Plan

Learning Objectives

1.

2.

3.

Make Decisions

1. Group size:

2. Assign to heterogeneous groups by:

3. Arrange the classroom as:

4. Prepare instructional materials of:

5. Assign roles of:

Tell Your Students, In Language They Understand

1. Academic tasks:

2. Positive interdependence:

3. Individual accountability:

4. Criteria for success:

5. Desired behaviors:

Monitor And Process

1. Monitor for:

2. Provide task assistance when:

3. Intervene to teach skills when:

4. Recognize appropriate learning and behaviors by:

5. Observer(s) will be:

6. Observation form includes:

7. Close lesson by:

8. Evaluate student learning by:

9. Process by:

Individualistic Lesson Plan

Learning Outcomes

1.

2.

Make Decisions

1. Arrange the classroom as:

2. Prepare instructional materials of:

Tell Your Students, In Language They Understand

1. Academic task:

2. No interdependence:

3. Criteria for success:

4. Desired behaviors:

Monitor And Process

1. Monitor for:

2. Provide task assistance when:

3. Reinforce appropriate learning and behavior by:

4. Close lesson by:

5. Evaluate student learning by:

◀ Competitive Lesson Plan ▶

Learning Objectives

1.

2.

Make Decisions

1. Assign students to homogeneous triads by:

2. Prepare instructional materials as:

3. Arrange the classroom as:

Tell Your Students, In Language They Understand

1. Academic task:

2. Negative interdependence:

3. Individual accountability:

4. Criteria for success:

5. Desired behaviors:

Monitor And Process

1. Monitor for:

2. Provide task assistance when:

3. Intervene to teach competitive skills when:

4. Close lesson by:

5. Evaluate student learning by:

6. Process by:

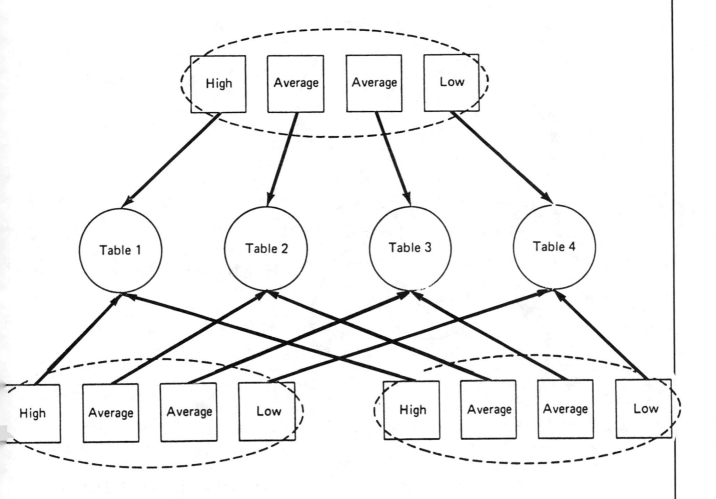

Figure 7.1

Assignment to Tournament Tables

Figure 7.2

Bumping Process

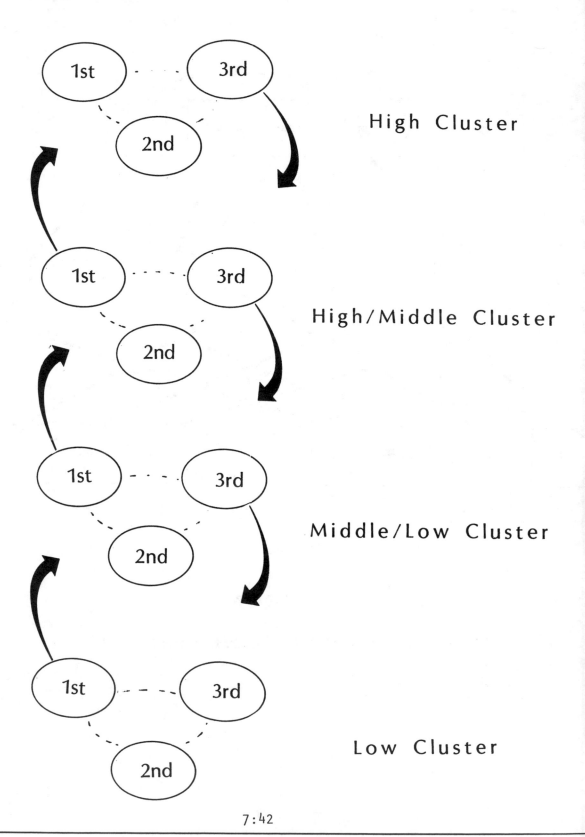

High Cluster

High/Middle Cluster

Middle/Low Cluster

Low Cluster

Rules of Play

A. To start the game shuffle the cards and place them face down on the table. Play is in a clockwise rotation.

B. To play, each player in turn takes the top card from the deck, reads it aloud, and does one of two things:

1. Says he does not know or is not sure of the answer and asks if another player wants to answer. If no one wants to answer, the card is placed on the bottom of the deck. If a player answers, he follows the procedure below.

2. Answers the question immediately and asks if anyone wants to challenge the answer. The player to his right has the first chance to challenge. If he does not wish to challenge, then the player to his right may challenge.

    a. If there is no challenge, another player should check the answer:

        1. If correct, the player keeps the card.

        2. If incorrect, the player must place the card on the bottom of the deck.

    b. If there is a challenge and the challenger decides not to answer, the answer is checked. If the original answer is wrong, the player must place the card on the bottom of the deck.

    c. If there is a challenge and the challenger gives an answer, the answer is checked.

        1. If the challenger is correct, he receives the card.

        2. If the challenger is incorrect, and the original answer is correct, the challenger must give up one of the cards he has already won (if any) and place it on the bottom of the deck.

        3. If both answers are incorrect, the card is placed on the bottom of the deck.

C. The game ends when there are no more cards in the deck. The player who has the most cards is the winner.

∽ Vocabulary Exercise: Lesson 1 ∽

Learn the following words and be ready to teach them to your group. See if you can fill in the blank, then check your answers below.

1. *in* is a prefix meaning **no** or **not**
   somnia is a Latin word meaning **sleep**
   insomnia means that a person _____

2. *lent* at the end of a word often means **inclined to**
   somnolent means _____

3. *facient* is a root meaning **causing to become something**
   somnifacient means hypnotic or _____

4. *amble* or *ambulate* means **to walk**
   somnambulate means _____

5. *pre* is a prefix meaning **before** or **in front**
   preamble, as a verb, literally means _____
   preamble, as a noun, means **introduction** (it comes before)

6. *per* is a prefix meaning **over** or **through**
   perambulate means _____

ANSWERS	**SAMPLE SENTENCES**
1. can not sleep (sleeplessness)	David has *insomnia*.
2. inclines to sleep (sleepy)	Roger is often *somnolent*.
3. tending to produce sleep	Is either of the brothers *somnifacient*?
4. to walk in your sleep	Some people *somnambulate*.
5. to walk before or in front	The *preamble* comes before the story.
6. to walk over or through (stroll)	Let's *perambulate* the park.

TEST: When you feel you know the words, cover the exercise and check yourself with this test. Match the word with the definition.

_____ 1. insomnia (ĭn-sŏm´ nē-ə)   a. introduction

_____ 2. somnolent (sŏm´ nə-lənt)   b. sleepy

_____ 3. somnifacient (sŏm´ nə-fā´ shənt)   c. sleeplessness

_____ 4. somnambulate (sŏm-năm´ byə-lāt)   d. to stroll

_____ 5. preamble (prē´ ăm-bəl)   e. to walk in your sleep

_____ 6. perambulate (pə-răm´ byə-lāt)   f. tending to produce sleep

Review if you are uncertain of the answers.

7:44

✍ Vocabulary Exercise: Lesson 2 ✍

Learn the following words and be ready to teach them to your group. See if you can fill in the blank, then check your answers below.

1. *mis* is a prefix meaning **wrong, wrongly, bad,** or **badly**
    nomer is a word part meaning **name**

    misnomer means _____

2. *miso* or *mis* is also a prefix meaning **hates**
    gyn means **woman**
    ist means **a person who**

    misogynist, then, is _____

3. *mis* means **hates**
    anthrope is a root word meaning **mankind**

    a *misanthrope* is a person who _____

4. *phil* means **love** or **like**

    a *philanthrope* is a person who _____

5. *harmonic* means **music** or **harmony**

    philharmonic means _____

6. *circum* is a prefix meaning **round, around,** or **surrounding**
    locution means **speaking** or **talking**

    circumlocution means _____

ANSWERS	**SAMPLE SENTENCES**
1. wrong name	She called him by a *misnomer.*
2. a person who hates women	He is a *misogynist.*
3. hates mankind or people	He is also a *misanthrope.*
4. loves mankind or people	She is a *philanthrope.*
5. loving music	He belongs to a *philharmonic* society.
6. speaking in a roundabout way; talking in circles	The governor used *circumlocution* in his speech.

TEST: When you feel you know the words, cover the exercise and check yourself with this test. Match the word with the definition.

_____   1. misnomer   (mĭs-nō-mər)   a. a person who loves mankind

_____   2. misogynist   (mĭ-sŏj´ ə-nĭst)   b. a person who hates mankind

_____   3. misanthrope   (mĭs´ ən-thrŏp)   c. a person who hates women

_____   4. philanthrope   (fĭ-lăn´ thrə-pē)   d. talking in circles

_____   5. philharmonic   (fĭl-här-mŏn´ ĭk) e. wrong name

_____   6. circumlocution   f. loving music
                (sûr-kəm-lō-kyoo-shən)

✍ Vocabulary Exercise: Lesson 3 ✍

Learn the following words and be ready to teach them to your group. See if you can fill in the blank, then check your answers below.

1. *claustro* means a **small, enclosed place**
   phobia means **fear**

   claustrophobia means _____

2. *agora* means a **big** or **open place**

   agoraphobia means _____

3. *mania* means **madness**
   a *maniac* is a **person with madness**
   pyro means **fire**

   a *pyromaniac* is _____

4. *klepto* means **thief**

   kleptomaniac is a _____

5. *acro* means **high places**

   acrophobia means _____

6. *scholiono* is from a Greek word meaning **school**

   scholionophobia is _____

ANSWERS	SAMPLE SENTENCES
1. fear of small, enclosed places	The boy has *claustrophobia*.
2. fear of big, open places	The girl has *agoraphobia*.
3. a person with a madness for fires	The *pyromaniac* set fire to the building.
4. a person with a madness to steal	The *kleptomaniac* was caught stealing.
5. fear of high places	They both have *acrophobia*.
6. fear of school	Hopefully, very few people suffer from *scholionophobia*.

TEST: When you feel you know the words, cover the exercise and check yourself with this test. Match the word with the definition.

_____ 1. claustrophobia (klôs-trə-fō´ bē-ə)

_____ 2. agoraphobia (ăg-ə-rə-fō´ bē-ə)

_____ 3. acrophobia (ăk-rə-fō´ bē-ə)

_____ 4. pyromaniac (pī-rō-mā´ nē-ăk)

_____ 5. kleptomaniac (klĕp-tə-mā´ nē-ăk)

_____ 6. scholionophobia (skō´ lē-ō-nō-phō´ bē-ə)

a. a person who has a madness for fires
b. a person who has a madness to steal
c. fear of big, open places
d. fear of small, enclosed places
e. fear of high places
f. fear of school

∞ Vocabulary Exercise: Lesson 4 ∞

Learning the following words and be ready to teach them to your group. See if you can fill in the blank, then check your answers below.

1. *mono* is a prefix meaning **one**
    tone means **tone**

    monotone means _____

2. *gamy* is a word part meaning **marriage**

    monogamy means having _____

3. *poly* is a prefix meaning **many**

    polygamy means having _____

4. *gyny* is a word part meaning **women** or **wives**

    polygyny means having _____

5. *bi* is a prefix meaning **two**
    andry is a suffix meaning **husbands**

    biandry means having _____

6. *bigamy* means having _____

ANSWERS	SAMPLE SENTENCES
1. one tone	He spoke in a *monotone*.
2. one marriage	She practices *monogamy*.
3. many marriages	She believes in *polygamy*.
4. many wives	He believes in *polygyny*.
5. two husbands	She believes in *biandry*.
6. two marriages	He practices *bigamy*.

TEST: When you feel you know the words, cover the exercise and check yourself with this test. Match the word with the definition.

_____ 1. monotone (mŏn´ ə-tōn)   a. having one marriage partner

_____ 2. monogamy (mə-nŏg´ ə-mē)   b. having two marriage partners

_____ 3. polygamy (pə-lĭg´ ə-mē)   c. having more than two marriage partners

_____ 4. polygyny (pə-lĭj´ ə-nē)   d. having several wives; having many wives

_____ 5. bigamy (bĭg´ ə-mē)   e. one tone

_____ 6. biandry (bī-an´ drē)   f. having two husbands

CURRICULUM ADAPTATION

Changing lesson plans to include cooperative interaction can be time-consuming at first. Here is a quick lesson plan worksheet which can be used initially to ensure all the critical elements of cooperative learning are incorporated into your lessons. As you use groups more often, this form can be used as a quick self-check.

SUBJECT AREA

I.   DECISIONS

    LESSON: _____

    GROUP SIZE: _____

    ASSIGNMENT TO GROUPS : _____

    MATERIALS: _____

II.   SET THE LESSON

    WHAT IS/ARE:

Academic Task:	Criteria for Success:

*Positive Interdependence:	*Individual Accountability:	*Expected Behaviors:

III.   *MONITORING

    WILL BE DONE BY: Teacher _____   Teacher/Student _____

    FOCUS WILL BE ON: Whole Class _____   Individual Groups _____   Individuals _____

    OBSERVATION SHEET INCLUDES THE BEHAVIORS OF: _____

    _____

    _____

    *PROCESSING/FEEDBACK: _____

    _____

    _____

----
*An essential element of cooperative groups   7:48

What Is Leadership?

What is a leader? What is leadership? Are leaders born, or are they made? Does effective leadership originate in a person or in a set of actions and behaviors? The concepts **leader** and **leadership** have been defined in more different ways than almost any other concept associated with group structure. Curiosity about leaders is not contained to social scientists. A preoccupation with leadership occurs throughout countries with an Anglo-Saxon heritage. The **Oxford English Dictionary** notes the appearance of the word **leader** in the English language as early as 1300. The word **leadership**, however, did not appear until about 1800. When one reads the historical as well as the current literature on leaders and leadership it seems as if there are as many different definitions as there are persons who have attempted to define the concepts. Perhaps an example will help clarify who a leader is and what leadership is.

Before Benjamin Franklin reached thirty years of age he had been chosen public printer for the colony of Pennsylvania, had founded the famous and influential Junto Club, created and published **Poor Richard's Almanac** (the most widely read publication in America), had founded the first circulating library, and had been elected grand master of the Freemasons Lodge of Pennsylvania. The next year he inaugurated the first fire-fighting company in Pennsylvania and was chosen clerk of the Pennsylvania Assembly. He was one of the most successful businessmen in the colonies, but had enough interest in scholarship and research to be the founder (at age thirty-seven) of the American Philosophical Society. He continued to serve in a variety of leadership posts in politics, the army, science, diplomacy, and education (founding the academy that became the University of Pennsylvania). At eighty he led the group enterprise of writing the Constitution of the United States. A biographer noted, "Nobody could approach him without being charmed by his conversation, humor, wisdom, and kindness" (Fay, 1929).

How would you explain Benjamin Franklin's success as a leader? Was it due to his (pick only one):

Completing the Task and Maintaining Good Relationships

1. Inborn, genetic traits?

2. Style of leadership?

3. Ability to influence others?

4. Occupation of positions of authority?

5. Ability to provide appropriate and helpful behaviors in diverse situations?

In selecting one of these alternatives, you have decided on a theory of small group leadership.

Trait Theories Of Leadership

Perhaps Benjamin Franklin was one of the greatest leaders of the 18th-Century because he was genetically superior to his contemporaries. Throughout history many people have believed that leaders are born, not made, and that great leaders are discovered, not developed. Especially in times of great social upheaval and trouble many people have looked for a great leader who has unique, inborn traits. This is the "great-person" theory of leadership. Royalty, members of elite social groups, older siblings, and early maturing children are likely to believe in this approach to leadership.

There are two problems with the trait theory of leadership. First, an unlimited number of leadership traits may be identified. Second, different traits may be needed under different conditions. Third, "great" leaders are identified after the fact, but who will become a "great" leader cannot be predicted ahead of time.

Leadership Styles

Perhaps Benjamin Franklin became a leader through his style of relating to others. Even casual observation of leaders in action reveals marked differences in their styles of leadership. Some leaders seem autocratic: They dictate orders and determine all policy without involving group members in decision making. Some leaders seem democratic: They set policies through group discussion and decision, encouraging and helping group members to interact, requesting the cooperation of others, and being considerate of members' feelings

and needs. Finally, some leaders take a laissez-faire approach: They do not participate in their group's decision making at all.

There are two major problems with the style theory of leadership. First, an unlimited number of styles may be identified. Second, different styles are effective under different conditions.

Influence Theory Of Leadership

Benjamin Franklin may have been an outstanding leader because he knew how to influence people. A **leader** may be defined as a group member who exerts more influence on other members than they exert on him or her. Influence seems to be greater when a leader justifies his or her demands as being good for the group, has the power to punish members who do not do as he or she has asked, and has a legitimate right to make demands of subordinates. There is a reciprocal role relationship between leaders and followers in which an exchange or transaction takes place. Without followers there can be no leader, and without a leader there can be no followers. The leader and the followers both give something to and receive something from each other. Influence over others is purchased at the price of allowing oneself to be influenced by others. Leaders persuade and inspire members to follow their views of what needs to be done in order to achieve a group's goals and to cooperate with each other in doing so.

Position Approach To Leadership

Perhaps Benjamin Franklin was known as a leader simply because he was appointed to various leadership positions. Leadership in organizations begins with the formal role structure which defines the hierarchy of authority. **Authority** is legitimate power vested in a particular position to ensure that individuals in subordinate positions meet the requirements of their organizational role. Because organizational law demands that subordinates obey their superiors in matters of role performance, a person with authority will influence his or her subordinates.

There are two problems with this approach to leadership. First, it is unclear how a person is picked to be placed in a position of authority. It does not have to be for leadership ability. Second, the role behavior of subordinates is also influenced by peers and outsiders who have no direct authority over them.

The Distributed-Actions Theory of Leadership

Not the cry, but the flight of the wild duck, leads the flock to fly and follow.

Chinese Proverb

Perhaps Benjamin Franklin became a renowned leader because he was able to vary his behavior systematically from situation to situation so as to provide the appropriate leadership actions at the appropriate time. There is currently a consensus among social scientists that leadership skills and competencies are not inherited from one's ancestors, that they do not magically appear when a person is assigned to a leadership position, and that the same set of competencies will not provide adequate leadership in every situation. Different situations require different approaches to leadership.

Groups have at least two basic objectives: to complete a task and to maintain effective collaborative relationships among the members. The **distributed-actions theory of leadership** emphasizes that certain functions need to be filled if a group is to meet these two objectives. It defines leadership as the performance of acts that help the group to complete its task and to maintain effective working relationships among its members. For a group to complete its task successfully, group members must obtain, organize, and use information to make a decision. This requires members to engage in the **task-leadership actions** of contributing, asking for, summarizing, and coordinating the information. Members have to structure and give direction to the group's efforts and provide the energy to motivate efforts to make the decision. For any group to be successful, such task-leadership actions have to be provided.

But it does no good to complete a task if the manner of doing so alienates several group members. If a number of group members refuse to come to the next meeting, the group has not been successful. Thus, members must pay attention to maintaining good working relationships while working on the task. The task must be completed in a way that increases the ability of group members to work together effectively in the future. For this to happen, certain **maintenance-leadership actions** are needed. Members have to encourage one another to participate. They have to relieve tension when it gets too high, facilitate communication among themselves, and evaluate the emotional climate of the group. They have to discuss how the group's work can be improved, and they have to listen carefully and respectfully to one another. These leadership actions are necessary for the maintenance of friendly relationships among members and indeed, for the success of the group.

Leadership actions tend to be performed by the individuals most concerned with achieving the group's goals. Among the survivors of the plane crash in the Andes (Read, 1974), Marcelo took responsibility for organizing the group into work squads and controlled the rationing of their meager food supplies. Marcelo turned out to be an admirable leader in terms of getting many necessary tasks accomplished such as finding drinking water and caring for the injured. But he did not satisfy the emotional needs of the group. By the ninth day, the survivors' were becoming more and more depressed and discouraged and Marcelo began crying silently to himself at night. Several members, as if to offset Marcelo's inability to cheer up the survivors, become more positive and friendly, actively trying to reduce conflict. The only surviving female (Liliana Methol), for example, became a "unique source of solace" for the men and seemed to take the place of their mothers and sweethearts. One of the younger boys "called her his god-mother, and she responded to him and the others with comforting words and gentle optimism" (Read, 1974, p.74). In this extreme setting, where the lives of the group's members were at stake, both task and maintenance leadership actions were required.

The distributed-actions theory of leadership includes two basic ideas: (1) any member of a group may become a leader by taking actions that help the group complete its task and maintain effective collaborative relationships; (2) any leadership function may be fulfilled by different members performing a variety of relevant behaviors. Leadership, therefore, is specific to a particular group in a particular situation. Under specific circumstances any given behavior may or may not be helpful; under another set it may impair the effectiveness of the group. For example, when a group is trying to define a problem, suggesting a possible solution may not be helpful; however, when the group is making various solutions to a defined problem, suggesting a possible solution may indeed be helpful.

From the perspective of this theory, leadership is a learned set of skills that anyone with certain minimal requirements can acquire. Responsible group membership and leadership both depend on flexible behavior, the ability to diagnose what behaviors are needed at a particular time in order for the group to function most efficiently, and the ability to fulfill these behaviors or to get other members to fulfill them. A skilled member or leader, therefore, has to have diagnostic skills in order to be aware that a given function is needed in the group, and he or she must be sufficiently adaptive to provide the diverse types of behaviors needed for different conditions. In addition, an effective group member or leader must be able to utilize the abilities of other group members in providing the actions needed by the group.

For at least three reasons, it is usually considered necessary for the behaviors that fulfill group functions to be distributed among group members. **First**, if members do not participate, then their ideas, skills, and information are not being contributed. This hurts the group's effectiveness. The **second** reason is that members are committed to what they help build. Members who participate become more committed to the group and what the group has done. Members who remain silent tend not to care about the group and its effectiveness. The more members feel they have influenced the group and contributed to its work, the more committed they will be to the group. The **third** reason is that active members often become worried or annoyed about the silent members and view them as unconcerned about task completion. Unequal patterns of participation can create maintenance problems within the group.

Sometimes actions within a group not only help it to operate but serve oneself as well. Such individually oriented behavior sometimes involves issues of personal identity (Who am I in this group? Where do I fit in?), personal goals and needs (What do I want from this group? Are the group's goals consistent with my personal goals?), power and control (Who will control what we do? How much power and influence do I have?), and intimacy (How close will we get to each other? How much can I trust the other group members?).

The distributed-actions theory of leadership is one of the most concrete and direct approaches available for improving a person's leadership skills and for improving the effectiveness of a group. People can be taught the diagnostic skills and behaviors that help a group accomplish its task and maintain effective collaborative relationships among its members. There is, however, some criticism of the approach. There are so many different actions members can take to help in task achievement and group maintenance that specific ones are hard to pin down. What constitutes leadership then depends on the view of the person who is listing the leadership behaviors.

Organizational Leadership

The distributed-actions theory of leadership deals with leading small groups or teams. No matter what the size of the group, it is helpful. Leading a school or school district, however, requires a more complex theory of leadership (see Johnson & Johnson, 1989b). To lead a school, you must face five issues:

1. **How to challenge the status quo** of the traditional competitive/individualistic, mass-production organizational structure that emphasizes "lone rangers." It just does not work well any more.

2. **How to inspire a clear mutual vision of the cooperative school.** What the school should and could be must be clarified and a clear mission that all members are committed to achieving must be developed. Faculty need a set of goals to guide their efforts. It is the long-term promise of achieving something worthwhile and meaningful that powers an individual's drive toward greater expertise.

3. **How to empower members through cooperative teamwork.** Structuring faculty (and students) into cooperative teams enables each individual member to take action to increase his or her expertise and effectiveness, both technically and interpersonally. To be effective, a cooperative team must be careful structured to include positive interdependence, face-to- face promotive interaction, individual accountability, social skills, and group processing.

4. **How to lead by example** by (a) using cooperative procedures and (b) taking risks to increase competence. You begin leadership be becoming a role model who exemplifies the organizational and leadership values you believe are important.

5. **How to encourage the heart** of members to persist and keep striving to improve their technical and interpersonal expertise. Within cooperative enterprises, genuine acts of caring draw people together and forward. Love of their work and each other is what inspires members to commit more and more of their energy to achieving the mutual vision.

These leadership issues are thoroughly covered in **Leading the Cooperative School** (Johnson & Johnson, 1989b).

Post-Test

*Join another individual. Take the post-test, **discussing** each question, arriving at one answer that **both** individuals agree is most correct. Then **combine** with another pair and repeat the procedure, making sure that all four individuals agree on the answer to each question.*

*To help **you** learn the task and maintenance actions, match the following terms with their definitions.*

Task Actions

_____ 1. **Information and Opinion Giver**

_____ 2. **Information and Opinion Seeker**

_____ 3. **Direction and Role Definer**

_____ 4. **Summarizer**

_____ 5. **Energizer**

_____ 6. **Comprehension Checker**

Maintenance Actions

_____ 7. **Encourager of Participation**

_____ 8. **Communication Facilitator**

_____ 9. **Tension Reliever**

_____ 10. **Process Observer**

_____ 11. **Interpersonal Problem Solver**

_____ 12. **Supporter and Praiser**

A. **Makes sure all group members understand what each other says.**

B. **Pulls together related ideas or suggestions and restates them.**

C. **Offers facts, opinions, ideas, feelings, and information.**

D. **Expresses acceptance and liking for group members.**

E. **Uses observations of how the group is working to help discuss how the group can improve.**

F. **Lets members know their contributions are valued.**

G. **Asks for facts, opinions, ideas, feelings and information.**

H. **Asks others to summarize discussion to make sure they understand.**

I. **Encourages group members to work hard to achieve goals.**

J. **Calls attention to tasks that need to be done and assigns responsibilities.**

K. **Helps resolve and mediate conflicts.**

L. **Tells jokes and increases the group fun.**

Match the following statements with the task or maintenance action they best seem to fill.

A. *Does everyone in the group under-stand Helen's ideas?*

Task Actions

B. *How about giving our report on yoga while standing on our heads?*

_____ 1. **Information and Opinion Giver**

_____ 2. **Information and Opinion Seeker**

C. *Edye's idea seems like Buddy's; I think they could be combined.*

_____ 3. **Direction and Role Definer**

D. *I think we should openly dis-cuss the conflict between Dave and Linda to help resolve it.*

_____ 4. **Summarizer**

E. *Before we go on, let me tell you how other groups have solved this task.*

_____ 5. **Energizer**

_____ 6. **Comprehension Checker**

F. *We need a time-keeper. Keith, why don't you do that?*

G. *I really enjoy this group. I especially enjoy Roger's sense of humor.*

Maintenance Actions

H. *I think we'd find a good solution if we put a little more work into it.*

_____ 7. **Encourager of Participation**

_____ 8. **Communication Facilitator**

I. *Frank, tell us what we've said so far to see if you understand it correctly.*

_____ 9. **Tension Reliever**

J. *We seem to be suggesting solutions before we're ready. Let's define the problem first.*

_____ 10. **Process Observer**

_____ 11. **Interpersonal Problem Solver**

K. *I don't understand. What do you mean?*

_____ 12. **Supporter and Praiser**

L. *Helen, I'd like to hear what you think about this; you have such good ideas.*

EXERCISE

MATERIALS

Warm-Up Exercise:
OUR IDEAL LEADERS

The purpose of this exercise is to identify the traits possessed by ideal leaders in our society. The procedure is as follows:

1. Form heterogeneous triads.

2. Each group is to:

   a. read the assignment sheet that appears below.

   b. pick at least five great leaders who have lived

   in the last fifty years.

   c. list the qualities of each that made him or her great.

   d. decide by consensus the ten most important qualities

   of a great leader.

IDEAL LEADERS
Assignment Sheet

Every society identifies traits characteristic of ideal leaders. The ancient Egyptians, for example, attributed three qualities of divinity to their king: "Authoritative utterance is in thy mouth, perception is in thy heart, and thy tongue is the shrine of justice." An analysis of leaders in Homer's Iliad resulted in four sets of ideal leadership qualities admired by ancient Greeks: justice and judgment (Agamemnon), wisdom and counsel (Nestor), shrewdness and cunning (Odysseus), and valor and action (Achilles). What are the qualities we most admire in our outstanding leaders?

∽ UNDERSTANDING YOUR LEADERSHIP ACTIONS ∾
Questionnaire

Each of the following items describes a leadership action.
For each question mark:

5   if you always behave that way
4   if you frequently behave that way
3   if you occasionally behave that way
2   if you seldom behave that way
1   if you never behave that way

WHEN I AM A MEMBER OF A GROUP:

5-4-3-2-1   1. I offer facts and give my opinions, ideas, feelings, and information in order to help the group discussion.

5-4-3-2-1   2. I warmly encourage all members of the group to participate. I am open to their ideas. I let them know I value their contributions to the group.

5-4-3-2-1   3. I ask for facts, information, opinions, ideas, and feelings from the other group members in order to help the group discussion.

5-4-3-2-1   4. I help communication among group members by using good communication skills. I make sure that each group member understands what the others say.

5-4-3-2-1   5. I give direction to the group by planning how to go on with the group work and by calling attention to the tasks that need to be done. I assign responsibilities to different group members.

5-4-3-2-1   6. I tell jokes and suggest interesting ways of doing the work in order to reduce tension in the group and increase the fun we have working together.

5-4-3-2-1   7. I pull together related ideas or suggestions made by group members and restate and summarize the major points discussed by the group.

5-4-3-2-1   8. I observe the way the group is working and use my observations to help discuss how the group can work together better.

LEADERSHIP QUESTIONNAIRE (continued)

5-4-3-2-1 9. I give the group energy. I encourage group members to work hard to achieve our goals.

5-4-3-2-1 10. I promote the open discussion of conflicts among group members in order to resolve disagreements and increase group cohesiveness. I mediate conflicts among members when they seem unable to resolve them directly.

5-4-3-2-1 11. I ask others to summarize what the group has been discussing in order to ensure that they understand group decisions and comprehend the material being discussed by the group.

5-4-3-2-1 12. I express support, acceptance, and liking for other members of the group and give appropriate praise when another member has taken a constructive action in the group.

Your Leadership Actions

In order to obtain a total score for task actions and maintenance actions, write the score for each item in the appropriate column and then add the columns.

Task Actions

_____ 1. Information and opinion giver

_____ 3. Information and opinion seeker

_____ 5. Direction and role definer

_____ 7. Summarizer

_____ 9. Energizer

_____ 11. Comprehension checker

_____ TOTAL FOR TASK ACTIONS

Maintenance Actions

_____ 2. Encourager of participation

_____ 4. Communication facilitator

_____ 6. Tension reliever

_____ 8. Process observer

_____ 10. Interpersonal problem solver

_____ 12. Supporter and praiser

_____ TOTAL FOR MAINTENANCE ACTIONS

∽ Task-Maintenance Patterns ∾

(**6, 6**) Only a minimum effort is given to getting the required work done. There is general noninvolvement with other group members. The person with this score may well be saying: "To hell with it all!" Or he or she may be so inactive in the group as to have no influence whatsoever on other group members.

(**6, 30**) High value is placed on keeping good relationships within the group. Thoughtful attention is given to the needs of other members. The person with the score helps create a comfortable, friendly atmosphere and work tempo. However, he or she may never help the group get any work accomplished.

(**30, 6**) Getting the job done is emphasized in a way that shows very little concern with group maintenance. Work is seen as important, and relationships among group members are ignored. The person with this score may take an army-drillmaster approach to leadership.

(**18, 18**) The task and maintenance needs of the group are balanced. The person with this score continually makes compromises between task needs and maintenance needs. Though a great compromiser, this person does not look for or find ways to creatively integrate task and maintenance activities for optimal productivity.

(30, 30) When everyone plans and makes decisions together, all the members become committed to getting the task done as they build relationships of trust and respect.

∽ Task-Maintenance Grid ∾

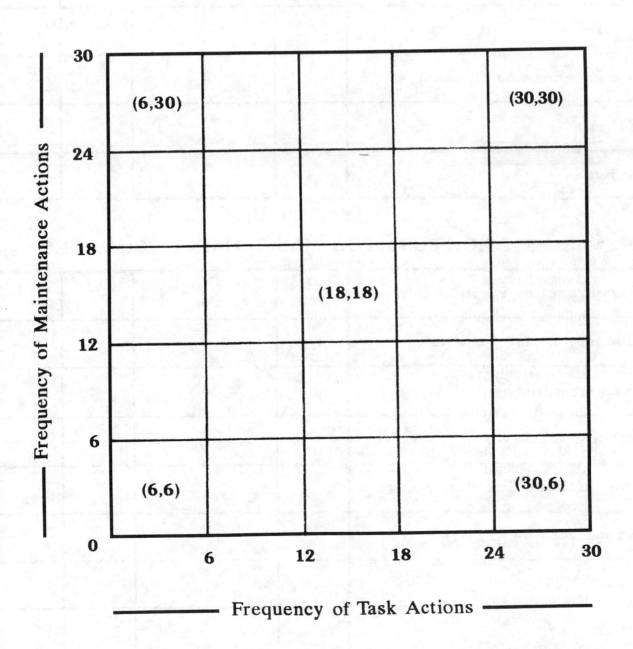

⟟ **OBSERVATION FORM FOR TASK BEHAVIORS** ⟟

1 **Information and Opinion Giver**					
3 **Information and Opinion Seeker**					
5 **Direction and Role Definer**					
7 **Summarizer**					
9 **Energizer**					
11 **Comprehension Checker**					
Other					
Other					

⟟ **OBSERVATION FORM FOR MAINTENANCE BEHAVIORS** ⟟

2 **Encourager of Participation**					
4 **Communication Facilitator**					
6 **Tension Reliever**					
8 **Process Observer**					
10 **Interpersonal Problem Solver**					
12 **Supporter and Praiser**					
Other					
Other					

8:16   Reprinted from: Human Relations and Your Career: A Guide to Interpersonal Skills (3rd ed.)
by David W. Johnson. Englewood Cliffs, NJ: Prentice-Hall, 1991.

SURVIVAL: The Situation

You have just crash-landed in the woods of northern Minnesota and southern Manitoba. It is 11:32 am in mid-January. The light plane in which you were traveling crashed on a lake. The pilot and copilot were killed. Shortly after the crash, the plane sank completely into the lake with the pilot's and copilot's bodies inside. None of you are seriously injured and you are all dry.

The crash came suddenly, before the pilot had time to radio for help or inform anyone of your position. Since your pilot was trying to avoid a storm, you know the plane was considerably off course. The pilot announced shortly before the crash that you were twenty miles northwest of a small town that is the nearest known habitation.

You are in a wilderness area made up of think woods broken by many lakes and streams. The snow depth varies from above the ankles in windswept areas to knee-deep where it has drifted. The latest weather report indicated that the

temperature would reach minus twenty-five degrees Fahrenheit in the daytime and drop to minus forty at night. There is plenty of dead wood and twigs in the immediate area. You are dressed in winter clothing appropriate for city wear -- suits, pants, street shoes, and overcoats or jackets.

While escaping from the plane the several members of your group salvaged twelve items. Your task is to rank these items according to their importance to your survival, starting with 1 for the most important item and ending with 12 for the least important one.

You may assume that the number of passengers is the same as the number of persons in your group, and that the group has agreed to stick together.

WINTER SURVIVAL:
Ranking Exercise

Item	Your Ranking	Experts' Ranking	Difference Score
Ball of steel wool			
Newspapers (one per person)			
Compass			
Hand ax			
Cigarette lighter (without fluid)			
Loaded .45-caliber pistol			
Sectional air map made of plastic			
Twenty-by-twenty foot piece of heavy-duty canvas			
Extra shirt and pants for each survivor			
Can of shortening			
Quart of 100-proof whiskey			
Family-size chocolate bar (one per person)			
TOTAL			

DEVELOPING AND

MAINTAINING TRUST

Introduction

For cooperation to be stable and productive, group members must establish and maintain mutual trust. Trust is one of the hardest collaborative skills to understand and implement. In this chapter you will:

1. Diagnose your level of skill in building and maintaining trust in a group.

2. Develop a conceptual understanding of the nature of trust.

3. Develop a behavioral understanding of the nature of trust.

4. Plan how to teach trust skills to your students.

Developing and Maintaining Trust

I am afraid to tell you who I am, because, if I tell you who I am, you may not like who I am, and it's all that I have.

John Powell

An essential aspect of group effectiveness is developing and maintaining a high level of trust among group members. The more members trust each other, the more effectively they will work together (Deutsch, 1962, 1973; Johnson, 1974). Group effectiveness rests on every member's sharing resources, giving and receiving help, dividing the work, and contributing to the accomplishment of mutual goals. Such behaviors will occur when there is trust that everyone else is contributing to the group's progress and not using members' openness and sharing of resources for personal rather than group gain. Group members will more openly express their thoughts, feelings, reactions, opinions, information, and ideas when the trust level is high. When the trust level is low, group members will be evasive, dishonest, and inconsiderate in their communications. The development and maintenance of trust is discussed at length in Johnson (1990).

Trust is essential for relationships to grow and develop among group members. In order to build a productive group, members must create a climate of trust that reduces their own and other members' fears of betrayal and rejection and promotes the hope of acceptance, support, and confirmation. Trust is not a stable and unchanging personality trait. Trust is an aspect of relationships and constantly changes and varies. Everything group members do increases or decreases the trust level in the group.

What is trust and how do you create it? Trust is a word everyone uses, yet it is a complex concept and difficult to define. Perhaps the best definition is Deutsch's (1962), who proposed that trust includes the following elements:

1. You are in a situation where a choice to trust another person can lead to either beneficial or harmful consequences for your needs and goals. Thus, you realize there is a risk involved in trusting.

2. You realize that whether beneficial consequences or harmful consequences result depends on the actions of another person.

3. You expect to suffer more if the harmful consequences result than you will gain if the beneficial consequences result.

4. You feel relatively confident that the other person will behave in such a way that the beneficial consequences will result.

Making a choice to trust another member involves the perception that the choice can lead to gains or losses, that whether you will gain or lose depends upon the behavior of the other member, that the loss will be greater than the gain, and that the other member will probably behave in such a way that you will gain rather than lose. Sounds complicated, doesn't it? In fact, there is nothing simple about trust; it is a complex concept and difficult to explain. An example may help. Imagine you are a part of a cooperative learning group analyzing **Hamlet**. You begin to contribute to the discussion, knowing you will gain if you contribute good ideas that other members accept but lose if your ideas are laughed at and belittled. Whether you gain or lose depends on the behavior of other group members. You will feel more hurt if you are laughed at than you will feel satisfaction if your ideas are appreciated. Yet you expect the other group members to consider your ideas and accept them. The issue of trust is captured in the question every group member asks: "If I openly express myself, will what I say be used against me?"

Another example may help. Trust is when you lend your older brother your bicycle. You can gain his appreciation or lose your bike; which one happens depends on him. You will suffer more if your bike is wrecked than you will gain by his appreciation, yet you really expect him to take care of your bike. (Sad experience has led an unnamed person to recommend that you never lend your bike to your older brother!)

Building Interpersonal Trust

In order to work together effectively to achieve a mutual goal, individuals must establish mutual trust. Trust is established through a sequence of trusting and trustworthy actions (see Figures 9:1). If person A takes the risk of being self-disclosing, he may be either confirmed or disconfirmed, depending on whether Person B responds with acceptance or rejection. If Person B takes the risk of being accepting, supportive, and cooperative, she may be confirmed or disconfirmed, depending on whether Person A is disclosing or nondisclosing. To complete tasks and achieve goals, group members are required to disclose more and more of their ideas, thoughts, conclusions, feelings, and reactions to the immediate situations and to each other. Once they do, other group members are required to respond, hopefully with acceptance, support, and cooperativeness. If group members express an opinion and do not get the acceptance they need, they may withdraw from the group. If they are accepted, they will continue to risk disclosing their thoughts and observations and continue to develop their relationships with other members.

Interpersonal trust is **built** through risk and confirmation and is **destroyed** through risk and disconfirmation. Without risk there is no trust, and the relationship cannot move forward. The steps in building trust are:

1. Person A takes a risk by disclosing his thoughts, information, conclusions, feelings, and reactions to the immediate situation and to Person B.

The Dynamics of Interpersonal Trust

	High acceptance, support, and cooperativeness	Low acceptance, support, and cooperativeness
High openness and sharing	PERSON A { Trusting / Confirmed PERSON B { Trustworthy / Confirmed	PERSON A { Trusting / Disconfirmed PERSON B { Untrustworthy / No risk
Low openness and sharing	PERSON A { Distrusting / No risk PERSON B { Trustworthy / Disconfirmed	PERSON A { Distrusting / No risk PERSON B { Untrustworthy / No risk

	Low Acceptance	High acceptance
High openness and sharing	Trusting But Untrustworthy	Trusting And Untrustworthy
Low openness and sharing	Distrusting And Untrustworthy	Distrusting But Trustworthy

2. Person B responds with acceptance, support, and cooperativeness and reciprocates Person A's openness by disclosing her own thoughts, information, conclusions, feelings, and reactions to the immediate situation and to Person A.

An alternative way in which trust is built is:

1. Person B communicates acceptance, support, and cooperativeness toward Person A.

2. Person A responds by disclosing his thoughts, information, conclusions, feelings, and reactions to the immediate situation and to Person B.

Being Trusting And Trustworthy

In a cooperative group, the crucial elements of trust are openness and sharing on the one hand and acceptance, support, and cooperative intentions on the other. Working cooperatively with others requires openness and sharing which in turn are determined by the expression of acceptance, support, and cooperative intentions in the group. **Openness** is the sharing of information, ideas, thoughts, feelings, and reactions to the issue the group is pursuing. **Sharing** is the offering of your materials and resources to others in order to help them move the group toward goal accomplishment. **Acceptance** is the communication of high regard for another person and his contributions to the group's work. **Support** is the communication to another person that you recognize her strengths and believe she has the capabilities she needs to manage productively the situation she is in. **Cooperative intentions** are the expectations that you are going to behave cooperatively and that every group member will also cooperate in achieving the group's goals.

The level of trust within a group is constantly changing according to members' ability and willingness to be trusting and trustworthy. **Trusting behavior** may be defined as the willingness to risk beneficial or harmful consequences by making oneself vulnerable to other group members. More specifically, trusting behavior involves your being self-disclosing and willing to be openly accepting and supportive of others. **Trustworthy behavior** may be defined as the willingness to respond to another person's risk taking in a way that ensures that the other person will experience beneficial consequences. This involves your acceptance of another person's trust in you. Expressing acceptance, support, and cooperativeness as well as reciprocating disclosures appropriately are key aspects of being trustworthy in relationships with other group members. In considering members' trustworthy behavior, you should remember that **accepting and supporting the contributions of other group members does not mean that you agree with everything they say.** You can express acceptance and support for the openness and sharing of other members and at the same time express different ideas and opposing points of view.

Acceptance is probably the first and deepest concern to arise in a group. Acceptance of others usually begins with acceptance of oneself. Group members need to accept themselves before they can fully accept others. **Acceptance is the key to reducing anxiety and fears about being vulnerable.** Defensive feelings of fear and distrust are common blocks to the functioning of a person and to the development of constructive relationships. Certainly, if a person does not feel accepted, the frequency and depth of participation in the group will decrease. To build trust and to deepen relationships among group members, each member needs to be able to communicate acceptance, support, and cooperativeness.

The key to building and maintaining trust is being trustworthy. The more accepting and supportive you are of others, the more likely they will disclose their thoughts, ideas, theories, conclusions, feelings, and reactions to you. The more trustworthy you are in response to such disclosures, the deeper and more personal the thoughts a person will share with you. When you want to increase trust, increase your trustworthiness.

The major skills necessary for communicating acceptance, support, and cooperativeness involve the expression of warmth, accurate understanding, and cooperative intentions. There is considerable evidence that the expression of warmth, accurate understanding, and cooperative intentions increases trust in a relationship, even when there are unresolved conflicts between the individuals involved (Johnson, 1971; Johnson & Matross, 1977; Johnson & Noonan, 1972). The procedures for communicating feelings such as warmth and in communicating that one is listening and accurately understands what the other is saying are covered in the chapter on communication skills. Cooperative intentions are expressed by comments indicating that you want to work together to achieve a mutual goal.

When you reciprocate self-disclosures, you increase trust and influence the other person to be even more self-disclosing. Reciprocating self-disclosures makes oneself vulnerable to rejection, and the mutual vulnerability resulting when all members actively participate in a group increases members' trust that all other members will be accepting and supportive of the others.

Destroying Trust

For trust to develop, one person has to let down his or her guard and become vulnerable to see whether the other person abuses that vulnerability. Many such tests are necessary before the trust level between two people becomes very high. A series of positive encounters may be necessary before trust is high. **It often takes, however, just one betrayal to establish distrust and, once established, distrust is extremely resistive to change.** Distrust is difficult to change because it leads to the perception that despite the other person's attempts to "make up," betrayal will recur in the future.

Creating distrust is not a good idea for several reasons. **First**, when group members distrust other members to do their share of the work, for example, they will loaf themselves rather than risk looking like a "sucker" who did the bulk of the work (Kerr, 1983). **Second**, when group members cannot trust each other, they often compete simply to defend their own best interests. Such competition is self-defeating in the long run, for it initiates a negative cycle. Distrust creates competition which creates greater distrust which creates greater competition. **Third**, distrust creates destructive conflict among group members. But to know how to maintain trust in a relationship it is important to be aware of the actions that make you look untrustworthy.

There are three types of behavior that will decrease trust in a relationship. The **first** is the use of rejection, ridicule, or disrespect as a response to the other's openness. Making a joke at the expense of the other person, laughing at his disclosures, moralizing about her behavior, being evaluative in your response, or being silent and poker-faced all communicate rejection and will effectively silence the other person and destroy some of the trust in the relationship. The **second** is the nonreciprocation of openness. To the extent that you are closed and the other members are open, they will not trust you. If a group member is open and you do not reciprocate, she will often feel overexposed and vulnerable. The **third** type of behavior that will decrease trust in a relationship is the refusal to disclose your thoughts, information, conclusions, feelings, and reactions after the other person has indicated considerable acceptance, support, and cooperativeness. If a group member indicates acceptance and you are closed and guarded in response, he will feel discounted and rejected.

Reestablishing Trust After It Has Been Broken

How can trust, once lost, be regained? The following guidelines may help. To reestablish trust, group members should:

1. Increase positive outcome interdependence by establishing cooperative goals that are so compelling that everyone will join in to achieve them. Such goals are often referred to as superordinate goals.

2. Increase their resource interdependence so that it is clear that no one person has a chance for succeeding on their own.

3. Openly and consistently express their cooperative intentions.

4. Reestablish credibility by making certain that their actions match their announced intentions. They must always follow up on their word.

5. Be absolutely and consistently trustworthy in their dealing with each other. Acceptance and support of other members are critical.

6. Periodically "test the waters" by engaging in trusting actions and making themselves vulnerable to the other members.

7. Apologize sincerely and immediately when they inadvertently engage in untrustworthy actions.

8. Strive to build a "tough but fair" reputation by:

    a. Initially and periodically responding cooperatively to other members who act competitively (even when they know in advance that the others plan to compete).

    b. Using a **tit-for-tat** strategy that matches the other person's behavior if the others continue to compete. When the competitors realize that their competitiveness is self-defeating and the best they can hope for is mutual failure, they may start cooperating.

Trusting Appropriately

Trust is not always appropriate. There are times when you will think it inadvisable to disclose your thoughts, feelings, or reactions to another person. There are people you undoubtedly know who would behave in very untrustworthy ways if you made yourself vulnerable to them. To master the skills in building and maintaining trust, therefore, you need to be able to tell when it is appropriate to be trusting and when it is not. A person must develop the capacity to size up situations and make an enlightened decision about when, whom, and how much to trust others. Remember not to reveal yourself so fast to another person that he is overpowered and bewildered. And remember there are situations in which trust is inappropriate and destructive to your interests.

Never trusting and **always** trusting are inappropriate. Trust is appropriate only when you are relatively confident that the other person will behave in such a way that you will benefit rather than be harmed by your risk, or when you are relatively sure the other person will not exploit your vulnerability. In some situations, such as competitive ones, trust is not appropriate. When you have a mean, vicious, hostile boss who has taken advantage of your openness in the past, it is inappropriate to engage in trusting behavior in the present.

Trusting As A Self-Fulfilling Prophecy

Tom joins a new group expecting the members to dislike and reject him. He behaves, therefore, in a very guarded and suspicious way toward the other group members. His actions cause them to withdraw and look elsewhere for a friendly companion. "See," he then says, "I was right. I knew they would reject me." Sue, who joins the same group at the same time Tom does, expects the members to be congenial, friendly, and trustworthy. She initiates warmth and friendliness, openly discloses her thoughts and feelings, and generally is accepting and supportive of the other members. Consequently, she finds her fellow members to be all that she expected. Both Tom and Sue have made a self-fulfilling prophecy.

A **self-fulfilling prophecy** is, in the beginning, a false definition of a situation that evokes a new behavior, one that makes it possible for the originally false impression to come true. The assumptions you make about other people and the way in which you then behave often influence how other people respond to you, thus creating self-fulfilling prophecies in your relationships. People usually conform to the expectations others have for them. If other people feel that you do not trust them and expect them to violate your trust, they will often do so. If they believe that you trust them and expect them to be trustworthy, they will often behave that way. The perceptions of others as untrustworthy is probably a major source of tensions leading to conflict. The history of labor/management strife, interracial violence, war, and revolution demonstrates the power of distrust. The lack of trust helps create conflict, and conflict leads to increased distrust. There is often a vicious circle of distrust causing conflict which increases distrust which increases conflict.

In building trust in a relationship, your expectations about the other person may influence how you act toward that person, thus setting up the possibility of a self-fulfilling prophecy. There is a lot to be said for assuming that other people are trustworthy.

Personal Proclivity To Trust

While trust exists in relationships, not in people, there has been some attempt to measure individual differences in willingness to trust others. Rotter (1971) developed the **Interpersonal Trust Scale** to distinguish between people who have a tendency to trust others and those who tend to distrust. A high truster tends to say, "I will trust a person until I have clear evidence that he or she cannot be trusted." A low truster tends to say, "I will not trust a person until there is clear evidence that they can be trusted." High trusters tend to be more trustworthy than will low trusters. High trusters, compared with low trusters, are (a) more likely to give others a second chance, respect the rights of others, and be liked and sought out as friends (by both low and high trust people), and (b) less likely to lie and be unhappy, conflicted, or maladjusted.

Helpful Hints About Trust

1. **Trust is a very complex concept to understand and teach to your students.** It may take a while before they fully understand it.

2. **Trust exists in relationships, not in someone's personality.** While some people are more naturally trusting than others, and it is easier for some people to be trustworthy than others, trust is something that occurs **between** people, not **within** people.

3. **Trust is constantly changing as two people interact.** Everything you do affects the trust level between you and the other person to some extent.

4. **Trust is hard to build and easy to destroy.** It may takes years to build up a high level of trust in a relationship, then one destructive act can destroy it all.

5. **The key to building and maintaining trust is being trustworthy.** The more accepting and supportive you are of others, the more likely they will disclose their thoughts, ideas, theories, conclusions, feelings, and reactions to you. The more trustworthy you are in response to such disclosures, the deeper and more personal the thoughts a person will share with you. When you want to increase trust, increase your trustworthiness.

6. **Trust needs to be appropriate. Never** trusting and **always** trusting are inappropriate.

7. **Cooperation increases trust, competitive decreases trust.** Trust generally is higher among collaborators than among competitors.

8. **Initial trusting and trustworthy actions within a group can create a self-fulfilling prophecy.** The expectations you project about trust often influence the actions of other group members toward you.

EXERCISE

MATERIALS

Understanding Your Trust Actions

The following are a series of questions about your behavior in your group. Answer each question as honestly as you can. There are no right or wrong answers. It is important for you to describe your behavior as accurately as possible.

1. I offer facts, give my opinions and ideas, provide suggestions and relevant information to help the group discussion.

   NEVER 1 ··· 2 ··· 3 ··· 4 ··· 5 ··· 6 ··· 7 ALWAYS

2. I express my willingness to cooperate with other group members and my expectations that they will also be cooperative.

   NEVER 1 ··· 2 ··· 3 ··· 4 ··· 5 ··· 6 ··· 7 ALWAYS

3. I am open and candid in my dealings with the entire group.

   NEVER 1 ··· 2 ··· 3 ··· 4 ··· 5 ··· 6 ··· 7 ALWAYS

4. I give support to group members who are on the spot and struggling to express themselves intellectually or emotionally.

   NEVER 1 ··· 2 ··· 3 ··· 4 ··· 5 ··· 6 ··· 7 ALWAYS

5. I keep my thoughts, ideas, feelings, and reactions to myself during group discussions.

   NEVER 1 ··· 2 ··· 3 ··· 4 ··· 5 ··· 6 ··· 7 ALWAYS

6. I evaluate the contributions of other group members in terms of whether their contributions are useful to me and whether they are right or wrong.

   NEVER 1 ··· 2 ··· 3 ··· 4 ··· 5 ··· 6 ··· 7 ALWAYS

Understanding Your Trust Actions

7. I take risks in expressing new ideas and current feelings during a group discussion.

   NEVER 1 ·· 2 ·· 3 ·· 4 ·· 5 ·· 6 ·· 7 ALWAYS

8. I communicate to other group members that I am aware of, and appreciate their abilities, talents, capabilities, skills, and resources.

   NEVER 1 ·· 2 ·· 3 ·· 4 ·· 5 ·· 6 ·· 7 ALWAYS

9. I offer help and assistance to anyone in the group in order to bring up the performance of everyone.

   NEVER 1 ·· 2 ·· 3 ·· 4 ·· 5 ·· 6 ·· 7 ALWAYS

10. I accept and support the openness of other group members, supporting them for taking risks, and encouraging individuality in group members.

    NEVER 1 ·· 2 ·· 3 ·· 4 ·· 5 ·· 6 ·· 7 ALWAYS

11. I share any materials, books, sources of information, or other resources I have with the other group members in order to promote the success of all members and the group as a whole.

    NEVER 1 ·· 2 ·· 3 ·· 4 ·· 5 ·· 6 ·· 7 ALWAYS

12. I often paraphrase or summarize what other members have said before I respond or comment.

    NEVER 1 ·· 2 ·· 3 ·· 4 ·· 5 ·· 6 ·· 7 ALWAYS

13. I level with other group members.

    NEVER 1 ·· 2 ·· 3 ·· 4 ·· 5 ·· 6 ·· 7 ALWAYS

14. I warmly encourage all members to participate, giving them recognition for their contributions, demonstrating acceptance and openness to their ideas, and generally being friendly and responsive to them.

    NEVER 1 ·· 2 ·· 3 ·· 4 ·· 5 ·· 6 ·· 7 ALWAYS

Your Trust Behavior

In order to get a total score, write the number you circled for each question in the following tables. Reverse the scoring for the starred questions. (If you circled 2, write 6; if you circled 1, write 7; 4 remains the same.)

TRUST **Openness and Sharing**	**TRUSTWORTHINESS** **Acceptance and Support**
1. _____	2. _____
3. _____	4. _____
* 5. _____	* 6. _____
7. _____	8. _____
9. _____	10. _____
11. _____	12. _____
13. _____	14. _____
TOTAL: _____	**TOTAL:** _____

The coordinates become . . .

(_____ , _____)

Johnson Trust Diagram

Always expresses acceptance, support, & cooperative intentions to other members

Expresses acceptance, support & cooperative intentions more often than not

Expresses rejection, nonsupport, & competitive intentions more often than not

Always expresses rejection, nonsupport, & competitive intentions to other members

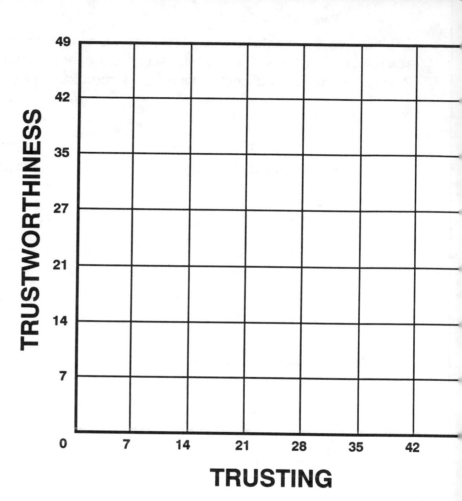

TRUSTWORTHINESS

49
42
35
27
21
14
7
0

0   7   14   21   28   35   42

TRUSTING

Never is open with ideas and information and never shares materials and resources

More closed and non sharing than not

More open and sharing than not

Always is open with ideas and always shares materials and resources

Trust Post-Test

Join another individual. Take the post-test, discussing each question, arriving at one answer that both individuals agree is most correct. Then combine with another pair and repeat the procedure, making sure that all four individuals agree on the answer to each question.

Test your understanding of building trust by answering **true** or **false** to the following statements.

____ 1. Trust involves a risk that can lead to either harmful or beneficial consequences.

____ 2. Your own behavior determines whether there are beneficial or harmful consequences from your trusting actions.

____ 3. When you trust another person, you will gain more from the beneficial consequences than you will suffer from the harmful ones.

____ 4. When you engage in trusting behavior, you are relatively confident that the other person will be accepting.

____ 5. In responding to another person's self-disclosures, you should be non-committal and nonjudgmental.

____ 6. It does not matter if the other person reciprocates your self-disclosures or not.

____ 7. When someone self-discloses, he or she will feel disconfirmed if the other person is not accepting.

____ 8. When people communicate acceptance, then you can risk trusting them.

____ 9. An example of trusting behavior would be Jane telling Frank about a personal problem.

____ 10. An example of trustworthy behavior would be Frank listening non-committally to Jane.

____ 11. Trust is necessary for stable cooperation.

____ 12. An ingredient of trust is the awareness that you are taking a chance of gaining or losing by it.

Trust Post-Test (continued)

Match the following elements of trust with their definitions:

    a. Openness

    b. Sharing

    c. Acceptance

    d. Support

    e. Cooperative intentions

    f. Trusting behavior

    g. Trustworthy behavior

_____ 13. The communication of high regard for another person and his contributions to the group.

_____ 14. Offering your materials and resources to others to help obtain the goal.

_____ 15. The expectation that you and the group members will help each other.

_____ 16. Sharing information, ideas, thoughts, feeling, and reactions to the issue.

_____ 17. Openness and sharing with others.

_____ 18. Expressing acceptance, support, and cooperative intentions.

_____ 19. Communicating that you recognize another person's strengths and believe she is capable.

Genetic Traits Task

Working as a group, estimate the number of people in your school who possess each of the following genetic traits. Establish the frequency of occurrence of each genetic trait, first in your group, then in the entire room. On the percentage of occurrence in your group and the room, estimate the number of people in your school who possess each trait.

1. Dimples in the cheeks versus no dimples.

2. Brown (or hazel) eyes versus blue, gray, or green eyes.

3. Attached versus free earlobes (an earlobe is free if it dips below the point where it is attached).

4. Little-finger bend versus no bend (place your little fingers together with your palms toward you--if your little fingers bend away from each other at the tips, you have the famous "little finger bend").

5. Tongue roll versus no tongue roll (if you can curl up both sides of your tongue to make a trough, you have it, and it's not contagious).

6. Hairy versus nonhairy middle fingers (examine the backs of the middle two fingers on your hands and look for hair between the first and second knuckle).

7. Widow's peak versus straight or curved hairline (examine the hairline across your forehead and look for a definite dip or point of hair extending down toward your nose).

OBSERVATION SHEE

Directions for Use: (a) Put names of group members above each column. (b) Put a tally mark in the appropriate box each time a group member contributes. (c) Make notes on the back when interesting things happen which are not captured by the categories. (d) It is a good idea to collect one (or more) good things that each group member does.

		Student A	Student B	Student C	Student D	Student E	TOTALS
1	CONTRIBUTES IDEAS						
2	DESCRIBES FEELINGS						
3	PARAPHRASES						
4	EXPRESSES SUPPORT, ACCEPTANCE, AND LIKING						
5	ENCOURAGES OTHERS TO CONTRIBUTE						
6	SUMMARIZES						
7	RELIEVES TENSION BY JOKING						
8	GIVES DIRECTION TO GROUP'S WORK						
	TOTALS						

9:20 Trusting: 1, 2; Trustworthy-Acceptance: 3, 4; Trustworthy-Reciprocation: 1, 2; Leadership-Task: 1, 2, 6, 7; Leadership-Maintenance: 3, 4, 5, 8; Communication: 1, 2, 3 (and, technically, all the rest); Conflict-Resolution: 1, 2, 3

NSURING EFFECTIVE

OMMUNICATION

Introduction: Communication Skills

Betsy is frustrated. She is a member of a cooperative group that includes Meredith, who is the bossiest student in the class. Whenever Betsy tries to contribute to the group's work, Meredith interrupts her and takes over. No one else gets to contribute their ideas and conclusions. Betsy wants to be an equal participant in the group but believes that Meredith will not let her. What is she to do?

Communicating is the first step in cooperating. Unless people can communicate with each other, they cannot cooperate. Although it is very difficult to find a definition of communication with which everyone will agree, it is clear that communication is the exchange or sharing of thoughts and feelings through symbols that represent approximately the same conceptual experience for everyone involved. In emphasizing communication skills to students, it is possible to divide these skills into two categories, sending and receiving. Each student must be able to send messages that correctly represent her ideas, beliefs, feelings, opinions, reactions, needs, goals, interests, resources, and a host of other things; the skills needed to send these messages we will lump under "sending skills." Each student must also be able to receive messages accurately so that he can understand the other person's ideas, beliefs, feelings, and so on; the skills needed to receive these messages we will lump under "receiving skills." Through sending and receiving, two students can clarify their mutual goals, plan how they are going to proceed to accomplish their goals, provide relevant information and intuitions to each other, reason together, coordinate their behavior, share their resources, give help and assistance to each other, and spark each other's creativity. Thus it is upon sending and receiving skills that we shall focus in this section. What are important sending skills? The following are some of the most crucial (Johnson, 1973).

1. **Clearly and unambiguously communicate your ideas and feelings.** Clearly "own" your message by (a) using personal pronouns such as "I" and "my" and (b) letting others know what your thoughts and feelings are. Students "disown" their messages when they use expressions such as "most people," "some people," "our group," making it difficult to tell whether they really think and feel what they are saying or are simply

repeating the thoughts and feelings of others. Besides using personal statements, often you will want to use behavior descriptions. A **behavior description** includes:

a. A **personal statement** that refers to "I," "me," "my," or "mine."

b. A **behavioral description statement** that includes the specific behaviors you have observed and does **not** include any judgment or evaluation or any inferences about the person's motives, personality, or attitudes. In addition, cooperation includes discussing how the relationship can be changed so the two of you can work together better. During such conversations, you will need to make relationship statements. A **relationship statement** describes some aspect of the way the two of you are interacting with each other. A good relationship statement indicates clear ownership (refers to I, me, my, or mine) and describes how you see the relationship. "I think we need to talk about our disagreement yesterday," is a good relationship statement.

2. **Make your messages complete and specific.** Include clear statements of all necessary information that the receiver needs in order to comprehend the message. Being complete and specific seems obvious, but often people will not communicate the frame of reference they are using, the assumptions they are making, their intentions in communicating, or the leaps in thinking they are making. Thus, although listeners may hear the words, they will not comprehend the "meaning" of the message.

3. **Make your verbal and nonverbal messages congruent with each other.** Every face-to-face communication involves both verbal and nonverbal messages. Usually these messages are congruent, so by smiling and expressing warmth nonverbally, a person can be saying that she has appreciated your help. Communication problems arise when a person's verbal and nonverbal messages are contradictory; if a person says, "Here is some information that may be of help to you" with a sneer and in a mocking tone of voice, the meaning you receive is confused by the two different messages being simultaneously sent.

4. **Ask for feedback concerning the way in which your messages are being received.** In order to communicate effectively, you must be aware of how the receiver is interpreting and processing your messages. The only way to be sure is to seek feedback continually as to what meanings the receiver is attaching to your messages.

Being skilled in sending messages is only half of what is needed to communicate effectively; one must also have receiving skills. **Receiving skills** include providing feedback concerning the reception of another person's message; this feedback facilitates clarification and continued discussion. The major purpose for providing such feedback is to communicate one's desire to understand completely the ideas and feelings of the sender. The major barrier to effective communication is the tendency most people have to judge, evaluate, approve, or disapprove of the messages they are receiving. For instance, the receiver may respond nonverbally or openly with, "I think you're wrong," "I don't like what you said," "I think you're right," or "That is the greatest (or worst) idea I have ever heard!" Such evaluative receiving will make the

sender defensive and cautious, thereby decreasing the openness of the communication. Thus, it is highly important for the receiver to indicate that he wants to understand the sender and will not evaluate the sender's messages until full understanding is reached. The specific receiving skills are paraphrasing, perception checking for feelings, and negotiating for meaning.

5. **Paraphrase accurately and nonevaluatively the content of the message and the feelings of the sender.** The most basic and important skill involved in receiving messages is paraphrasing. To **paraphrase** is to restate the words of the sender, and it should be done in a way that indicates an understanding of the sender's frame of reference. The basic rule to follow in paraphrasing is: You can speak up for yourself only after you have first restated the ideas and feelings of the sender accurately and to the sender's satisfaction.

6. **Describe what you perceive to be the sender's feelings.** Sometimes it is difficult to paraphrase the feelings of the sender if they are not described in words in the message. Thus a second receiving skill is the perception check for the sender's feelings. This check is made simply by describing what you perceive to be the sender's feelings. This description should tentatively identify the sender's feelings without expressing approval or disapproval and without attempting to interpret or explain the causes of the feelings. It is simply saying, "Here is what I understand your feelings to be. Am I accurate?"

7. **State your interpretation of the sender's message, and negotiate with the sender until there is agreement on the message's meaning.** Often the words contained in a message do not carry the actual meaning. A person may ask, "Is it safe to drive this

fast?" and mean, "Please slow down." A person may say, "That's a good suggestion," and mean, "I will ignore what you are saying and get rid of you by giving a superficial response." Sometimes paraphrasing the content of the message will do little to communicate your understanding of the message. In such a case, you **negotiate the meaning of the message.** You may wish to preface your response to the sender with, "What I think you mean is..." If you are accurate, you then continue the discussion; if you are inaccurate, the sender restates the message until you can state what the essential meaning of the message is. Keep in mind that it is the process that is important in negotiating meaning, a variety of introductory phrases will be used. Be tolerant of others who are using the same phrases over and over as they are developing this skill.

The sending and receiving skills described above seem very simple to most people. Yet they are very difficult to master fully and are indispensable when interacting with others. You should practice them consciously until they are as automatic as saying good morning.

Describing Your Feelings

Expressing and controlling your feelings is one of the most difficult aspects of interpersonal relationships. It is also one of the most important. It is through experiencing and sharing feelings that close relationships are built and maintained. Feelings provide the cement holding relationships together as well as the means for deepening relationships and making them more effective and personal. **Feelings are internal physiological reactions to your experiences.** You begin to tremble, sweat, or have a surge of energy. Your heart may beat faster. Tears may come. Although feelings are internal reactions, they do have outward signs. Sadness is inside you, but you may frown or cry on the outside. Anger is inside you. But you may stare and shout at the person you are angry with. Feelings are always internal states, but you use overt behaviors to communicate your feelings to other people.

It is often difficult to express feelings, especially within conflict situations. Whenever there is a risk of being rejected or laughed at, expressing feelings becomes very difficult. The more personal the feelings, the greater the risk you may feel. It is also difficult to hide your feelings from other people. You may cry when you do not want to, get angry when it is best not to, or even laugh at a time that disturbs others. If you are angry and upset, typically the people you work with and the people around you will know. When you do not recognize, accept, and express your feelings a number of difficulties may arise. Relationships may deteriorate, conflicts may fester, bias may creep into your judgments, and the insecurities of your students and colleagues may increase. For many reasons it is often best to communicate your feelings directly when conflicts are building.

There are two ways of communicating feelings: verbally and nonverbally. If you want to communicate clearly, your verbal and your nonverbal expression of feelings must agree or be congruent. Many of the communication difficulties experienced in relationships spring from giving contradictory messages to others by indicating one kind of feeling with words, another with actions, and still another with nonverbal expressions.

Communicating your feelings depends on your being aware of your feelings, accepting them, and being skillful in expressing them constructively. When you are unaware or unaccepting of your feelings, or when you lack skills in expressing them, your feelings may be communicated indirectly through:

1. **Labels**: "You are rude, hostile, and self- centered" versus "When you interrupt me I get angry."

2. **Commands**: "Shut up!" versus "I'm annoyed at what you just said."

3. **Questions**: "Are you always this crazy?" versus "You are acting strangely, and I feel worried."

4. **Accusations**: "You do not care about me!" versus "When you do not pay attention to me I feel left out."

5. **Sarcasm**: "I'm glad you are early!" versus "You are late; it has delayed our work, that irritates me."

6. **Approval**: "You are wonderful!" versus "I like what you did."

7. **Disapproval**: "You are terrible!" versus "I do not like what you did."

8. **Name calling**: "You are a creep!" versus "You are embarrassing me."

Such indirect ways of expressing feelings are common. But they are ineffective because they do not give a clear message to the receiver. And the receiver often will feel rejected and "put down" by the remarks. We are taught how to describe our ideas clearly and correctly. But we are rarely taught how to describe our feelings clearly and correctly. We express our feelings, but we do not usually name and describe them. Here are four ways you can describe a feeling.

1. **Identify or name it**: "I feel angry." "I feel embarrassed." "I like you."

2. **Use sensory descriptions that capture how you feel**: "I feel stepped on." "I feel like I'm on cloud nine." "I feel like I've just been run over by a truck." Because we do not have enough names of labels to describe all our feelings, we make up ways to describe them.

3. **Report what kind of action the feeling urges you to do**: "I feel like hugging you." "I feel like slapping your face." "I feel like walking on your face."

4. **Use figures of speech as descriptions of feelings**: "I feel like a stepped-on toad." "I feel like a pebble on the beach."

You describe your feelings by identifying them. A description of a feeling must include:

1. **A personal statement** - refer to "I," "me," "my," or "mine."

2. **A feeling name, simile, action urge, or figure of speech.**

Anything you say can convey feelings. Even the comment, "It's a warm day," can be said so that it expresses resentment or irritation. To build and maintain a friendship or any relationship, you must be concerned with communicating your feelings clearly and accurately, especially the feelings of warmth, affection, and caring. If you convey your feelings by commands, questions, accusations, or judgments, you will tend to confuse the person with whom you are interacting. When you want to express your feelings, your ability to describe them is essential for effective communication.

When you describe your feelings, expect at least two results. First, describing your feelings to another person often helps you to become more aware of what it is you actually do feel. Many times we have feelings that seem ambiguous or unclear to us. Explaining them to another person often clarifies our feelings to ourselves as well as to the other person. Second, describing your feelings often begins a dialogue that will improve your relationship. If other people are to respond appropriately to your feelings, they must know what the feelings are. Even if the feelings are negative, it is often worthwhile to express them. Negative feelings are signals that something may be going wrong in the relationship, and you and the other person need to examine what is going on in the relationship and figure out how it may be improved. By reporting your feelings, you provide information that is necessary if you and the other person are to understand and improve your relationship. When discussing your relationship with another person, describing your feelings conveys maximum information about what you feel in a more constructive way than giving commands, asking questions, making accusations, or offering judgments.

Some general rules to follow in expressing feelings are:

1. When the other person expresses a feeling toward you, use the communication skills of paraphrasing and checking perceptions to show you understand how she is feeling.

2. Always describe your feelings.

3. Always describe without evaluation the actions of the other person that influenced your feelings.

4. Avoid irrational assumptions that lead to negative feelings.

5. When a person expresses a feeling toward you, always respond with a feeling. Feelings need to be answered by feelings, not by silence, uninvolved understanding, or ridicule.

6. When it can be done in a helpful way, express your feelings. Hidden feelings usually cause problems in the future.

Checking Your Perception Of Another's Feelings

After you have described your view of the situation and your feelings about it, the next step is to ask the other person to do the same. Sometimes other people will clearly describe their feelings and other times they will express them in ambiguous and confusing ways. In order to respond you will have to clarify how they really feel.

Feelings are internal reactions, and we can tell what people are feeling only from what they tell us and from their overt actions. Overt actions include such things as smiles, frowns, shouts, whispers, tears, and laughter. When other people describe their feelings to us, we can usually accept their feelings to be what they say they are. But if other people express their feelings indirectly (such as through sarcasm) or nonverbally (such as through a frown), we often need to clarify how they actually feel. **A basic rule in interpersonal communication is that before you respond to a person's feelings, you need to check to make sure you really know what the other person actually feels.**

The best way to check whether or not you accurately understand how a person is feeling is through a perception check. A **perception check** has three parts:

1. You describe what you think the other person's feelings are.

2. You ask whether or not your perception is accurate.

3. You refrain from expressing approval or disapproval of the feelings.

"You look sad. Are you?" is an example of a perception check. It describes how you think the person is feeling, then it asks the person to agree with or correct your perception, and it does both without making a value judgment about the feeling. A perception check communicates the message, "I want to understand your feeling: is this the way you feel?" It is an invitation for other people to describe their feelings more directly. And it shows you care enough about the person to want to understand how the person feels. Perception checking will help you avoid actions you later regret because they are based on false assumptions about what the other person is feeling.

Checking out out impressions of how others are feeling is an important communication skill. Our impressions are often biased by our own fears, expectations, and present feelings. If we are afraid of anger and expect other people to be angry, then we may think other people are about to reject us. We frequently misperceive how other people are feeling, and it is therefore essential that we check out our perceptions before taking action.

Different Shoes, Different Perspectives

Juanita and Betsy work together as laboratory technicians in a large hospital. Juanita comes from a well-off middle-class family. Betsy's parents had a hard struggle sending their daughter through college. Juanita and Betsy buy tickets for a state lottery in which they could win up to $50,000. When the drawing is held, they learn that they are both winners. Juanita says, "Hey, I won $50,000 in that lottery. Imagine that." Then she continues eating lunch and reading a magazine. Betsy starts jumping up and down shouting, "I won! I won! I won $50,000!" She throws her arms around her friend, crying and laughing in her excitement.

Why did Juanita and Betsy react so differently to the news that they had each won $50,000 in a state lottery?

You see things from your shoes. I see things from my shoes. From your shoes, a person you work with is sexy, attractive, desirable; from my shoes, the person is only so-so. From your shoes that movie is fantastic; from my shoes, it certainly is! Sometimes we see things the same. Sometimes we see things differently.

Different people have different perspectives. Misunderstandings often occur because we assume that everyone sees things from the same perspective as we do. If we like Italian food, we assume that all our friends like Italian food. If we are interested in sports, we assume that everyone is interested in sports. If we get angry when someone laughs at our behavior, we assume that everyone will get angry when they are laughed at. If we think our boss is stupid, we are surprised when a coworker thinks the boss is brilliant. As children, we can see things only from our perspective. As we become adults, we learn that different people have different perspectives, and we learn how to understand other people's perspectives.

You can have different perspectives at two different times. When you are a tired clerk who wants to go home to get ready for an important date, a customer's behavior may seem unreasonable. When you are a manager who is trying to increase sales, the same customer behavior may seem very understandable. On Monday, if a clerk overcharges you, you may laugh it off. But on Tuesday, when you have been overcharged at the last three stores you have visited, a careless clerk may make you angry. If you have been lifting 100-pound bags of cement and someone tosses you a 40-pound bag, it will seem very light. But if you have been lifting 20-pound bags, the 40-pound bag will seem

very heavy. As your job role, experiences, assumptions, and values change, your perspective will change.

The same message can mean two entirely different things to two different people. If you provoke your coworker, she may laugh. But if you provoke your boss, she may get angry and fire you! Different perspectives mean the message will be given different meanings. From one perspective, the same message may be interpreted as friendly teasing or as hostile insubordination.

To be skilled in communicating, you need to understand the perspective of the receiver. **When you are deciding how to phrase a message, you need to take into account:**

1. The receiver's perspective.

2. What the receiver already knows about the issue.

3. What further information the receiver needs and wants about the issue.

To be skilled in communicating, you need to understand the sender's perspective. **When deciding what a message means, you need to take into account:**

1. The sender's perspective.

2. The meaning of the message from the sender's shoes.

There is nothing more helpful for effective communication than being skilled in seeing things from the other person's perspective. Try standing in someone else's shoes. It will really improve your communication with that person.

Let Me Tell You What You Just Said

There is no skill more important in a relationship than being a good listener (see Johnson, 1986, 1987). A good listener is always liked and is always sought out for conversations. Listening skills are a major asset for your career. If you are a good listener, you have it made.

The keystone to good listening is **paraphrasing**. Restating, in your own words, what the person says, feels, and means improves communication in several ways. First, it helps you avoid judging and evaluating. When you are restating, you are not passing judgment. Second, restating gives the sender direct feedback as to how well you understand the messages. If you do not fully understand, the sender can add messages until you do. If you are interpreting the message differently from the way he intended it, the sender can clarify. Being able to clarify and elaborate are important for making sure communication is taking place.

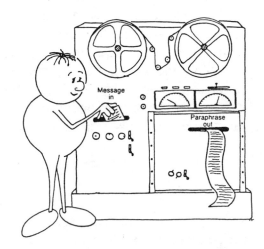

Third, paraphrasing communicates to the sender that you want to understand what he is saying. It shows that you care about him enough to listen carefully, that you are interested, that you take what he is saying seriously, and that you want to understand. Finally, paraphrasing helps you get into the sender's shoes: It helps you see the message from the sender's perspective. By restating the message as accurately and fairly as possible, you begin to see things from the sender's point of view.

The simple act of paraphrasing is perhaps the most powerful thing you can do to reduce conflict and misunderstandings. It works by correcting inaccuracies in communication. It also indicates empathy--trying to see things from the sender's shoes.

Paraphrasing is often a simple restatement of what has been said. At first, it may feel dumb to restate what another person has said. It may feel awkward and unnatural until you get used to doing it. But the speaker will be grateful for a chance to clarify or add to his original statement, and he will feel grateful for being understood.

Paraphrasing becomes harder when it includes feelings as well as ideas. And it is not limited to only the words the sender uses. Nonverbal cues are also important. Examples of paraphrasing are given in the following conversation.

Paraphrasing may sound simple. But it is often difficult to do. To be skilled in communicating, you must be skilled in paraphrasing. It has very powerful and constructive effects. It is one of the most essential skills of effective communication.

This does not mean that you will want to paraphrase every statement made by anyone who speaks to you. Some statements aren't important enough to bother with. When someone says hello, there is no need to paraphrase. When someone says "Look at that!" there is no need to paraphrase. Paraphrasing is for important messages: When you are not sure what the sender means, when your boss is giving important instructions, or when someone is being very emotional, you paraphrase. In the middle of a conflict, when you want the sender to feel understood, or when you want to be absolutely sure what is being said before you reply, you paraphrase. Paraphrasing is essential in important conversations.

When you use paraphrasing, there is a rhythm to your statements. The rhythm is, You said . . .; I say . . . First you say what the sender said (You said). Then you reply (I say).

Remember the **paraphrasing rule. Before you can reply to a statement, restate what the sender says, feels, and means correctly and to the sender's satisfaction.**

General Guidelines for Paraphrasing

1. Restate the sender's expressed ideas and feelings in your own words rather than mimicking or parroting her exact words.

2. Preface paraphrased remarks with, "You think...," "Your position is...," "It seems to you that...," "You feel that...," and so on.

3. Avoid any indication of approval or disapproval.

4. Make your nonverbal messages congruent with your verbal paraphrasing; look attentive, interested, and open to the sender's ideas and feelings, and show that you are concentrating upon what the sender is trying to communicate.

5. State as accurately as possible what you heard the sender say and describe the feelings and attitudes involved.

6. Do not add to or subtract from the sender's message.

7. Put yourself in the sender's shoes and try to understand what it is she is feeling and what her message means.

EXERCISE

MATERIALS

WHO OWNS THIS?

Purpose

A basic communicatio skill is to speak for yourself by taking ownership for your thoughts, feelings, and needs. The sender can be speaking for him- or herself, for no one, or for someone else. The purpose of this exercise is to give you some practice in recognizing who owns the thoughts, feelings, or needs in a message.

Procedure

1. Working alone, read each of the statements listed below and write your answers. Put an "S" for each statement in which the sender is speaking for him- or herself, a "N" for each statement in which the sender is speaking for no one, or an "O" for each statement in which the sender is speaking for someone else.

2. Working as a group of three, decide whether each statement is an "S," "O," or "N." Discuss any disagreements among members until all members agree on the answers. Then rephrase the "O" and "N" statements to make them "S" statements.

Statements

_____ 1. Everyone here hates the boss.
_____ 2. I love you.
_____ 3. Rumor has it that you are a beautiful person.
_____ 4. We think school is groovy.
_____ 5. I feel nervous when you look at me that way.
_____ 6. You make people feel good just by smiling at them.
_____ 7. I can tell by looking at your face that you feel terrible.
_____ 8. No one would skip this class.
_____ 9. You think I have big feet and it is not true!
_____ 10. Bill thinks you are strange.
_____ 11. I am really excited about my grade!
_____ 12. Most people would be angry if you did that to them.
_____ 13. My teacher thinks I am great!
_____ 14. I believe in the United States of America.
_____ 15. I need more time to think about it.

• • • ● Describing ● ● • •

Purpose

The purpose of this lesson is to give you some practice in describing another person's behavior without passing judgment.

Procedure

1. Working alone, read each of the statements listed below and write your answers. Put a "D" for each statement that **describes** a person's behavior, a "J" for each statement that **judges** a person's behavior.

2. For a group of three and review members' answers. Discuss any disagreements until all members agree on each answer.

Statements

_____ 1. Sam interrupted Sally when she tried to talk about the Minnesota Twins.
_____ 2. Mark is very sincere.
_____ 3. Sue never understands what Jack is saying.
_____ 4. Sally is rude and ungrateful.
_____ 5. Sam changed the subject.
_____ 6. Jane's trying to make me mad.
_____ 7. It is a great day today.
_____ 8. That is the fourth time that you finished one of my sentences.
_____ 9. Sam and Mark have made the most statements during this exercise.
_____ 10. Jane is very shy.
_____ 11. I do not like Sally.
_____ 12. Sam has not made a statement for the past three sessions.
_____ 13. During class yesterday, you sat staring into space for the first half-hour.
_____ 14. Today on my way to school I saw three butterflies.
_____ 15. Linda has a great sense of humor.

10:15

• • • •

"You and Me" -- Relationship Statements

Procedure

The purpose of this exercise is to give you some practice in differentiating between good and poor relationships statements. Form groups of three. Read each of the Relationship Statements listed below. Write one answer that all members agree is correct. Put an "R" for each good relationship statement that describes how the speaker sees the relationship. Put a "J" for a poor relationship statement that judges, an "O" for a poor relationship statement that speaks for the other person, or a "P" for a statement that is about a person, not a relationship. **Rewrite the poor relationship statements to make them good ones.** Check your triad's answers against the correct answers. Discuss any statements the group missed until all members understand it.

Statements

_____ 1. We really enjoyed ourselves last night.

_____ 2. Our relationship is really lousy!

_____ 3. For the past two days, you have not spoken to me. Is something wrong?

_____ 4. You look sick today.

_____ 5. You really make me feel appreciated and liked.

_____ 6. You are angry again. You are always getting angry.

_____ 7. We are great at communicating.

_____ 8. I think we need to talk about our disagreement yesterday.

_____ 9. I think you can finish that job today.

_____ 10. I feel you are making nasty comments. Are you angry with me?

_____ 11. You really are mean and vicious!

_____ 12. My big brother is going to beat you up if you do not stop doing that!

_____ 13. I am concerned that when we go to lunch together we are often late for work in the afternoon.

_____ 14. You really seem happy about your promotion.

_____ 15. This job stinks!

_____ 16. I am confused by your behavior. Last week you were really friendly to me. This week you have not even said hello once.

···❧❳[**Describing, Not Evaluating**]❲❧···

To define a conflict, you must tell the other person what you want. How you say what you want has positive or negative effects on how the conflict turns out.

Defining a conflict is like lacing your shoes. If you start out wrong, the whole thing gets messed up. Make the conflict over the other person's actions, not over his or her personality. If you call the other person names, insult or blame him or her, the conflict will probably turn out badly.

If you describe the conflict, then the conflict will probably turn out well. Describing needs to be caring, non-threatening, and non-judgmental. The words you use can make the other person angry at you or can make the other person want to resolve the conflict.

Using the person's name shows respect and caring.

Working as a pair, write a "D" by the statements that describe and write a "E" by the statements that evaluate:

_____ 1. You are a mean person!

_____ 2. Sam. I don't like it when you call me a name.
Do you want to tell me what's wrong?

_____ 3. You are a rotten bully!

_____ 4. Bob. I don't like being pushed. Please stop.

_____ 5. You're an evil witch!

_____ 6. Jane. I'm sorry when you say things about me that aren't true.
Please tell me why you are angry.

Try your skill at describing, not evaluating. Working as a pair, write your answer to each of the following:

1. A friend "snoops" into your things: _____

_____

_____.

2. A classmate teases you: _____

_____

_____.

3. A classmate blames you for not working hard enough:

_____

_____.

Your Challenge

With your partner, create a role play using one of the above situations.

10:18

Describing Your Feelings

The objectives of this exercise are to help you recognize when you are displaying feelings without describing them, to explain how you may express your feelings verbally in a way that communicates them effectively, and to give you a chance to practice the latter. In the list below, each of the ten items consists of two or three statements. One statement is a description of a feeling; the others are expressions that do not describe the feelings involved. The procedure for the exercise is:

1. Divide into groups of three.

2. **Work individually**. In item 1 put a "D" before the sentence that describes the sender's feelings. Put a "No" before the sentence that conveys feeling but does not describe what it is. **Mark the answers for item 1 only**; do not go on to item 2 yet.

3. **Work cooperatively**. Compare your answers to item 1 with those of the other two members of your triad. Discuss the reasons for any differences. Then turn to the answers that follow the list and read the answer for item 1. Discuss the answer in your triad until you all understand the point.

4. Repeat steps 2 and 3 for item 2. Then continue the same procedure for each item until you have completed all ten.

Describing Your Feelings (continued)

Questions

_____ 1. a. Stop driving this fast! Slow down right now!
_____ 1. b. Your driving this fast frightens me.

_____ 2. a. Do you have to stand on my foot?
_____ 2. b. You are so mean and vicious you don't care if you cripple me for life!
_____ 2. c. I am annoyed at you for resting your 240-pound body on my foot.

_____ 3. a. I feel ecstatic about winning the Reader's Digest Sweepstakes!
_____ 3. b. This is a wonderful day!

_____ 4. a. You're such a helpful person.
_____ 4. b. I really respect your ideas; you're so well informed.

_____ 5. a. Everyone here likes to dance with you.
_____ 5. b. When I dance with you I feel graceful and relaxed.
_____ 5. c. We all feel you're a great dancer.

_____ 6. a. If you don't start cleaning up after yourself, I'm moving out!
_____ 6. b. Did you ever see such a messy kitchen in your life?
_____ 6. c. I am afraid you will never do your share of housework.

_____ 7. a. This is a very interesting book.
_____ 7. b. I feel this is not a very helpful book.
_____ 7. c. I get very excited when I read this book.

_____ 8. a. I do not feel confident enough to contribute anything to this group.
_____ 8. b. I'm not worthwhile enough to contribute anything to this group.

_____ 9. a. I'm a born loser; no one will ever like me!
_____ 9. b. Sue is a rotten creep! She laughed at my score on the test!
_____ 9. c. I'm depressed because I flunked that test.

_____ 10. a. I feel warm and comfortable in my group.
_____ 10. b. Someone in my group always seems near when I need company.
_____ 10. c. I feel everyone cares that I'm a part of this group.

Describing Your Feelings (continued)

Answers

1. **a. No.** Commands like these communicate strong feelings, but they do not name the feeling that underlies the commands.

1. **b. D.** This statement both expresses and names a feeling. The person communicates the feeling by describing himself as frightened.

2. **a. No.** A feeling is implied through a question, but the specific feeling underlying the question is not described.

2. **b. No.** This statement communicates considerable feeling through an accusation, but it is not clear whether the accusation is based on anger, hurt, fear, or some other feeling.

2. **c. D.** The person describes the feeling as annoyance. Note that the speaker also "owns" the feeling by using the personal pronoun "I."

3. **a. D.** The speaker describes herself as feeling ecstatic.

3. **b. No.** This statement communicates positive feelings without describing what they are. The speaker appears to be commenting on the weather when in fact the statement is an expression of how the speaker feels. We cannot tell whether the speaker is feeling proud, happy, caring, accepted, supported, or relieved.

4. **a. No.** The speaker makes a value judgment communicating positive feelings about the other person, but the speaker does not describe the feelings. Does the speaker admire the other person or like the other person, or is the speaker only grateful?

4. **b. D.** The speaker describes the positive feelings as respect.

5. **a. No.** This statement does name a feeling (likes) but the speaker is talking for everyone and does not make clear that the feeling is personal. A description of a feeling must contain "I," "me," "my," or "mine" to make clear that the feelings are within the speaker. Does it seem more friendly for a person to say, "I like you," or "Everybody likes you?"

5. **b. D.** The speaker communicates clearly and specifically the feeling the speaker has when dancing with the other person.

5. **c. No.** First, the speaker does not speak for herself, but rather hides behind the phrase "we feel." Second, "You're a great dancer" is a value judgment and does not name a feeling. Note that merely placing the word feel in front of a statement does not make the statement a description of feeling. People often say feel when they mean think or believe.

6. **a. No.** This statement communicates general and ambiguous negative feelings about the person's behavior. It refers to the condition of the apartment or house and the speaker's future behavior, but not to the speaker's inner feelings.

6. **b. No.** The speaker is trying to communicate a negative feeling through a rhetorical question and a value judgment. Although it is clear the feeling is negative, the specific feeling is not described.

6. **c. D**. The speaker describes fear as the negative feeling connected with the other person's housework.

Note: Notice that in a and b the feelings could easily have been interpreted as anger. Many times the expression of anger results from an underlying fear. Yet when the receiver tries to respond, she may understand that the other person is angry without comprehending that the basic feeling to be responded to is a feeling of fear.

7. **a. No.** The speaker communicates a positive value judgment that conveys feelings, but the specific feelings are not described.

7. **b. No.** The speaker uses the words "I feel" but does not then describe or name a feeling. Instead, the speaker gives a negative value judgment. What the speaker actually meant was "I believe" or "I think" the book is not very good. People commonly use the word feel when they mean think or believe. Consider the difference between, "I feel you don't like me" and "I believe (think) you don't like me."

7. **c. D.** The speaker describes a feeling of excitement while reading this book.

Note: Many times people who say they are unaware of what they feel--or who say they don't have any feelings about something--state value judgments about recognizing that this is the way their positive or negative feelings get expressed. Many times useless arguments can be avoided if we are careful to describe our feelings instead of expressing them through value judgments. For example, if Joe says the book is interesting and Fred says it is boring, they may argue about which it "really" is. If Joe, however, says he was excited by the book and Fred says he was frustrated by it, no argument should follow. Each person's feelings are what they are. Of course, discussing what it means for Joe and Fred to feel as they do may provide helpful information about each person and about the book.

8. **a. D.** Speaker communicates a feeling of incompetence.

8. **b. No.** Warning! This statement is potentially hazardous to your health! Although it sounds much the same as the previous statement, it states that the speaker actually is incompetent. The speaker has passed a negative value judgment on himself and labeled himself as incompetent.

Note: Many people confuse feeling with being. A person may feel incompetent yet behave very competently or a person may feel competent and perform very incompetently. A person may feel hopeless about a situation that turns out not to be hopeless once his behavior is given an appropriate focus. A sign of emotional maturity is that a person does not confuse feelings with the reality of the situation. An emotionally mature person knows he can perform competently, even though he feels incompetent. He does not let his feelings keep him from doing his best because he knows the difference between feelings and performance and knows that the two do not always match.

9. **a. No.** The speaker has evaluated herself-- passed a negative value judgment on herself by labeling herself a born loser.

9. **b. No.** This statement also communicates a negative value judgment, but against another person rather than of oneself. Although the statement contains strong feelings, the feelings are not specifically named or described.

9. **c. D.** The speaker states she feels depressed. Statements a and c highlight the important difference between passing judgment on yourself and describing your feelings.

Note: Feelings are constantly changing and are by no means written in concrete once they occur. To say that you are now depressed does not imply that you will or must always feel the same. If you label yourself as a born loser, however, you imply a permanence to a feeling of depression by defining it as a trait rather than as a temporary affective response. You can feel anger without being an angry person. You can feel shy without being a shy person. Many people try to avoid new situations and activities by labeling themselves. "I'm not artistic," "I'm not a good public speaker,'""I can't participate in groups," are examples. If we could recognize what our feelings are beneath such statements, maybe we would be more willing to risk doing things we are somewhat fearful of.

Describing Your Feelings (continued)

10. **a. D.** The speaker communicates a feeling by describing it and taking ownership of it.

10. **b. No.** The speaker communicates a positive feeling but does not take direct ownership of it and does not say whether the feeling is happiness, gratefulness, supportiveness, or what.

10. **c. No.** Instead of "I feel" the speaker should have said "I believe." The last part of the statement really tells what the speaker believes the others feel about her. It does not tell what the speaker feels. Expressions a and c relate to each other as follows: "Because I believe that everyone cares whether I am part of this group, I feel warm and comfortable.

BODY TALK

BODY LANGUAGE is another way of communicating. As you react to different situations, your body takes on certain positions.

Picture yourself at times when you feel the emotions listed below. Describe how your body looks when you feel these ways.

Embarrassment _____

_____

Nervousness _____

_____

Excitement _____

_____

Boredom _____

_____

Now draw a line from each face below to the feeling it shows.

Embarrassment

Nervousness

Excitement

Boredom

Anger

Happiness

10:25

Is This the Way You Feel?

To negotiate effectively and to communicate clearly, you need to check your perceptions of other people's feelings. Working in a pair, put a:

PC for each perception check.

J for each statement that makes a judgment about the other person.

O for each statement that speaks for the other person rather than for yourself.

Q for each question that does not include a description of your perceptions of the other person's feelings.

Agree on each answer. Then combine with another pair and compare answers. Discuss each statement until everyone agrees.

Statements

_____ 1. Are you angry with me?

_____ 2. You look as if you are upset about what Sally said. Are you?

_____ 3. Why are you mad at me?

_____ 4. You look as if you feel put down by my statement. That's stupid!

_____ 5. What is it about your teacher that makes you resent her so much?

_____ 6. Are your feelings hurt again?

_____ 7. You look unhappy. Are you?

_____ 8. Am I right that you feel irritated that nobody commented on your suggestion?

Your Point of View

Everyone has his or her own point of view. Some people like Chinese food. Some people don't. If you like Chinese food you tend to assume that everyone does. If you like to be teased you assume that everyone likes to be teased.

In resolving conflicts it is important to understand the other person's point of view. An example of the need to understand other's points of view is given below. Read the story with your partner.

⤙ The Wise Men and the Elephant ⤚

Once upon a time, there were six wise men who lived in the same town. All six wise men were blind. One day, an elephant was brought to the town. The six men wanted to know what the elephant looked like. So they went to the elephant and started to touch it. The first one touched the elephant's big, flat ear. He felt it move slowly back and forth. "The elephant is like a fan," the first man cried. The second man felt the elephant's legs. "The elephant is like a tree," he cried. The third man was feeling the elephant's tail. "You are both wrong," he cried. "The elephant is like a rope." The fourth man was holding the elephant's trunk. "You are all wrong," he said. "The elephant is like a snake." The fifth man was touching one of the elephant's tusks. "The elephant is like a spear!" he yelled. "No, No!" the sixth man cried. "The elephant is like a high wall!" He was feeling the elephant's side. "Fan!" "Tree!" "Rope!" "Snake!" "Spear!" "Wall!" The six blind men shouted at each other for an hour. And they never agreed on what an elephant looked like.

10:27

YOUR POINT OF VIEW Exercise

Working in your pair, answer the following questions. They join another pair and share your answers.

1. Which blind man was right? _____

_____

2. What was their conflict based on? _____

_____

3. Were they really "wise"? How do you tell if someone is wise? _____

_____

4. How could the wise men have discovered what an elephant really looks like?

_____

5. What is the moral of the story? What does the story tell you about solving conflicts?

_____

———————————————◆———————————————

In your pair, rewrite the ending of the story to make it come out with a good solution to the conflict.

_____

_____

_____

_____

_____

Our Point of View:
Blind Spots

In the story, "The Wise Men And The Elephant" each of the six blind men argued about how an elephant looked. Their perceptions were based on their "blindness." At times, all of us suffer from "blind spots" because we tend to look at things from our own feelings, experiences, needs, and values.

Half full . . .
or half empty?

Puzzle pieces . . .
or a hidden word?

Air conditioner on ceiling . . .
or corner out of a cube?

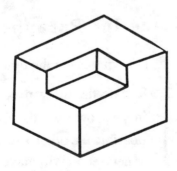

In your pair, discuss each of the pictures above.

1. Does everyone see the pictures in the same way?

2. How do you think "blind spots" affect conflicts?

3. Can "blind spots" cause prejudice?

4. What are three ways "blind spots" can be overcome?

 Choose an idea you feel strongly about. Interview other students to get different points of view. How did their perceptions differ from yours? Do you find evidence of "blind spots"?

Paraphrasing

1. Pick a real conflict that a member of the class is experiencing and identify four good alternative agreements. Number the agreements from "1" to "4" and then number the four corners of the room from "1" to "4."

2. Class members think of which option would make the best agreement. After considering the pro's and con's of each option, each students writes down their choice and the reasons why it is the best option on the sheet of paper.

3. All members of the class signify their choice by going to the corner of the room that represents the option they have chosen. They pair up with another student who made the same choice, compare and combine their reasons, and make a list of three reasons why their option is the best agreement. Each student needs a copy of the reasons.

4. Form groups of four (one student from each corner). Divide each group into pairs (student 1 meets with student 2, student 3 meets with student 4). One student presents their reasons. The other student listens carefully and then paraphrases the reasons. If the paraphrase is not accurate or complete, the student presenting corrects the paraphraser. The two students then reverse roles. Follow the rules for good paraphrasing. When both partners have paraphrased accurately and fully, switch partners (1 with 3, 2 with 4) and do present/paraphrase again. Switch partners again (1 with 4, 2 with 3) so that each student paraphrases the three other positions.

5. Students then decide if they wish to change their minds and choose a different option. The teacher asks students to go to the corner they now think would be the best option to agree to. The teacher counts how many students in each corner. The procedure may be repeated if there is time.

Rules for Paraphrasing

1. Put yourself in the other person's shoes.

2. Restate the other person's ideas and feelings in your own words. State as correctly as possible the other's reasons for believing his or her option will make the best agreement.

3. Start your remarks with, *You want...*, *You feel...*, and *You think...*

4. Show understanding and acceptance by nonverbal behaviors: tone of voice, facial expressions, gestures, eye contact, and posture.

From Their Shoes

The purpose of this exercise is to provide some practice in phrasing messages so they are appropriate to the receiver's perspective. The procedure is:

1. Form into groups of four and read the story entitled "The Typists," which follows below. As a group, write out what Jim might say to Sally, John Adams, and Dr. Elizabeth Smith. Then read the story entitled "The Laboratory Technicians." Write out what Edythe might say to Buddy, Helen, Dr. Smith, and Mrs. Jonathan.

2. In your group, discuss the following questions:
   a. How do your group's answers compare with the answers of the other groups?
   b. What did you learn about making messages appropriate to the perspective of the receiver?
   c. How do you find out what another person's perspective is?

The Typists

Sally and Jim are typists for a small publishing firm. Sally and Jim often tease each other about who is the faster typist. Their boss, John Adams, asks Jim to type a manuscript for one of their authors, whose name is Dr. Elizabeth Smith.

Dr. Smith is a well-known authority in mathematical psychology. The manuscript is very complicated. It contains a great many mathematical equations that are hard to type. It contains a lot of psychological jargon that Jim does not understand. It has handwritten notes all over it that are impossible for him to read. Dr. Smith, for example, has written sentences filled with psychological jargon, in small and sloppy handwriting and in ink that is smeared all over the page. It takes Jim hours trying to figure out what the handwritten notes say. Since he does not know what half the words mean, he cannot be sure whether he has typed the notes correctly or not. The math included in the manuscript, furthermore, is very complicated. It all has to be double checked to make sure it is correctly typed. This has taken hours and hours of proofreading and correcting mistakes. All in all, Jim hates the manuscript. But he is working hard to finish it correctly. To top it all off, Jim is using an old typewriter that is difficult to type on. He asked his boss, John, for a new one several weeks ago, but so far John has not tried to get him one.

One morning Sally looks over at Jim, smiles, and says, "That manuscript is really taking you a long time to type. How come?" Then John walks in and asks, "Jim, I have other typing for you to do and you're still working on Dr. Smith's manuscript. Why is it taking you so long?" Then Dr. Smith phones Jim and says, "Look! I have to revise the manuscript before next month! I need a clean, typed copy immediately. Why haven't you finished it?"

Taken from: Reaching Out: Interpersonal Effectiveness and Self-Actualization
(4th ed.) by David W. Johnson. Englewood Cliffs, NJ: Prentice-
Hall, 1990.

From Their Shoes (continued)

If you were Jim, would you say the same thing to Sally, John, and Dr. Smith? If you phrased your answers differently, what would you take into account about the persons? In phrasing his messages to each person, Jim might take into account:

1. Who the person is
2. What his or her position in the company is
3. How much the person knows about the condition and content of the manuscript
4. What the nature of the relationship between Jim and the person is
5. How appropriate it is to be fully honest about:
   a. Jim's feelings about the manuscript
   b. The facts about why it is so hard to type

The Laboratory Technicians

Buddy and Edythe are laboratory technicians in a large hospital. They have worked with each other for just a few days and do not know each other very well. One morning their supervisor, Helen, asks them to do a rush job on a blood sample. Helen is Edythe's older sister. Helen states that Dr. Smith is very worried about the patient. The tests, therefore, have to be done perfectly. The patient's name is Mrs. Jonathan. Edythe has never met either Dr. Smith or Mrs. Jonathan.

Edythe quickly conducts a series of blood tests. The results indicate that Mrs. Jonathan has blood cancer. As she finishes writing up the results of the tests, Buddy comes over and asks, "What'd you find?" Then Helen rushes in and asks, "What were the results of the blood tests for Dr. Smith?" Dr. Smith then calls on the phone for a quick report from Edythe. Finally, later in the day, Mrs. Jonathan calls up Edythe and says, "Look! I'm the person paying the bills! I want to know the results of my blood tests! And don't tell me to ask Dr. Smith! I already did and he won't tell me!"

If you were Edythe, would you say the same thing to Buddy, Helen, Dr. Smith, and Mrs. Jonathan? If the answer is no, what would you take into account in replying to each person? You might want to take the following factors into consideration:

1. Who the person is
2. What his or her position in the hospital is
3. How much the person knows about blood tests and blood cancer
4. What the nature of the relationship between Edythe and the person is
5. How appropriate it is to be fully honest about the results of the blood tests

11 BUILDING A CLIMATE FOR ACCEPTANCE OF DIFFERENCES

Introduction

One of the most important and long-standing goals of American education is to promote constructive relationships and positive attitudes among heterogeneous students. Almost every school district has acceptance of differences as one of their stated goals for students. Legislation exists that proclaims it is unlawful to segregate any student unless it is absolutely necessary. Ethnic minorities, handicapped students, non-English-speaking students, and even the subtle discouragement of females from interest in science and math are examples of areas where students need to be integrated with a wide variety of peers. Acceptance of differences is a central issue for all students. This chapter, however, focuses on the mainstreaming of handicapped students into the regular classroom.

Mainstreaming

Mainstreaming begins when a handicapped student walks into the regular classroom and faces his or her new classmates for the first time. While the handicapped child may feel apprehensive and afraid, the nonhandicapped children may be experiencing discomfort and uncertainty. There is strain on both sides and no guarantee that the students will feel any more comfortable with each other as time passes. Mainstreaming carries the risk of making relationships between handicapped and nonhandicapped students worse. The way in which student-student interaction is structured during instruction largely determines whether mainstreaming results in positive or negative relationships between handicapped and nonhandicapped students.

Placing handicapped students in the regular classroom is the beginning of an opportunity to influence handicapped students' lives deeply by promoting constructive relationships between them and their nonhandicapped peers. **Like all opportunities, however, main-**

streaming carries the risk of making things worse as well as the possibility of making things better. If mainstreaming goes badly, handicapped students will experience increased stigmatization, stereotyping, and rejection. Even worse, they may be ignored or treated with paternalistic care. If mainstreaming goes well, true friendships and positive relationships will develop between handicapped and nonhandicapped students. The essential question is, what does the regular classroom teacher do to ensure that mainstreaming goes well? The answer to this question goes beyond constructive teacher-student interaction and providing students with appropriate instruction materials. The answer is found in how relationships among students are structured.

Mainstreaming is based on the assumption that placing heterogeneous students (in terms of handicapping conditions) in the same school and classroom will facilitate positive relationships and attitudes among the students. Yet, there is considerable disagreement as to whether there are conditions under which physical proximity between handicapped and nonhandicapped students will lead to constructive relationships. The lack of theoretical models and apparently inconsistent research findings have left the impression that mainstreaming may not be working and may not be constructive. One of the key factors identified by the research as determining whether mainstreaming promotes positive or negative relationships among heterogenous students is whether students cooperate, compete, or work independently on their academic assignments. By structuring positive, negative, or no interdependence among heterogeneous students during academic learning situations, teachers can influence the pattern of interaction among students and the interpersonal attraction that results (Deutsch, 1962; Johnson & Johnson, 1975, 1984a; Johnson, Johnson, & Holubec, 1986).

It is when handicapped students are liked, accepted, and chosen as friends that mainstreaming becomes a positive influence on the lives of both handicapped and nonhandicapped students.

Any definition of mainstreaming that does not recognize the importance of relationships for handicapped students with nonhandicapped peers is incomplete. It is nonhandicapped peers who provide handicapped children and adolescents with entry into the normal life experiences of their age groups, such as going to dances, taking buses, going to movies, shopping, knowing what is "cool" and what is not, and dating. **Constructive peer relationships are not only an absolute necessity for maximal achievement and healthy social and cognitive development, they may be the primary relationships within which development and socialization take place.** Handicapped students especially need access to highly motivated and appropriately behaving peers.

11 : 2

Placing a handicapped student in the corner of a classroom and providing individualistic learning experiences is not effective mainstreaming. Mainstreaming is successful only if it includes the integration of handicapped students into friendships with nonhandicapped peers (Johnson, 1979; Johnson & Johnson, 1978). Thus, a definition of mainstreaming is as follows:

Mainstreaming is the provision of an appropriate educational opportunity for all handicapped students in the least restrictive alternative, based on individualized educational programs, with procedural safeguards and parent involvement, and aimed at providing handicapped students access to, and constructive interaction with, nonhandicapped peers.

Mainstreaming is not something you do for a few students. It is something you do for every student in your class. The instructional procedures needed for the constructive mainstreaming of handicapped students also benefit the shy student sitting over by the window, the overaggressive student who seeks acceptance through negative behaviors, the bright but stereotyped student sitting in the front row, and the average student in the center of the classroom who needs very little help and is often neglected. All students need to be accepted and benefit from a classroom where it is acceptable to be different. We have also found in our research that when nonhandicapped students collaborate with handicapped peers on instructional tasks, the result is increased empathy, altruism, and ability to view situations from a variety of perspectives. Even the most well-adjusted and hard-working students benefit from the instructional techniques associated with mainstreaming when it is conducted with some competence.

What Difference Does It Make?

When a teacher wishes to mainstream handicapped students into instructional situations with nonhandicapped peers, learning can be organized in one of three ways (Deutsch, 1962; Johnson & Johnson, 1991): (a) cooperatively (positive goal interdependence), (b) competitively (negative goal interdependence), and (c) individualistically (no goal interdependence). Each way of structuring learning goals promotes a different pattern of interaction among students. Compared with competitive and individualistic learning situations, working cooperatively with peers:

1. Creates a pattern of positive interaction in which there is:

   a. More direct face-to-face interaction among students.

   b. An expectation that one's peers will facilitate one's learning.

   c. More peer pressure toward achievement and appropriate classroom behavior.

   d. More reciprocal communication and fewer difficulties in communicating with each other.

   e. More actual helping, tutoring, assisting, and general facilitation of each other's learning.

   f. More open-mindedness to peers and willingness to be influenced by their ideas and information.

   g. More positive feedback to and reinforcement of each other.

   h. Less hostility, both verbal and physical, expressed towards peers.

2. Creates perceptions and feelings of:

   a. Higher trust in other students.

   b. More mutual concern and friendliness for other students, more attentiveness to peers, more feelings of obligation to and responsibility for classmates, and a greater desire to win the respect of other students.

   c. Stronger beliefs that one is liked, supported, and accepted by other students, and that other students care about how much one learns and want to help one learn.

   d. Lower fear of failure and higher psychological safety.

   e. Higher valuing of classmates.

f. Greater feelings of success.

Considerable evidence exists that cooperative learning experiences, compared with competitive and individualistic ones, promote more positive relationships between handicapped and nonhandicapped students (Johnson & Johnson, 1975, 1978, 1983, 1984b, 1985a, 1989a; Johnson, Johnson & Maruyama, 1983). A meta-analysis reviewed all available studies comparing the three types of instructional situations on relationships among students (98 studies conducted between 1944 and 1982) and found that these results held among handicapped and nonhandicapped students, students from different ethnic groups, and homogeneous students (Johnson & Johnson, 1989a; Johnson, Johnson, & Maruyama, 1983).

The theoretical framework behind the meta-analysis provides a basis for some generalizations about cooperative learning where students participate in experiences designed to include mutual goals and responsibilities for learning. Handicapped students are stigmatized and viewed by peers in negative and prejudiced ways. Physical proximity alone does not change this negative view. Nonhandicapped students may view their handicapped peers more negatively or more positively. Whether the relationships between handicapped and nonhandicapped become more negative or more positive depends on how the teacher structures classroom learning. When learning situations are structured cooperatively, and handicapped and nonhandicapped students work together in the same learning groups, then they interact in positive ways, feel supported and encouraged to achieve, gain an understanding of each other's perspectives, build a differentiated and realistic view of each other, accept themselves as their peers accept them, feel academically successful, and develop a positive relationship with each other. When learning situations are structured competitively or individualistically, handicapped and nonhandicapped students do not interact with each other, feel disconnected and rejected by each other, are inaccurate in their perspective-taking, have monopolistic and oversimplified views of each other, have low self-esteem, are relatively unsuccessful academically, and have negative relationships with each other.

As nonhandicapped students work closely with handicapped peers, the boundaries of the handicap become more and more clear. While handicapped students may be able to hide the extent of their disability when they are isolated, intensive interaction in a cooperative learning situation promotes a realistic as well as differentiated view of handicapped students and their disabilities. If a handicapped member of a learning group cannot read or speak clearly, the other members of the learning group become highly aware of that fact. With interaction, however, there also comes a decrease in the primary potency of the handicap and a decrease in the stigmatization connected with the handicapped person.

11 : 5

Along with the more realistic and dynamic perception of each other, a direct consequence of cooperative experiences is that nonhandicapped students' acceptance of and liking for handicapped peers increases when interaction occurs within a context of positive goal interdependence, and the self-attitudes of both nonhandicapped and handicapped students also become more positive (Deutsch, 1962; Johnson & Johnson, 1989a).

Both competitive and individualistic learning activities provide little or no information about handicapped peers, thus allowing initial stereotypes to continue. What little information is available is likely to confirm existing stereotypes that handicapped peers are "losers" and "different". The boundaries of the handicap are not clarified and the labeled handicap maintains its primary potency and the stereotype can even become stronger. It does not make any sense to mainstream handicapped students into the regular classroom and have them compete with the other students. That does not build acceptance. It is equally ludicrous to mainstream students into the regular classroom to work alone, individualistically, where they are seen, but no interaction takes place. The only interaction pattern which builds acceptance of differences and positive relationships between handicapped and nonhandicapped students is cooperation.

Integrating Handicapped Students Into Cooperative Learning Groups

When handicapped students are mainstreamed into cooperative learning groups, there are sometimes student anxieties and concerns that teachers need to respond to so the process runs more smoothly and is more effective. Careful attention to positive interdependence, individual accountability, collaborative skills, and group processing usually solve such problems. Three of the most common problems are the handicapped students being fearful and anxious, the nonhandicapped students being concerned about having their grades affected, and the handicapped students being passively uninvolved. Methods for dealing with such problems have been identified and practiced in successful programs.

Anxious Handicapped Students

Many handicapped students may be fearful and anxious about participating in a cooperative learning group with nonhandicapped peers. Their anxiety may be alleviated through the following actions:

1. **Explain the procedures the learning group will follow.**

2. **Give the handicapped students a structured role so that they understand their responsibilities.** Even if a student cannot read, he or she can listen carefully and summarize what everyone in the group is saying, provide leadership, help to keep the group's work organized, and so forth. There is always some way to facilitate group work, no matter what handicap a student may have.

3. **Enlist the aid of a special education teacher to coach the handicapped students in the behaviors and collaborative skills needed within the cooperative group.** Pretraining in collaborative skills and periodic sessions to monitor how well the skills are being implemented will increase the handicapped student's confidence.

4. **Enlist the aid of a special education teacher to pretrain the handicapped student in the academic skills needed to complete the group's work.** Try to give the handicapped student a source of expertise the group will need.

Anxious Nonhandicapped Students

Many nonhandicapped students may be concerned that the handicapped student will lower the overall performance of their group. The three major ways of alleviating their concern are as follows:

1. **Train nonhandicapped students in helping, tutoring, teaching, and sharing skills.** The special education teacher may wish to explain to the group how best to teach the handicapped group member. Many teaching skills, such as the use of praise and prompting, are easily taught to students.

2. **Make the academic requirements for the handicapped students reasonable.** Ways in which lessons can be adapted so the students at different achievement levels can participate in the same cooperative group are to:

11 : 7

    a. Use different criteria for success for each group member.

    b. Vary the amount each group member is expected to master.

    c. Give group members different assignments, list, work, or problems and then use the average percentage worked correctly as the group's score.

    d. Use improvement scores for the handicapped students. If it is unclear how to implement these procedures, consult with the special education teacher to decide what is appropriate for the specific handicapped student.

3. **Give bonus points to the groups that have handicapped members.** This will create a situation in which nonhandicapped students want to work with their handicapped classmates to receive the bonus points.

Passively Uninvolved Handicapped Students

When handicapped students are turning away from the group, not participating, not paying attention to the group's work, saying little or nothing, showing no enthusiasm, or not bringing their work or materials, the teacher may wish to

1. **Jigsaw materials so that each group member has information the others need.** If the passive uninvolved student does not voluntarily contribute his or her information, the other group members will actively involve the student.

2. **Divide up roles and assign the passively uninvolved student one that is essential to the group's success.**

3. **Reward the group on the basis of their average performance, which will encourage other group members to derive strategies for increasing the problem member's involvement.**

What About Teacher/Teacher Cooperation?

Cooperation is powerful for teachers as well as students and will produce the same positive outcomes (Johnson & Johnson, 1980). It is important for successful mainstreaming that the relationships between regular education and special education teachers be positive and cooperative (we arc in this sink or swim together). In the districts where these positive relationships exist, and both teachers are concerned about structuring heterogeneous, cooperative groups in the classroom, mainstreaming becomes a positive force. And yet, the reality of many school settings is that teachers work alone, do their job independently, and perhaps even compete with one another. Cooperation among staff in the school setting should be structured with some care and rewarded. Some advice for doing so includes:

1. **Maintaining contact.** Contact between regular classroom and special education teachers needs to be scheduled and informal. The meetings in which the IEP's for individual handicapped students are written provide a place where the positive interdependence of shared goals for the student are formed. It is essential that both teachers assume responsibility for the student and believe that they share responsibility for the plan.

2. **Establishing a division of labor.** This is a resource interdependence that specifies each teacher's role in the mainstreaming effort. **The basic role of the regular classroom teacher is:**

   a. Structuring cooperative lessons which place handicapped and nonhandicapped students into the same group.

   b. Observing students as they work.

   c. Identifying problems in the cognitive and social functioning of all group members, both handicapped and nonhandicapped.

   The **special education teacher** can also engage in supportive acitivites such as the following:

   a. Train all students in the social skills (e.g., leadership and communication skills they need to function effectively as part of a cooperative learning group).

b. Give special tutoring to collaborating pairs of students (one handicapped and one nonhandicapped) in how to function effectively in their cooperative learning group and to help each other to learn more and behave appropriately.

c. Provide the regular classroom teacher with guidelines on how much each mainstreamed student can realistically achieve so that group scores can be adjusted to encourage maximal achievement and to avoid penalizing nonhandicapped students.

d. Be available for unforeseen problems in building and maintaining accepting and supportive relationships between handicapped and nonhandicapped students.

3. **In order to work together effectively, the regular and special education teachers should talk regularly to plan their joint teaching activities and evaluate their efforts.** At regularly scheduled meetings, the teachers can discuss each student being mainstreamed, refer the student for further evaluation when it is warranted, and plan interventions to improve the functioning of the student's cooperative groups when it is needed. Collaboration takes planning and it needs to be evaluated. One of the most difficult things to find (and one of the most valuable) is time for teachers to meet with each other to plan and evaluate their collaborative activities.

4. **The regular and special education teachers should reap the benefits of their collaboration; they should celebrate their successes and appreciate each other's efforts to promote more positive and supportive relationships among students, and be rewarded for their efforts by administrators.**

Summary

The central question in mainstreaming is, "How will handicapped and nonhandicapped students interact with each other?" Placing handicapped students in the regular classroom is the beginning of an opportunity but, like all opportunities, it carries a risk of making things worse as well as the possibility of making things better. Physical proximity of handicapped and nonhandicapped students does not guarantee positive attitudes and increased acceptance; increased prejudice and rejection may be the result. The crucial factor in whether a process of acceptance or a process of rejection occurs in the classroom is the kind of student-student interaction fostered by the teacher. Cooperative interactions between handicapped and nonhandicapped students encourage the positive social interaction.

Cooperative instruction is based on a set of practical strategies which any teacher can master. It does not require the regular classroom teacher to become an expert in special education. The model described in this chapter provides a natural way for regular and special education teachers to work together as a team in planning for cooperative learning.

One of the better ways to build a collaborative relationship between teachers, especially special education and regular classroom teachers, is to inservice them as a team in the use of cooperative learning groups so that they strengthen their own relationship and examine their own cooperative skills as they are learning about how to do the same for handicapped and nonhandicapped students. Cooperation among teachers and administration is needed for mainstreaming to be successful and if it begins during the inservice, it will more likely occur in the school setting.

When handicapped students are mainstreamed into the regular classroom, the primary goal is to involve them in constructive relationships with nonhandicapped peers. When cooperative learning is emphasized, that goal is accomplished along with several other important instructional outcomes. With the amount of research evidence available, it is surprising that classroom practice is so oriented toward individualistic and competitive learning. It is time for the discrepancy to be reduced between what research indicates is effective and what teachers actually do in practice.

Whether or not mainstreaming results in positive or negative outcomes for handicapped and nonhandicapped students depends on how teachers structure classroom learning. If positive cross-handicapped relationships are to be established and the achievement and social development of both handicapped and nonhandicapped students are to be maximized, learning situations should be structured cooperatively, not competitively or individualistically. For cooperative learning to be most effective, positive interdependence, individual accountability, training in collaborative skills, and processing of how effectively the group is working have to occur. The specific procedures teachers need to structure cooperative learning have been specified and validated through numerous research studies. Mainstreaming may be implemented successfully, and the predominant use of cooperative learning procedures serve to facilitate the special education experiences received by all students participating in the process.

EXERCISE

MATERIALS

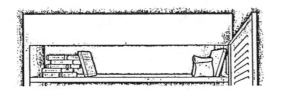

Cooperative Poetry: I, Too

EDYTHE JOHNSON HOLUBEC

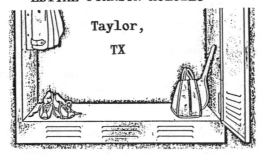

Taylor,

TX

Subject Area: English

Grade Level: Junior and Senior High

Lesson Summary: Students read a poem and answer questions about it.

Instructional Objectives: Students gain practice in reading and understanding poetry, in sharing their interpretations of a poem, and in listening to and considering other interpretations and other points of view.

Materials:

ITEM	NUMBER NEEDED
Copy of I, Too (with discussion questions and agreement form)	One per student
Role cards	One set per group
Observation form	One per group

Time Required: One class period

 © Appears in **Structuring Cooperative Learning: The 1987 Lesson-Plan Handbook** by D. W. Johnson, R. T. Johnson, and Edythe Johnson Holubec. Edina, MN: Interaction Book Company, 1987.

≈ Decisions ≈

Group Size: Four (five if an observer is used)

**Assignment
to Groups:**   Teacher assigned, with a high, two medium, and a low achieving student in each group.   Also, each group should contain males and females and a mix of racial/cultural backgrounds.

Roles: **Encourager:** Watches to make certain all group members are contributing and invites silent members in by asking them for their opinions or help.

Reader: Reads the poems to the group.   Also serves as the **Praiser** who praises good ideas or helpful suggestions of group members.

Recorder: Records the group's answers and summarizes each answer until the group is satisfied with it.

Checker: Checks to make certain group members can explain each answer and the group's rationale for it.

Observer: (Optional) Does not take part in the discussion of the poem but observes the group's interactions, records the behaviors on the Observation Sheet, and reports to the group during the processing time.

≈ The Lesson ≈

Instructional Task:

Your task will be to read a poem and answer the questions. I want you to come up with three possible answers for each question, then circle your favorite.

Positive Interdependence:

I want one set of answers from the group that you all agree upon.

Individual Accountability:

I will ask each of you sometime during the class period to give me the rationale for your group's answers.

Criteria for Success:

Your group will start with a grade of 100 on this assignment. I will pick someone at random to explain one of your group's answers to me. If s/he can do that, you will keep your score. If not, you will lose 10 points. I will check at least three of you on at least three of the questions.

Expected Behaviors:

I want to see each of you contributing and helping your group, listening to your group members with care, and pushing the group to look for all the possibilities before deciding on an answer. Also, your group will get a set of role cards. Pass them out randomly, read your role, and make certain you know how to do it before the Reader starts reading the poem. The Observer will report on how well s/he saw you performing your roles during the processing time. (If necessary, go over the roles to make certain the students understand them.)

～ Monitoring and Processing ～

Monitoring: Circulate among and listen to the groups. Check to make certain the groups are doing the task right (coming up with at least three possible answers, then agreeing on their favorite) and that group members are performing their roles.

11:15

Intervening: Feel free to interrupt while the groups are working. Push groups to explore interesting answers and elaborate on superficial ones. Praise examples of good group skills. If you see an interaction problem, encourage the group to stop and solve it before continuing.

Closing: After the groups have finished answering the questions, have a class discussion over the answers. Pick group members at random to explain answers, keeping track of contributors and groups and grading groups accordingly. List the groups' answers on the board, then see if the class can decide on answers all members agree on.

Processing: After the class discussion, have the groups get back together to process. Have the observer report on what he/she saw and show each group their marks on the observation sheet. Then have the groups write down their answers to the following questions:

1. *What behaviors did we do well?*
2. *What behaviors do we need to improve upon?*
3. *How well did we perform our roles?*
4. *What would help us perform our roles better?*

If there is time, have the groups share some of their answers with the whole class.

◄ Observation Sheet ►

	Group Members			
Contributes Ideas				
Encourages Others				
Praises Good Ideas				
Summarizes				
Pushes Deeper				

Other Helpful Behaviors Noticed:

I, Too

By Langston Hughes

I, too, sing America.

I am the darker brother.
They send me to eat in the kitchen
When company comes,
But I laugh,
And eat well,
And grow strong.

Tomorrow,
I'll be at the table
When company comes.
Nobody'll dare
Say to me,
"Eat in the kitchen,"
Then.

Besides,
They'll see how beautiful I am
And be ashamed -

I, too, am America.

---

1. What are the emotions expressed by the poem?

2. What do you think/feel about what the poem says?

3. What are the three key words in the poem?
   (Be able to defend your choice.)

4. What is the poem saying?

To group members: When you sign your name for the answers to these questions, it means that you have participated in the assignment and understand the questions and the answers. You also must agree with the answers and be able to explain them.

The lesson developed around this poem was originated by Edythe Johnson Holubec, a high school English teacher in Taylor, TX (and David and Roger's sister).

12 FACULTY WORKING COOPERATIVELY WITH COLLEAGUES

Introduction

> *To have joy one must share it. Happiness was born a twin.*
>
> Indian Proverb

The school is an organization and, similar to all organizations, it has to achieve its goals, maintain effective working relationships among members, and adapt to changes in its community, country, and world. Like all organizations, schools must adapt to changes in their environment or risk fading away like the dinosaurs. The dinosaur presumably made good day-to-day adaptations to its environment. It probably made a pretty good choice of what leaves to eat off what trees and selected the most desirable swamps in which to slosh. At a tactical level of decision, we have no reason to believe that these giant beasts were not reasonably competent. But, when faced with major changes in (a) the earth's climate and (b) competition from other animal life, the dinosaur was unable to make the fundamental changes required to adapt to the new environment conditions. Schools may now be faced with new environmental conditions that require them to do what the dinosaur could not.

To adapt to changing conditions in the community, society, and world, and to ensure that the school continuously develops as an organization, individuals within a school must **diagnoses** how effectively the school is functioning and then **intervene** to improve its effectiveness. Fundamental changes in current environmental conditions require fundamental changes in the organizational structure of the school. Structural change requires the redesign of work, a new organizational culture, and changes in the attitudes and competencies of administrators, faculty, and students. The required changes in schools parallel the changes in organizational structure taking place within business and industry throughout the world.

For decades business and industrial organizations have functioned as "mass manufacturing" organizations that divided work into small component parts performed by individuals who worked separate from and, in many cases, in competition with peers. Personnel were considered to be interchangeable parts in the organizational machine. Such an organizational structure no longer seems effective and many companies are turning to the high productivity generated by teams.

Most schools have also been structured as mass manufacturing organizations. Teachers work alone, in their own classrooms, with their own set of students, and with their own set of curriculum materials. Students could be assigned to any faculty member because teachers were interchangeable parts in the education machine and, conversely, an teacher could be given any student to teach. Schools need to change from a mass- manufacturing competitive/individualistic organizational structure to a "high performance" cooperative team-based organizational structure. The new organizational structure is generally known as "the cooperative school."

The Organizational Structure Of Schools

Two are better than one, because they have a good reward for their toil. For if they fall, one will lift up his fellow; but woe to him who is alone when he falls and has not another to lift him up...And though a man might prevail against one who is alone, two will withstand him. A threefold cord is not quickly broken.

Ecclesiastes 4:9-12

Schools are not buildings, curriculums, and machines. **Schools are relationships and interactions among people** (Johnson & Johnson, 1989b). How the interpersonal interaction is structured determines how effective schools are. There are three ways that faculty relationships may be structured: competitively, individualistically, and cooperatively. Faculty effectiveness depends on the interpersonal interactions being oriented toward cooperatively achieving the goals of the school. Schools must be cooperative places. The **cooperatively structured school** consists of cooperative learning within the classroom and cooperative efforts within the faculty. In other words, the organizational structure of schools must change from a competitive/individualistic mass-manufacturing structure within which faculty work alone to a high-performance team-based organizational structure in which faculty work in teams. Such a change will not be easy in many cases as the organizational structure of the school traditionally has discouraged collegiality among teachers and severely limited their opportunities to cooperate with each other.

Schools are **loosely coupled** organizations in which teachers and administrators function far more independently than interdependently, with little or no supervision, engaging in actions that do not determine or affect what others do, and engage in actions that seem isolated from their consequences (Johnson & Johnson, 1989b). Teachers have been systematically isolated from one another during most of the school day. And that isolation often results in teachers experiencing an amorphous and diffuse competition with their peers.

A cooperative school structure begins in the classroom. Faculty typically cannot promote isolation and competition among students and be collaborative with colleagues. What is promoted in the instructional situations tends to dominate relationships among faculty. Teachers who regularly tell students, "Do not copy," "I want to see what you can do, not your neighbor," "Let's see who is best," and "Who is the winner," will in turn tend to approach their colleagues with the attitudes of, "Don't copy from me," and "Who is the best teacher in our department?" The cooperative context that is necessary for faculty to learn from their colleagues begins in the classroom. Teachers may be expected to:

1. Structure the majority of learning situations cooperatively (see Johnson, Johnson, & Holubec, 1990). Cooperative learning requires that the teacher carefully creates positive interdependence, face-to-face promotive interaction, individual accountability, social skills, and group processing.

2. Teach students the leadership, decision-making, communication, trust-building, and conflict-resolution skills they need to function effectively within cooperative learning groups (see Johnson, 1990, 1991; Johnson & F. Johnson, 1991).

The use of cooperative learning will increase student achievement, build better working relationships among students and between the teacher and the students, and increase the school's ability to respond flexibly to new demands from and changing conditions in the community. In addition, by structuring cooperative learning and teaching students how to work effectively within cooperative teams, teachers themselves learn the skills and attitudes required to work cooperatively with their colleagues.

The second level in creating a cooperative school is to form colleagial support groups, task forces, and ad hoc decision- making groups within the department and school (Johnson & Johnson,

1989b). The cooperative interaction among faculty should be as carefully structured as is the cooperative interaction among students in the classroom. All faculty should be involved in cooperative teams that meet regularly to work on meaningful tasks. The more faculty use cooperative learning, furthermore, the more likely they are to be productive members of faculty teams.

The third level in creating a cooperative school is to implement administrative cooperative teams within the school (Johnson & Johnson, 1989b). The president should organize administrators into cooperative teams similarly to how faculty organize students into cooperative learning groups. All administrators should be involved in cooperative teams that meet regularly and work on meaningful tasks. If administrators compete to see who is the best, they are unlikely to be able to promote cooperation among faculty. The more the school faculty work in cooperative teams, the easier it will be for faculty to use cooperative learning and vice versa.

What is good for students is even better for faculty. The research that validates the use of cooperative learning in the classroom also validates the use of cooperative faculty teams at the departmental or school level. To increase the cooperation among faculty, faculty members may be organized into three different types of cooperative teams: colleagial support groups to encourage and support each other's efforts to use cooperative learning, task forces to make recommendations about how to deal with schoolwide issues such as curriculum revision, and ad hoc decision-making groups to involve all faculty members in the important school decisions. The organizational structure of the classroom, department, and school are then congruent. Each level of cooperative teams supports and enhances the other levels.

Colleagial Support Groups

The success of a school largely depends on the success teachers have in educating students. The success of teachers in educating students depends on (a) how committed teachers are to continually increasing their instructional expertise and (b) the amount of physical and psychological energy teachers commit to their work. The commitment of physical and psychological energy to achieve the goal of improving one's instructional expertise is heavily influenced by the degree to which colleagues are supportive and encouraging. **Teachers generally teach better when they experience support from their peers.** In most schools, however, such support is hard to achieve. As a result, teachers may feel harried, isolated, and alienated. Yet there is a human need to work cooperatively and intimately with supportive people. Colleagial support groups provide teachers with the opportunity to share ideas, support each other's efforts to use cooperative learning, and encourage each other.

A **colleagial support group** consists of two to five teachers who have the goal of improving each other's instructional expertise and promoting each other's professional growth (Johnson & Johnson, 1989b). Colleagial support groups should be small and members should be heterogeneous. **Colleagial support groups are first and foremost safe places where:**

1. Members like to be.

2. There is support, caring, concern, laughter, camaraderie, and celebration.

3. The primary goal of improving each other's competence in using cooperative learning is never obscured.

The purpose of this colleagial support group is to work jointly to improve continuously each other's expertise in using cooperative learning procedures or, in other words, to:

1. Provide the help, assistance, support, and encouragement each member needs to gain as high a level of expertise in using cooperative learning procedures as possible.

2. Serve as an informal support group for sharing, letting off steam, and discussing problems connected with implementing cooperative learning procedures.

3. Serve as a base for teachers experienced in the use of cooperative learning procedures to teach other teachers how to structure and manage lessons cooperatively.

4. Create a setting in which camaraderie and shared success occur and are celebrated.

Colleagial support groups succeed when they are carefully structured to ensure active participation by members and concrete products (such as lesson plans) that members can actually use. The structure must clearly point members toward increasing each other's expertise in implementing cooperative learning to prevent meetings from degenerating into gripe sessions, destructive criticism of each other, or amateur therapy. Members need to believe they sink or swim together, ensure considerable face-to- face discussion and assistance takes place, hold each other accountable to implement cooperative learning in between meetings, learn and use the interpersonal and small group skills required to make meetings productive, and periodically initiate a discussion of how effective the colleagial support group is in carrying out its mission. Task-oriented discussion, planning, and problem solving, as well as empathy and mutual support, should dominate the meetings.

The three key activities of a colleagial support group are (Little, 1981):

1. Frequent professional discussions of cooperative learning in which information is shared, successes are celebrated, and problems connected with implementation are solved.

2. Coplanning, codesigning, copreparing, and coevaluating curriculum materials relevant to implementing cooperative learning in the classrooms of the members.

3. Coteaching and reciprocal observations of each other teaching lessons structured cooperatively and jointly processing those observations.

Professional Discussions

> *Knowing is not enough; we must apply. Willing is not enough; we must do.*
>
> Goethe

What most teachers find very useful is opportunities to talk to each other about teaching. Within the colleagial support groups there is frequent, continuous, increasingly concrete and precise talk about the use of cooperative learning pro-

cedures. Through such discussion members build a concrete, precise, and coherent shared language that can describe the complexity of using cooperative learning procedures, distinguish one practice and its virtues from another, and integrate cooperative learning procedures into other teaching practices and strategies that they are already using. Through such discussions, teachers will exchange successful strategies and materials. They will focus on solving specific problems members may be having in perfecting their use of cooperative learning strategies. Most of all, teachers' comprehension and deeper-level understanding of the nature of cooperative learning will be enhanced by explaining how they are implementing it to their colleagues.

Expertise in using cooperative learning begins with conceptual understanding of what it is. Teachers must conceptually understand (a) the nature of cooperative learning, (b) how to implement the cooperative learning step-by-step, and (c) the results expected from the effective implementation of cooperative learning. Teachers must also think critically about the strategy and adapt it to their specific students and subject areas. They must retain what they have learned, integrate it into their conceptual networks about teaching, and conceptually combine cooperative learning with their existing teaching strategies. Such conceptual understanding is enhanced when teachers **orally summarize, explain, and elaborate** what they know about the cooperative learning to colleagues. Oral reviews consolidate and strengthen what is known and provide relevant feedback about the degree to which mastery and understanding have been achieved. The way people conceptualize material and organize it cognitively is markedly different when they are learning material for their own benefit from when they are learning material to teach to others (Murray, 1983). Material being learned to be taught or explained to others is learned at a higher conceptual level than is material being learned for one's own use. Such discussions, furthermore, enable the listeners to benefit from others' knowledge, reasoning, and skills. The concept of "gatekeeper," for example, was created to explain the process of information flow through an organization. A **gatekeeper** is a colleague who is sought out to explain what a new strategy is and how it may be used. It is within colleagial support groups that faculty exchange understandings of what cooperative learning is and how it may be used within their classes.

Joint Planning and Curriculum Design

Well begun is half done.

Aristotle

Once cooperative learning is understood conceptually, it must be implemented. If faculty are to progress through the initial awkward and mechanical stages to a routine-use, automatic level of mastery, they must (a) receive continual feedback as to the accuracy of their implementation and (b) be encouraged to persevere in their implementation attempts long enough to integrate cooperative learning into their ongoing instructional practice. Thus, productivity hinges on having colleagues to co- plan and co-teach lessons, observe one's implementation efforts, provide feedback, and encourage one to keep trying until the strategy is used routinely without conscious thought. Needless to say, such procedural learning usually does not take place within competitive and individualistic situations.

Members of professional support groups should frequently plan, design, prepare, and evaluate lesson plans together. This results in teachers sharing the burden of developing materials needed to conduct cooperative lessons, generating emerging understanding of cooperative learning strategies, making realistic standards for students and colleagues, and providing the machinery for each other to implement cooperative learning procedures. Teachers should leave each meeting of their colleagial support group with something concrete that helps them implement cooperative learning. The process of planning a lesson together, each conducting it, and then processing it afterwards is often constructive. This cycle of **coplanning, parallel teaching, coprocessing** may be followed by one of **coplanning, coteaching, coprocessing**.

The discussions and coplanning that take place within colleagial support groups ensures that teachers clarify their understanding of what cooperative learning is and create a support and accountability system to ensure that they try it out. The next steps in increasing expertise are to assess the consequences of using cooperative learning, reflecting on how well the lesson went, and teaching another cooperative lesson in a modified way. All of these steps benefit from the input and feedback from supportive colleagues. The more colleagues are involved in your teaching, the more valuable the help and assistance they can provide.

Reciprocal Observations

Members of colleagial support groups should frequently observe each other teaching lessons structured cooperatively and then provide each other with useful feedback. This observation and feedback provide members with shared experiences to discuss and refer to. The observation and feedback, furthermore, have to be reciprocal. **Teachers especially need to treat each other with the deference that shows they recognize that anyone can have good and bad days and that the mistakes they note in a colleague may be the same mistakes that they will make tomorrow.**

Guidelines to follow when observing the teaching of other colleagial support group members include:

1. Realize that you can learn from every other member of the group, regardless of his or her experience and personal characteristics.

2. Make sure observation and feedback is reciprocal.

3. Ask the person you're observing what he/she would like you to focus your attention on. This may include specific students the teacher may wish observed, specific aspects

of structuring interdependence or accountability, or some other aspect of cooperative learning.

4. Focus feedback and comments on what has taken place, not on personal competence.

5. Don't confuse a teacher's personal worth with her/his current level of competence in using cooperative learning procedures.

6. Be concrete and practical in your discussions about how effectively members are using cooperative learning procedures.

7. Above all, communicate respect for each other's overall teaching competence. We all have professional strengths and weaknesses. Recognize and respect those strengths in each other.

Working cooperatively with others brings with it camaraderie, friendship, warmth, satisfaction, and feelings of success. These are all to be enjoyed.

Selecting Teachers To Train

Once you have decided to form a colleagial support group, you must select colleagues to be members. Look for someone who is interested in trying cooperative learning, who will follow through and actually use cooperative learning, and who is your friend (or at least someone you would enjoy working with). Choose colleagues who are motivated to use cooperative learning, who are committed enough to persist until the group is successful, and who are supportive, caring, and interpersonally skilled. The teacher next door or across the hall (with whom you are already supporting each other's teaching efforts or are friends) is often the best one to start with.

Initiating Contact

After deciding whom you would like to work with, approach them very carefully (to establish a collaborative relationship). This is a touchy task as it is easy to drive colleagues away. Present the possibility of working together to improve your own use of cooperative learning as well as their'. Never

say "It is easy" or "Anyone can do it!" Be sure to be realistic about the length of time it will take to gain some expertise in using cooperative learning procedures and the amount of work it will take. And never say, "Have I got a good idea for you! Here is how we are going to change the way you teach!" Instead, ask for help in implementing cooperative learning in your classroom, use a soft approach of indicating an open door, make the cooperative (not expert-novice) relationship clear, and trade lessons.

Once you have picked one or more colleagues to work with and approached them about working together on implementing cooperative learning, you must know how to proceed. In essence, you must know how to help other people develop expertise in implementing cooperative learning.

Gaining Expertise In Using Cooperative Learning

Colleagial support groups are aimed at increasing faculty expertise in using cooperative learning. The professional discussions, coplanning of lessons, and reciprocal observing of each other's teaching all form a process within which faculty may progressively refine their ability to use cooperative learning procedures competently. More specifically, faculty progressively refine their competence in using cooperative learning by:

1. **Understanding conceptually what cooperative learning is and how it may be implemented in their classrooms.**

2. **Trying cooperative learning out in their classrooms with their students.** Faculty must be willing to take risks by experimenting with new instructional and managing strategies and procedures. Faculty risk short-term failure to gain long-term success in increasing their expertise by experimenting with new strategies and procedures. It is assumed that one's efforts will fail to match an ideal of what one wishes to accomplish for a considerable length of time until the new strategy is overlearned to a routine-use, automated level.

3. **Assessing how well cooperative learning lessons went and obtaining feedback on one's teaching from others.** Although the lesson may have not gone well, from the progressive refinement point of view failure never occurs. There are simply approximations of what one wants and with refining and fine- tuning of procedures and more practice the approximations get successively closer and closer to the ideal.

4. **Reflecting on what one did and how it may be improved.** The discrepancy between the real and the ideal is considered and plans are made about altering one's behavior in order to get a better match in the future.

Building

Expertise

5. **Trying cooperative learning out again in a modified and improved way.** Perseverance in using cooperative learning again and again and again is required until the teacher can teach a cooperative lesson routinely and without conscious planning or thought. Even at this point feedback should be attained, reflection on how to improve the implementation of cooperation, and refining and fine-tuning should take place until the teacher retires (or beyond).

As part of gaining expertise in using cooperative learning, teachers must:

1. **Take ownership of cooperative learning** and incorporate it into their professional identity. The more faculty use cooperative learning, and the more effort they expend implementing cooperative learning, the greater their feelings of success and the greater their ownership of cooperative learning.

2. **Train a colleague.** Expertise is never fully attained until one teaches what one knows to someone else.

Faculty do not become proficient in using cooperative learning procedures from attending a workshop or from reading this book. **Faculty become proficient and competent from doing.** For faculty to develop the expertise in cooperative learning procedures they need to structure a cooperative lesson routinely without conscious planning or thought, they have to use cooperative learning procedures frequently and regularly for several years. **Progressive refinement is not something you do once, it is a way of life!**

Be Inclusive, Not Exclusive

As your success in reaching out to and working with colleagues is recognized, colleagues will begin asking you to work with them next. Be open to such invitations. When you do not have time to meet all the requests, pair each new teacher with an experienced veteran that you have trained. Keep your study groups small. Each time a teacher you are training achieves some expertise in implementing cooperative learning, pair him or her with a teacher just expressing an interest in doing so. This matchmaking will allow the teacher with newly gained expertise to solidify what they have learned by teaching it to another person. Give guidance as to how to reach out effectively. Keep in contact with the colleagues you have trained and regularly provide support and assistance. Finally, periodically lead a celebration of the success they are having in implementing cooperative learning. A sense of purpose and accomplishment should be nurtured among the teachers you train.

Providing Leadership To Colleagial Support Groups

For colleagial support groups to flourish they must be structured, encouraged, and rewarded by administrators. The Department Chair or even the Dean becomes the team leader even though they may attend only periodically. In general, leadership is provided by (Johnson & Johnson, 1989b):

1. **Challenging The Status Quo**: The status quo is the competitive-individualistic mass-manufacturing structure that dominates schools and classrooms. In the classroom it is represented by the old paradigm that is using operationalized by lectures, whole class discussions, individual worksheets, and tests. Leaders challenge the efficacy of the status quo.

2. **Inspiring A Mutual Vision Of What The School Could Be**: Leaders enthusiastically and frequently communicate the dreams of establishing the new paradigm of teaching throughout the school. The leader is the **keeper of the dream** who inspires commitment to joint goals and objectives.

3. **Empowering Through Cooperative Teams**: This is the most important of all leadership activities. When faculty or students feel helpless and discouraged, providing them with a team creates hope and opportunity. It is social support from and accountability to valued peers that motivates committed efforts to achieve and succeed. In the classroom this means using cooperative learning. In the school this means using faculty teams.

4. **Leading By Example**: Leaders model the use of cooperative strategies and procedures and take risks to increase their professional competence. Actions must be congruent with words. What is advocated must be demonstrated publicly.

5. **Encouraging The Heart To Persist**: Long-term, committed efforts to achieve come from the heart, not the head. It takes courage and hope to continue to strive for increased knowledge and expertise. It is the social support and concrete assistance from teammates that provides the strength to persist and excel.

Within this general leadership model, there are specific actions that leaders need to take to supervise and enhance the effectiveness of cooperative teams.

1. **Be a coach, not an autocrat.**

2. **Assume that all team members are competent and motivated.** Respect their abilities and respect them as people.

3. **Confront lazy and maladapted members.** One of the surest ways to undermine a team is to ignore its nonperformers. The resentment by other members will quickly destroy the team's effectiveness. When faced with a nonperformer or an obstructor, the leader clarifies what is expected of a team member, notes where changes are needed, gives a timeframe to implement the changes, and sets a clear deadline.

4. **Know how to structure and promote controversy.** Constructive conflict is the key to making team meetings fun, interesting, and challenging. Members must honestly share their points of view which will inevitably result in disagreement and conflict. Leaders help make the conflict a source of creativity and enjoyment.

5. **Be a player.** The leader must be a willing worker, a player, who is ready to take part in team meetings and in the implementation of cooperative learning within the classroom. Be accountable for contributing your share of the work. Coteaching with team members and coplanning of class sessions creates a bond that gives the leader increased influence as well as emotional enjoyment.

6. **Form your own colleagial support group.** You have to want to be a part of a team. Just as students meet in cooperative learning groups, faculty should meet in colleagial support groups. Just as faculty meet in colleagial support groups, administrators should meet with each other to support each other's efforts to implement cooperative procedures and strategies. If you believe in cooperation, be part of a cooperative effort at your own level.

The way to succeed in the old paradigm is to stress personal individual triumphs over peers. The way to succeed in the new paradigm is to provide the support and encouragement peers need to challenge their competencies and gain new levels of expertise. Contributing to team efforts is becoming paramount at every rung of the ladder in modern organizations. Schools are no exception. Students and faculty have to want to belong to teams, they have to contribute their share of the work, and they must take positions and know how to advocate their views in ways that spark creative problem solving. To be a contributing team member you must be able to win a fair hearing for your ideas. Lone wolves who do not pull with their peers will increasingly find themselves the odd person out.

Colleagial support groups are not the only teams that faculty will belong to. There are also task forces and ad-hoc decision- making groups.

Schoolwide Task Forces

For many schoolwide issues (such as curriculum revision) task forces need to be organized (Johnson & Johnson, 1989b). Task forces carefully consider and research the issue and make a recommendation to the faculty as a whole. To be effective task forces need to collect valid and complete information about the problem, engage in controversy to ensure that all alternative solutions get a fair hearing, synthesize the best points from all perspectives, and make a free and informed choice of which alternative solution to adopt. Members must have continuing motivation to solve the problem so that a new recommendation may be made if the initial plan does not work.

Ad Hoc Decision-Making Groups

Within faculty meetings, ad hoc decision-making groups consider the recommendations of the task forces and decide whether to accept or modify the proposed solution (Johnson & Johnson, 1989b). Faculty members are assigned to temporary cooperative decision-making triads during a faculty meeting. The ad hoc groups consider the recommendation of the Task Force and decide whether to accept or modify the recommendation. Each ad-hoc group then reports its decision to the entire faculty, a discussion is held, and finally a faculty decision is made by consensus.

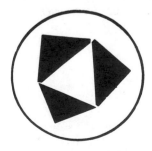

Conclusions

For things we have to learn before we can do them, we learn by doing them.

Aristotle

Traditionally, teachers have not been skilled in working effectively with adult peers. Blake and Mouton (1974) found that teachers and administrators lacked teamwork skills and were too ready to resolve differences by voting or by following the "official leader." They observed that educators were far less competent in working in small problem-solving groups than were industrial personnel. And they found that educators described themselves as being more oriented toward compromising quality of work for harmonious relationships, exerting minimal effort to get their job done, and being more oriented toward keeping good relationships than toward achieving the school's goals. Blumberg, May, and Perry (1974) found that teachers were ill-equipped behaviorally to function as part of a faculty, as they lacked the skills and attitudes needed for effective group problem-solving.

The lack of competence in being a constructive colleague, however, is not primarily the fault of teachers. The competitive/individualistic organizational structure existing in most schools discourages cooperation among faculty. In order to implement cooperative learning within school classrooms, it may also be necessary to implement cooperative teams among faculty. It is time that the school became a modern organization. In the real world, most of the important work is done by cooperative teams rather than by individuals. When teachers are isolated and alienated from their peers, they will also tend to be alienated from their work and, therefore, not likely to commit a great deal of psychological energy to their jobs or commit themselves to grow professionally by attaining increased expertise. Instead of requiring teachers to engage in quiet and solitary performance in individual classrooms, teachers should be organized into cooperative teams with an emphasis on seeking and accepting help and assistance from peers, soliciting constructive criticism, and negotiating by articulating their needs, discerning what others need, and discovering mutually beneficial outcomes. The structuring of cooperation among faculty would both support the use of cooperative learning and provide a congruent organizational structure throughout the school.

The cooperative school begins in the classroom with faculty use of cooperative learning. **What is good for students, however, is even better for faculty.** In a cooperative school, three types of cooperative groups need to be employed (Johnson & Johnson, 1989b):

1. **Colleagial support groups** to increase teachers' instructional expertise and success. Their purpose is to improve members' professional competence and ensure members' professional growth. Colleagial support groups begin when two or more teachers meet

together and talk about their efforts to implement cooperative learning. Participation in the colleagial support groups is aimed at increasing teachers' belief that they are engaged in a joint venture ("**We** are doing it!"), public commitment to peers to increase their instructional expertise ("I will try it!), peer accountability ("They are counting on me!"), sense of social support ("They will help and assist me!"), sense of safety ("The risk is challenging but not excessive!"), and self-efficacy ("If I exert the effort, I will be successful!").

The heart of school effectiveness is the faculty's teaching expertise. **Teachers progressively refine their expertise in implementing cooperative learning by being willing to take the risk of teaching cooperatively structured lessons, assessing the consequences of teaching lessons cooperatively, reflecting on how to improve implementation of cooperative learning, and teaching a modified lesson.** Teachers should then share what they have learned about implementing cooperative learning with colleagues. Gaining and maintaining expertise is an inter-personal process that requires supportive and encouraging colleagues.

2. **Task force groups** plan and implement solutions to schoolwide issues and problems such as curriculum revisions, recruiting students, and creating more of a learning community. These small problem-solving groups diagnose a problem, gather data about the causes and extent of the problem, consider a variety of alternative solutions, make conclusions, and present a recommendation to the faculty as a whole.

3. **Ad hoc decision-making groups** used during faculty meetings to involve all faculty members in important school decisions. Ad hoc decision-making groups are part of a small- group / large-group procedure in which faculty members listen to a recommendation, are assigned to small groups (usually three members), meet in the small groups and consider the recommendation, discuss the positive and negative aspects of the recommendation, report to the entire faculty their support or questions about the recommendation, and then decide as a faculty what the course of action should be. Such a procedure maximizes the participation and involvement of all faculty members in the school's decision making.

The most important aspect of providing leadership within a school involves empowering faculty by structuring them into cooperative teams. Individual faculty members can feel helpless and discouraged. Having them work with colleagues provides hope and opportunity. It is social support from and accountability to valued peers that motivates committed efforts to succeed. Just as students need to be placed in permanent base groups, faculty need to participate in permanent **colleagial support groups** whose purpose is to increase faculty members' instructional expertise and success.

EXERCISE

MATERIALS

INK

Committment Assessment

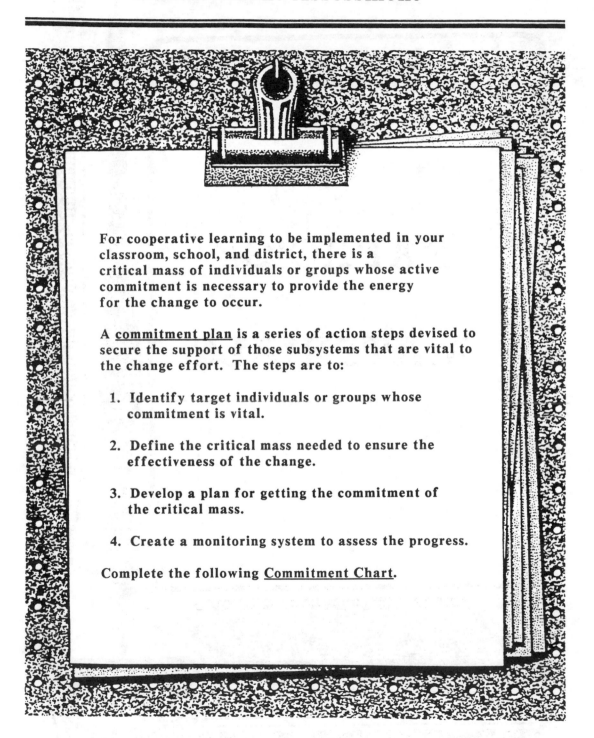

For cooperative learning to be implemented in your classroom, school, and district, there is a critical mass of individuals or groups whose active commitment is necessary to provide the energy for the change to occur.

A <u>commitment plan</u> is a series of action steps devised to secure the support of those subsystems that are vital to the change effort. The steps are to:

1. Identify target individuals or groups whose commitment is vital.

2. Define the critical mass needed to ensure the effectiveness of the change.

3. Develop a plan for getting the commitment of the critical mass.

4. Create a monitoring system to assess the progress.

Complete the following <u>Commitment Chart</u>.

COMMITMENT CHART

Key Players	No Commit- ment	Let It Happen	Help It Happen	Make It Happen
1.				
2.				
3.				
4.				
5.				
6.				
7.				
8.				
9.				
10.				
11.				
12.				
13.				
14.				
15.				

COPLANNING A LESSON

Your **tasks** are to: (1) coplan a lesson and (2) make a list of "best" advice for helping a colleague plan a cooperative learning lesson. Form a triad. Assign each member one of the following roles:

1. **Rookie** develops a lesson to teach.

2. **Veteran** helps the rookie develop the lesson, making sure that all parts of the model are in place.

3. **Observer** collects data on the specific behaviors engaged in by the rookie and veteran.

The **goal structure is cooperative**. The lesson is to be planned by the triad so that the rookie believes he or she can successfully teach the lesson (i.e., self-efficacy) and is energized and committed to doing so. The whole triad is responsible for a successful planning session.

R〉 Advice to Rookie

Plan a real lesson you are going to teach but have not yet structured cooperatively. Do **not** role play a "difficult" colleague. Be open to and seek direction and help from the veteran. Carefully write a complete lesson description/plan.

V〉 Advice to Veteran

1. **Establish positive goal and role interdependence.** Be a colleague rather than a tutor.

2. **Listen carefully,** paraphrase, give support, and encourage. Confirm the rookie's basic competence as a teacher.

Coplanning a Lesson (continued)

3. Focus. **Stay on task.** Make the logical progression of the lesson clear. Summarize at the end of each section of the lesson plan.

4. **Give rookie suggestions that include limited options.** Example: "In terms of group size, it is better to start small. Would you prefer groups of two, three, or four?"

5. **Be Socratic.** Ask questions that lead the rookie into making choices and decisions.

6. **Ensure that the rookie "owns" the lesson. Basic rule:** Better a good lesson that the rookie is excited about doing and feels ownership of than an excellent lesson that the rookie feels was imposed.

7. **Do not ignore potential problems** (problem students still will be problems).

8. **Provide for and be aware of the rookie's comfort.**

Advice to Observer

1. Observe specific behaviors such as giving ideas, asking questions, paraphrasing, encouraging, confirming competence, giving direction, and humor.

2. Watch for insights, rules, and strategies for collaborative planning (things to keep in mind while coplanning a lesson).

Processing

1. Whose lesson is it (veteran's or rookie's)?

2. Who talked the most?

3. What actions did each person emphasize? What actions were missing?

4. Was the rookie empowered and energized to conduct the lesson?

ASSUMPTIONS for INNOVATION

1. Divide the three assumptions (attached sheets) in your group so that each group member has one.

2. Study your assumption carefully so that you can:

   a. Summarize the assumption.

   b. List specific strategies or examples.

   c. Relate to your own situation.

3. Prepare to share that material with your group by:

   a. Outlining exactly what you want to share.

   b. Preparing something visual to illustrate your point (diagram, metaphor, etc.)

   c. Preparing a way to check to see if they understand.

4. Find someone in the room who has the same assumption you do and pair up. Practice what you are going to present and ask for feedback. Listen with care to your practice partner and give him/her feedback (positive, primarily). Borrow whatever you can from your partner.

5. Present your material in your group (checking their eyes, asking questions if necessary). Listen with care to the other presentations so that all three of you know all three assumptions well.

6. Write down suggestions and strategies for increasing the attitude of experimentation, sense of positive interdependence, and personal peer support within:

   a. Your school staff.

   b. Yourself.

POSITIVE INTERDEPENDENCE

There is little hope of implementing new ideas into a school unless there is an acceptance of positive interdependence among staff members. Positive interdependence is the perception that you are linked with others in a common effort so that you cannot succeed unless they do (and vice versa), and that their work benefits you and your work benefits them. It promotes a situation in which individuals work together in small groups to maximize the learning of all members, sharing their resources, providing mutual support, and celebrating their joint success. In such a situation, individuals perceive:

1. There is a **mutual, shared set of goals** that all group members accept and will work toward.

2. Group members share a **common fate** where they all gain or lose on the basis of the overall performance of group members.

3. Group members are **striving for mutual benefit** so that all members of the group will gain. There is the recognition that what helps other group members benefits me and what promotes my productivity benefits the other group members.

4. The **performance of group members is mutually caused** by all members. Each member views himself or herself as instrumental in the productivity of the other group members by sharing ideas and giving encouragement and views other group members as being instrumental in his or her success. This mutual causation results in mutual responsibility for the performance of each member and mutual obligation to the assistance and support of the other group members.

5. There is the **shared identity** of group membership. Besides being a separate individual, you are a member of a team or organization. The shared identity binds members together emotionally.

6. There is an expectation of **joint celebration** based on mutual respect and appreciation of the mutual success. Being part of a team effort brings camaraderie, belonging and pride. Feelings of success are shared and celebration is more powerful than individual feelings of success and individual celebration.

PERSONAL PEER SUPPORT

There is an assumption in the field of social psychology that states that when pressure is increased, the personal support must also be increased. This is true in a family setting, in a friendship and in an organization. If pressure to achieve is increased without personal support, you are likely to get complaints, scapegoating, and resistance. Innovation and change increase stress on staff members. That stress can result in resistance when staff members feel isolated and alone. Personal peer support can take many different forms, but is most evident in how staff interact with each other. If you are part of a supportive staff, you would expect to see staff:

1. Sharing ideas with each other and listening to each other with real care.

2. Expressing support and acceptance for each other professionally and personally, making it a low risk to share and problem solve in a staff group.

3. Expressing warmth and liking for each other as they work for mutual goals.

4. Enjoying the mutual celebration when members of a staff are successful and achieve mutual goals.

The more supportive the relationships among teachers, the more frequently they will cooperate with each other, the more productive their teaching will be, the more they will like each other and their jobs, and the higher their professional self-esteem will be. How well teachers instruct students, and the quality of life teachers experience within the schools, depends on how supportive teacher-teacher relationships are.

Being involved in supportive relationships with colleagues results in a feeling of belonging. Teachers' frustration is less because they have colleagues to talk to and problem solve with. No matter if staff members are adequate or a superior teachers, there is no doubt that they teach better when they experience support from their colleagues.

Staff members will be more creative and will cope with the increased stress of innovation and change more effectively, when they have peer support for trying new ideas, are listened to with respect, and are working with colleagues they care about toward mutual goals.

≋ AN ATTITUDE of EXPERIMENTATION ≋

One of the key times in implementing a new idea is when you first try out the new instruction strategy or procedure. Implementation of any new, significant procedure involves a struggle and the risk of some failures. Change always sounds easier on paper, in the planning, or in the training than it actually is. For the first few times the new strategies are tried, the results may be less than ideal. Teachers who lack a positive attitude toward experimentation will decide early that the implementation does not work and give up. Teachers who have an attitude of experimentation will tend to process why the new practice did not work as well as expected, fine-tune their procedures and persist.

Teaching does not foster an attitude of experimentation. Teachers are expected never to fail and, if they do, to hide the failure as something shameful (or proving that they are not as competent as the other teachers). Teachers are then placed in a bind where they are supposed to be innovative, but are also expected to master the new innovation perfectly the first time they try it. What is needed is a more healthy **attitude toward experimentation**.

1. Believe that teaching is a continuous process of developing more effective instructional procedures, modifying old ones, and integrating new procedures into one's standard practice.

2. Accept barriers and problems as a natural part of modifying teaching procedures (as opposed to believing they are proof that the new procedures will not work). Innovating always carries the risk of failure and of meeting roadblocks and barriers. It is always easier and safer in the short run to keep on doing things the same way they have always been done. The changes that make teaching more effective will take some work.

3. View roadblocks and problems as signs that adjustments are needed in the process. Setbacks and negative results that are not expected need to be viewed as temporary barriers rather than as permanent obstacles. Learning from mistakes is a talent found in teachers who are continuously trying to improve their teaching competence. They are always fine-tuning their practices and looking for better ones to try. When they try something that past data indicates should work, they persist in implementing it.

⋙ Suggestions and Strategies ⋙

Assumptions	School Staff	Me
. . **Attitude Of Experimenta- tion**		
. . **Positive Interdepen- dence**		
. . **Personal Peer Support**		

ONCLUSIONS

Old Vs. New Paradigm

> *Whether one believes in a religion or not, and whether one believes in rebirth or not, there isn't anyone who doesn't appreciate kindness and compassion...We must build closer relationships of mutual trust, understanding, respect, and help, irrespective of differences of culture, philosophy, religion, or faith.*
>
> The Dalai Lama, 1989 Nobel Peace Prize

Frank Koch, in **Proceedings**, the magazine of the Naval Institute, reported the following: Two battleships assigned to the training squadron had been at sea on maneuvers in heavy weather for several days. I was serving on the lead battleship and was on watch on the bridge as night fell. The visibility was poor with patchy fog, so the captain remained on the bridge keeping an eye on all activities. Shortly after dark, the lookout on the wing of the bridge reported, "Light, bearing on the starboard bow." "Is it steady or moving astern?" the captain called out. Lookout replied, "Steady, captain," which meant we were on a dangerous collision course with that ship. The captain then called to the signalman, "Signal that ship: We are on a collision course, advise you change course 20 degrees." Back came a signal, "Advisable for you to change course 20 degrees." The captain said, "Send, I'm a captain, change course 20 degrees." "I'm a seaman, second class," came the reply, "You had better change course 20 degrees." By that time the captain was furious. He spat out, "Send, I'm a battleship. Change course 20 degrees." Back came the flashing light, "I'm a lighthouse." We changed course.

A faculty member may feel like a captain of a battleship cruising through the seas too powerful to be challenged. When faced with the realities of the modern world, however, it is the faculty member who may find that he or she has to change course to stay afloat.

A **paradigm** is a theory, perspective, or frame of reference that determines how you perceive, interpret, and understand the world. The **old paradigm** of education views teaching as the transfer of faculty's knowledge to passive students while faculty classify and sort students in a norm-referenced, competitive way. It is based on John Locke's assumption that the untrained mind is like a blank sheet of paper on which faculty write. Quality is assured by (a) selecting only the most intelligent and hard- working students for admission and (b) inspecting them continually to weed out those who prove to be defective. Whether or not schools "add value" or just serve as a holding ground for students as they mature is unclear.

In teaching a paradigm shift is taking place. Minor modifications of current teaching practices will not solve the problems with instruction. A new approach is needed. The **new paradigm** views teaching as helping students construct their knowledge in an active way while working cooperatively with classmates so that students' talents and competencies are developed. Quality is assured by motivating students to exert extraordinary effort to learn, grow, and develop. This is largely done through creating cooperative learning situations in which students care about each other and inspire each other to work hard in actively gaining knowledge and expertise. Adding value becomes an important teacher focus through knowing students personally and being committed to their intellectual growth and general well-being.

The new paradigm is operationalized through the use of cooperative learning within the classroom and the formation of faculty cooperative teams. Cooperative learning is the instructional use of small groups so that students work together to maximize their own and each other's learning. There is considerable research demonstrating that cooperative learning produces higher achievement, more positive relationships among students, and

healthier psychological adjustment than do competitive or individualistic experiences. These effects, however, do not automatically appear when students are placed in groups. To be cooperative, learning groups must be carefully structured to include the five basic elements: positive interdependence to ensure that students believe they "sink or swim together," face-to-face promotive interaction to ensure that students help and assist each other, individual accountability to ensure that everyone does their fair share of the work, social skills to work effectively with others, and group processing to reflect on and improve the quality of group work. There are, furthermore, many different ways to structure cooperative learning. Three broad categories of cooperative learning strategies are **formal cooperative learning groups** that last for several class sessions to complete assignments, **informal cooperative learning groups** that last for only a few minutes for a brief discussion, **cooperative base groups** that last for a semester or more to provide overall academic assistance. One of the most important uses of formal cooperative learning groups in schools is through the use of **structured academic controversies**. Cooperation, furthermore, is just as powerful among faculty as it is among students. There needs to be an organizational restructuring from the existing competitive-individualistic college structure to a cooperative team-based school structure.

In order to understand the necessity of adopting the new paradigm to education it may be helpful to consider in a broader context the issue of schools providing quality education.

Mission, Product, Customers

The community stagnates without the impulse of the individual; the impulse dies away without the sympathy of the community.
William James, **Great Men and Their Environment**

To determine whether schools are adding value by giving students a high-quality education, the mission of the school has to be determined. The mission has to specify who the school's customers are and what the product is. There are at least two complementary ways to describe the mission of schools. **First**, the school may be viewed as an industry that produces and sells knowledge. The school's product is validated theory and its customers are those who need it. The **mission** of the school is to create and test theory through systematic programs of research. Concerns about **quality** focus on high well faculty develop sound theory, conduct systematic programs of reliable research to test the theory, operationalize the results into procedures consumers may use, and convince consumers to implement the procedures.

Second, the school may be viewed as a service organization that functions as a broker between (a) students and (b) employers and graduate schools. While schools serve both students and the people who hire its graduates, the more important of the two is the student, as the success of a school's graduates will determine the level of demand for future graduates. The "product" of a school is the education it provides and students are its primary consumers. The **mission** of a school, therefore, is to provide quality education to students in order that they will be hired by desirable or prestigious companies or enter prestigious graduate schools. This requires more than intellectual development. Students should also be moral, decent, loving, and loveable people. Concerns about **quality** focus on how well students are educated and trained. The harder it is to get a job or be admitted to college or technical training, the more pressure there is on schools to provide a quality education. In determining the quality of a school's educational program there are at least three factors to consider:

1. Do all teachers provide high-quality teaching? High-quality teaching may be defined as the skillful and effective use of the new (rather than the old) paradigm. Faculty cannot grow by mimicking the past. Cooperative learning must dominate the classroom. Other new instructional methods, processes, procedures, and practices have to be adopted.

2. What is the time it takes to develop and implement improvements in teaching? This may be the most critical factor in a school being successful. In general, cycle time must be continuously reduced.

3. Has a process of continuous improvement in instruction been institutionalized to keep teaching in general and the use of cooperative learning in particular at the state-of-the-art level?

In order to improve faculty's teaching, reduce cycle time, and ensure a process of continuous improvement in instruction, schools may wish to promote commitment to the new paradigm of teaching, use a benchmarking process to set goals, and adopt a cooperative-team organizational structure.

Changes In Attitudes And Thinking About Teaching

Collaboration operates through a process in which the successful intellectual achievements of one person arouse the intellectual passions and enthusiasms of others, and through a process in which a fact that was at first expressed by only one individual becomes a common intellectual possession instead of fading away into isolation.

Alexander Humboldt

To have high-quality instructional programs, faculty must change the way they think about teaching. The new paradigm must not only be adopted, but faculty must view it positively and be personally committed to implementing it within their classrooms. Faculty must believe that teaching in the old way harder and faster with more bells and whistles will not do. Faculty must believe in their hearts that it is a good idea to give up the "select and weed out" approach to instruction and replace it with the "development" approach. It is only through developing students' talents and competencies that schools add value through their instructional program.

Benchmarking And Goal Setting

> *Almost every evening, either I went to Braque's studio or Braque came to mine. Each of us **had** to see what the other had done during the day. We criticized each other's work. A canvas wasn't finished unless both of us felt it was.*
>
> Pablo Picasso (in a letter to Francoise Gilot)

> *The things Picasso and I said to one another during those years will never be said again, and even if they were, no one would understand them anymore. It was like being roped together on a mountain.*
>
> Georges Braque

The benchmarking process involves establishing operating targets based on best known practices. There are four steps to using the benchmark process to set organizational goals. **First, identify the "best in class" in the world** (search for the practices that will lead to superior performance of students, faculty, and administrators). **Second, set a goal to achieve that level of performance as a minimum** (establish operating targets based on the best possible practices). A school must benchmark its instructional program against the leading instructional programs in the world to determine where the school is today and what the faculty needs to do to maintain or reach "world-class" instruction. Doing so involves examining quality of instruction, its cost, its flexibility, and its speed of delivery. **Third, develop performance measures to evaluate every function's contribution toward reaching the school's goals**. These measures must go beyond student achievement. Ways to measure effort to achieve, team skills, ability to enhance team problem solving, commitment to quality work, and commitment to continuous improvement of competencies need to be developed to supplement the traditional focus on achievement tests. **Fourth, continue to move your benchmark higher as initial goals are reached**. Expertise is not a state, it is a process of progressive refinement of one's use of cooperative formal, informal, and base groups. Either faculty are improving their skills in implementing cooperative learning or else their skills are gradually deteriorating. Their expertise in using cooperative learning cannot stand still. Perfection is never reached but should be strived for in realistic steps.

The Japanese use the concept **Dantotsu**--striving to be the "best of the best"--to describe the benchmarking process. The steps of dantotsu are:

1. Know who your competitors are, especially internationally.

2. Benchmark.

3. Do not "mimic the past." New methods, processes, practices have to be uncovered and adopted.

4. Identify the "best of the best" in instructional procedures. The strategies and procedures identified have to fit together logically.

5. Conduct research on instructional methods and either adopt what is proven to be effective or adapt the good features of an instructional procedure to fit into your teaching.

An important aspect of the benchmarking process is having faculty see each other teach. Just as a ball-player needs to see other people play in order to form a frame-of-reference as to how good he or she is and where improvement is needed, faculty need to access their use of cooperative learning within a broad **frame-of- reference** based on observing many other faculty members using cooperative learning.

In order to form a frame-of-reference within which to set goals for improvement in one's use of cooperative learning, faculty members must understand (a) what cooperative learning is and (b) the basic elements of a well-implemented cooperative lesson. Otherwise, the fidelity of the implementation of cooperative learning may suffer. Most instructional innovations fade away because their implementation deteriorates and becomes approximate and sloppy. Cooperative learning will be in danger of deteriorating into traditional class-room grouping unless faculty pay attention to the exactness of its implementation. **Fidelity of use** depends on the inclusion of positive interdependence, face-to-face promotive inter-action, individual accountability, interpersonal and small group skills, and group processing. No matter if it is a cooperative formal, informal, or base group, or if the lesson is a structured academic controversy, these basic elements must be operationalized into the assignment.

Once a benchmarking process is established for setting and continually upgrading goals for world-class quality of instruction, schools will wish to modernized their organizational structure.

Modernizing Organizational Structure

> *Nothing new that is really interesting comes without collaboration.*
> James Watson, Nobel Prize Winner (codiscoverer of the double helix)

Ford Motor Company knew it had to do something different, dramatically different, to gain back market share from imports. A new mid-sized car was conceived to be Ford's best chance to do so. For years Ford had operated within a mass-manufacturing structure whose motto was "any color as long as it is black." Designers etched out sketches and gave them to manufacturing with the order "build it!" Sales inherited the car and had to figure out how to sell it. That was the way Ford had always built cars. But not this time. An interdisciplinary team was created made up of designers, engineers, manufacturing and financial executives, and sales and marketing people. Together they created the Taurus, a car whose sales neared one million units in its first four production years and which has consistently won praise from both auto experts and consumers.

Ford is not the only company to switch to cooperative teams. While there is an American myth of progress being spurred on by Lone Rangers, in today's corporations that image is about as current as bustles and spats. From Motorola to AT&T Credit Corporation, self-managing, multi-disciplinary teams are in charge of keeping the company profitable. And they are succeeding. Teams get things done.

Team development is at the core of the changes necessary to alter the way faculty and students think and work. It is the best way of developing the educating students the right way the first time. That does not mean that reorganizing students and faculty into teams will be easy. Changing the school culture while getting all faculty working together to educate students right the first time may be the biggest challenge facing any school.

There are two steps in moving from a competitive-individualistic mass-manufacturing organizational structure to a high-performance cooperative-team structure. The first step is using cooperative learning procedures extensively within the school's courses. The second step is organizing faculty into colleagial support groups that focus on the continuous improvement of the use of cooperative learning and instruction in general. These steps are taken not because they are popular, but because it is rational to do so. Currently available data indicates that a cooperative team-based organizational structure is more desirable for many reasons (see Chapter2) than is a competitive- individualistic mass-manufacturing organizational structure.

Data-Driven Change And Gaining Expertise

The amount of research data and the consistency of the findings provide irrefutable evidence that a team-based organizational structure will be more effective in producing quality instruction and achieving the school's mission. Barry Bennett (personal communication) summarizes the research as follows: "Imagine you are a doctor conducting heart surgery. You realize that if you use procedure "A" the patient has a 50 percent chance of survival and if you use procedure "B" the patient has a 75 percent chance of survival. Which procedure do you use? That difference is the difference in achievement between cooperative learning and competitive or individualistic instruction." Once a faculty member knows about cooperative learning, it is difficult not to use it.

Knowing from the research that cooperative learning is more effective than are competitive and individualistic instruction is the first step to change. The second is gaining expertise in using cooperative learning in your courses. To be an expert in cooperative learning you have to use it long enough to:

1. **Be able to take any lesson in any subject area and structure it cooperatively.**

2. **Use cooperative learning at the routine-use level** where it is implemented automatically without a great deal of conscious thought or planning. Cooperative learning then becomes a central part of a faculty member's professional identity and faculty members become willing to share their expertise with interested colleagues.

3. **Use cooperative learning at least 60 percent of the time.** A cooperative context needs to dominate the classroom and school. At least 60 percent of a student's day should be spent in cooperative learning experiences. Up to 40 percent of instruction should probably be individualistic and competitive experiences.

Gaining and maintaining such expertise is a long-term process requiring up to two years or more of hard work. Simply putting students in groups is not enough. The five basic elements of cooperative efforts (positive interdependence, face-to-face promotive interaction, individual accountability, social skills, and group processing) have to be implemented. This is not easy. **Gaining expertise in using cooperative learning takes at least one lifetime.** Faculty development programs are needed in order to ensure that cooperative learning (rather than traditional classroom grouping) is being used.

Programs to develop faculty expertise in structuring learning situations cooperatively requires procedural learning (very similar to learning how to perform brain surgery, how to fly an airplane, or how to play tennis) and being a member of an ongoing colleagial support group. **Procedural learning** exists when you study cooperative learning to:

1. Learn conceptually what cooperative learning is.

2. Translate your conceptual understanding of cooperative learning into a set of operational procedures appropriate for your students and subjects taught.

3. Teach cooperatively structured lessons regularly.

4. Eliminate errors in using cooperative learning so that you move through the initial awkward and mechanical stages of skill mastery.

5. Attain a routine-use, automated level of use of cooperative learning.

Procedural learning differs from simply learning facts and acquiring knowledge. It relies heavily on feedback about performance and modifying your implementation until the errors of performance are eliminated. Usually your efforts will fail to match the ideal of what you wish to accomplish for a considerable length of time until cooperative learning is overlearned at a routine-use, automated level. **Failure is part of the process of gaining expertise. Success is inevitable when failure is followed by persistent practice, feedback, and reflection on how to use cooperative learning more competently.** To gain expertise you need a colleagial support group made up of peers you like and trust. Gaining expertise takes learning partners who are willing to trust each other, talk frankly about their teaching, and observe each other's performance over a prolonged period of time to help each other identify and eliminate the errors being made in implementing cooperative learning. Unless you are willing to reveal your lack of expertise to obtain accurate feedback from trusted colleagues, teaching expertise cannot be gained. In order to commit the effort required to gain such expertise in the use of cooperative learning (which usually takes from one to two years of hard work) teachers need considerable support and help from colleagues. **Gaining expertise is not a solitary activity. It is a social process requiring a colleagial support group.**

Faculty Development And State-Of-The-Art Teaching

More and more companies, as they move into global competitiveness, see that the one thing that can make a difference in the world market is people. Raw material, technology, and systems are available to everybody. The right people can be a unique commodity. To be a world-class school and provide a world-class education, each faculty member must be developed to his or her highest potential as a teacher. To do so requires that faculty maintain a state-of-the-art use of cooperative learning.

The term **state-of-the-art** is an engineering concept that involves the set of heuristics describing best available practice. Like most heuristics it is difficult to define but easy to recognize. Take sound reproduction technology, for example. The current state-of-the-art is digital-audio tape (DAT), the previous "best available practice" and currently commercially available technology is Compact Disk. Before that it was phonograph record. Best available practice usually persists for a limited period of time, and is eventually replaced by a superior approach. The changes that have occurred in the development of cooperative learning represent a progressive refinement in the state-of-the-art. Improvement is expected to continue, since cooperative learning is a dynamic area in education and the research investigating its nature and use is continuing.

Approaches to implementing cooperative learning may be placed on a continuum with direct applications at one end and conceptual applications at the other. **Direct applications** consist of packaged lessons, curricula, and strategies that are used in a lock-step prescribed manner. Direct applications can be divided into three subcategories. Teachers can adopt a strategy (such as groups-of-four in intermediate math) that is aimed at using cooperative learning in a specific subject area for a certain age student (**the strategy approach**), they can adopt a curriculum package that is aimed at a specific subject area and grade level (**the curriculum package approach**), or they can replicate a lesson they observed another teach (**the lesson approach**). In essence, faculty are trained to use a specific cooperative activity, lesson, strategy, or curriculum package in a Step 1, Step 2, Step 3 manner without any real understanding of cooperation. Some of the more powerful strategies include the jigsaw method developed by Elliot Aronson and his colleagues (Aronson, 1978), the coop/coop strategy developed by Spencer Kagan (Kagan, 1988), the group project method developed by the Sharans (Sharan & Sharan, 1976).

The **conceptual approach** is based on an interaction among theory, research, and practice. The two conceptual approaches to cooperative learning have been developed by Elizabeth Cohen (1986) and the authors of this book (Johnson & Johnson, 1975/1991; Johnson, Johnson, & Holubec, 1984/1990). Cohen bases her conceptual principles on expectation-states theory while we base our conceptual principles on the theory of cooperation and competition Morton Deutsch derived from Kurt Lewin's field theory. Teachers are taught a general conceptual model of cooperative learning (based on the essential elements of positive interdependence, face-to-face interaction, individual accountability, social skills, and group processing--**the essential elements approach**) which they use to tailor cooperative learning specifically for their circumstances, students, and needs. Faculty are taught to apply a conceptual system to build cooperative activities, lessons, strategies, and curricula. Using the five basic elements of cooperation, faculty can (a) analyze their current curricula, students, and instructional goals and (b) design cooperative learning experiences specifically adapted for their instructional goals and the ages, abilities, and backgrounds of their students. Becoming competent in implementing the basic elements is a requirement for obtaining real expertise in cooperative learning. In essence, teachers are taught an **expert system** of how to implement cooperative learning that they use to create a unique adaptation to their specific circumstances, students, and needs. The resulting expertise is based on a metacognitive understanding of cooperative learning.

At the Cooperative Learning Center of the University of Minnesota we have focused on five interrelated activities: reviewing and synthesizing the research, developing theory, conducting systematic research to validate or disconfirm the theory, operationalizing the research into "state-of-the-art" cooperation procedures, and implementing cooperative learning and faculty teams in a network of colleges and school districts throughout the United States and other parts of the world.

The state-of-the-art use of cooperative learning has changed substantially since the initial conceptualization of the theory by Morton Deutsch in 1949. Deutsch's theorized that positive interdependence was the central feature of cooperation. Our understanding of positive interdependence has increased as the different ways of structuring it have been investigated (see Johnson & Johnson, 1989a). The other mediators of the effectiveness of cooperative learning are continually being redefined and calibrated, modifying how cooperative learning is best structured within classrooms. While the authors used formal, informal, and base groups in their teaching in the 1960s, the definition of each has been considerably refined and many of the specific operationalizations have been updated and fine-tuned in the 1970s and 1980s.

The dynamic nature of cooperative learning requires faculty development programs that last for several years. As a rule it takes at least three years of training and experience to become proficient in the integrated and flexible use of all types of cooperative learning. Our training programs are divided into training in the fundamentals of cooperative learning the first year, training in more integrated, refined, and advanced use of cooperative learning in the second year, and training in the use of structured academic controversies and peer mediation the third year (Johnson, Johnson, & Holubec,

1988, 1991; Johnson & Johnson, 1991). For administrators there is an additional year of training (Johnson & Johnson, 1989b). And since the theory and research are continually progressing, refresher training is recommended every few years.

Empowering Students To Be Peacemakers

Discipline problems plague classrooms and schools. Students bicker, threaten, tease, and harrass each other. Conflicts involving racial and cultural differences are increasing. Truancy is epidemic. Violence is escalating. Generally, conflicts among students and between students and staff occur with frequency and consume considerable teacher and administrator time.

Classroom and school discipline programs may be classified on a dimension from being based on external rewards and punishments that control and manage student behavior to being based on teaching students the competencies and skills required to resolve their interpersonal conflicts constructively, cope with stress and adversity, and behave in appropriate and constructive ways. At one end of the continuum the focus is on the faculty and staff controlling and managing student behavior. At the other end of the continuum the focus is on students regulating their own and their peers actions.

External Rewards/ 1--2--3--4--5--6--7 Competencies For
Punishments   Self-Regulation

Most discipline programs are clustered at the adult administering external rewards and punishment end of the continuum. Thus, it is up to the staff to monitor student behavior, determine whether it is or is not within the bounds of acceptability, and force students to terminate inappropriate actions. When the infractions are minor, the staff often arbitrate ("The pencil belongs to Mary, Jane be quiet and sit down.") or conjoule students to end hostilities ("Let's forgive and forget. Shake hands and be friends."). If that does not work, students may be sent to the principal's office for a stern but cursory lecture about the value of getting along, a threat that if the conflict continues more drasic action will ensue, and a final admonition to "Go and fight no more." If that does not work, time-out rooms may be used. Eventually, some students are expelled from school. Such programs teach students that adults or authority figures are needed to resolve conflicts. The programs cost a great deal in instructional and administrative time and work only as long as students are under surveillance. This approach does not empower students. Adults may become more skillful in how to control students, but students do not learn the procedures, skills and attitudes required to resolve conflicts constuructively in their personal lives at home, in school, at work, and in the community.

At the other end of the continuum are programs aimed at teaching students self-responsibility and self-regulation. **Self-regulation** is the ability to act in socially approved ways in the absence of external monitors. It is the ability to initiate and cease activities according to situational demands. Self- regulation is a central and significant hallmark of cognitive and social development. To regulate their behavior, students must monitor their own behavior, assess situations and take other people's perspectives to make judgments as to which behaviors are appropriate, and master the procedures and skills required to engage in the desired behavior. In interaction with other people, students have to monitor, modify, refine, and change how they behave in order to act appropriately and competently.

If students are to learn how to regulate their behavior they must have opportunities to (a) make decisions regarding how to behave and (b) follow through on the decisions made. Allowing students to be joint architects in matters affecting them promotes feelings of control and autonomy. Students who know how to manage their conflicts constructively and regulate their own behavior have a developmental advantage over those who do not. Ideally, students will be given the responsibility of regulating their own and their classmates' behavior so that teachers can concentrated on instruction rather than control.

Our peer mediation program teaches all students the joint problem solving and decision making competencies and skills they need to regulate their own and their classmates' behavior. Students received 30 minutes of training per day for 30 days. Students are taught to be peacemakers in three steps. First, they are taught how to negotiate. This coorients all students as to how conflicts should be resolved and gives them a set of procedures and skills to regulate their own behavior. Second, students are taught how to mediate their classmates' conflicts. Third, the teacher implements the peacemaker program. Each day two students are selected to be the class mediators. They are responsible for helping classmates resolve any conflicts they cannot negotiate a wise agreement to. The curriculum for this conflict training is **Teaching Students to be Peacemakers** (Johnson & Johnson, 1991). Students role-play and practice the procedures and skills involved in negotiating and mediating until they can negotiate and mediate at a routine-use level.

13 : 13

Long-Term Time Perspective

The importance of structuring cooperation throughout all levels of the school district becomes most apparent when a realistic time perspective is taken for learning from colleagues. The process of gaining expertise in teaching is no different than gaining expertise in any other field. It takes at least one lifetime. Professional growth is a complex, time-consuming, and difficult process that places both cognitive and emotional demands on teachers. A support system is needed to encourage and assist teachers in a long-term, multi-year effort to improve continually their professional competence. With only a moderately difficult teaching strategy, for example, teachers may require from 20 to 30 hours of instruction in its theory, 15 to 20 demonstrations using it with different students and subjects, and an additional 10 to 15 coaching sessions to attain higher- level skills (Shalaway, 1985). For a more difficult teaching strategy several years of training and support may be needed to ensure that teachers master it. Your commitment to implementing cooperative learning, and gaining expertise in using cooperative learning, needs to extend throughout your career.

Looking Forward

I couldn't have done it without the boys.
> Casey Stengel (after winning his ninth American League pennant in ten years)

Now that you have reached the end of this book you are at a new beginning. Years of experience in using cooperative learning in your classroom are needed to gain expertise in its use. While you are using cooperative learning there is much more to learn about its use. The addition of informal cooperative learning activities and long-term permanent base groups will increase the power and effectiveness of cooperation in your classroom. Teaching students more and more sophisticated social skills will improve how well they work together to maximize their learning. Supplementing the use of cooperative learning with appropriate competitions and individualistic assignments will further enrich the quality of learning within your classroom. Structuring academic controversies within your cooperative learning groups will move students to higher levels of reasoning and thinking while providing a considerable increase in energy and fun. Teaching students how to negotiate their differences and mediate each other's conflicts will accelerate their skills in managing conflicts within cooperative learning groups. Finally, moving cooperation up to the school level by organizing faculty into cooperative teams will create a congruent organizational structure within which both faculty and students will thrive.

 **Review and Celebration**

The greatest rewards come only from the greatest commitment.

Arlene Blum, Mountain Climber and Leader, American Women's Himalayan Expedition

Review of Progress

Meet in your base groups. The **task** is that each member has ten minutes to summarize what they have accomplished in implementing cooperative learning in their classrooms. the summary should include their personal learnings as recorded by their journal, the impact of the cooperative lessons on the students they were following for their case studies, the number and type of lessons they have conducted, and their overall experiences in teaching cooperative skills to students. Once all members have summarized their classroom implementation of cooperative learning, the group makes at least three conclusions about their experiences to share with the entire class. This is a **cooperative** activity, everyone should participate, listen carefully to groupmates, provide support and encouragement, and make the other members of your group feel appreciated for the effort they have made to implement cooperative learning into their classrooms and schools.

Sharing Successes

Stay in your base groups. Your **task** is to share your successes in implementing cooperative learning within your classroom and help each of your groupmates do the same. Work **cooperatively** in answering the following questions:

1. How have your students benefited from cooperative learning?

2. What cooperative lesson was most successful?

3. Which student benefited most from working cooperatively with classmates?

4. What cooperative lesson was most important to you personally?

Task 3: Cooperative Learning Review Quiz

Divide your base group into pairs. Your **task** is to take the Review Quiz and answer each question correctly. Work **cooperatively**. Each pair should take the quiz together, one answer for the two of you, with both members in agreement and able to explain each answer. When finished, reform as a base group and take the Review Quiz again. If there is any disagreement as to the answer to a question, find the page number in the book the answer appears on and clarify until all members are in agreement and can explain the answer.

Task 4: Basic Concepts Review

Meet in your base group and divide into pairs. Starting with Chapter1, identify the basic concepts within each chapter and ensure that both members of the pair can correctly define each one. When finished, reform as a base group and compare the concepts identified for each chapter and their definitions. If there is disagreement as to the definitions, identify what page the definition is on and clarify the definition until all members of the group agree and are able to explain it. Make sure that all members of your base group can define and explain each of the concepts.

Task 5: Planning Your Cooperative Learning Future

Your **tasks** are to (1) diagnosis where you now stand in gaining expertise in using cooperative learning and (2) make a plan for increasing your expertise. The diagnosis and plan must be in writing and signed by all other base group members.

Meet in your base group and work **cooperatively**. Ensure that each member of your base group has completed the above two tasks and that all members of the base group agree with each member's diagnosis and plan (noted by their signature at the bottom of each member's plan).

In diagnosing where you stand in gaining expertise in cooperative learning consider:

1. The long-term goals of being able to:

   a. Take any lesson in any subject area and teach it cooperatively.

   b. Use cooperative learning at the routine-use level.

   c. Use cooperative learning at least 60 percent of the time.

   d. Be a member of an ongoing colleagial support groups.

2. The amount of training you have received.

3. The amount of experience you have in using cooperative learning.

4. The effectiveness of your colleagial support group in encouraging and assisting members' implementation efforts.

5. Your ability to experiment, take risks, and generally stay on the edge of your comfort zone in order to increase your expertise.

6. The quality and quantity of the feedback you are receiving on your implementation efforts.

7. The quality and quantity of your reflections and problem solving on the feedback received.

8. Your persistence in trying it again and again.

9. Your experience in encouraging and assisting your colleague's efforts to implement cooperative learning.

What are your next steps in increasing your expertise in cooperative learning? Your plan should include a:

1. List of units coming up in which cooperative learning should be used.

2. List of cooperative skills you plan to teach to and work on with your students.

3. Plan for:

   a. Forming and maintaining a colleagial support group within your school building to focus on cooperative learning.

   b. Your own skill development in working cooperatively with colleagues.

    c. A **time schedule** as to when cooperative skills will be taught and perfected by your students while you provide opportunities for the use of the skills, feedback on how well each student is performing the skill, and encouragement for each student to continue practicing the skill.

    d. The phone numbers of the other members of your base groups and the time of the month you will call each one and give him or her a report on your progress.

Task 6: Whole Class Review By Drawing Names

The purpose of this activity is to provide a fun review of the course. The instructor will ask a question and then draw a participant's name from a hat. The participant named will then be required to give an interesting and truthful answer.

Task 7: Thanking Your Learning Partners

Seek out the people who have helped you learn how to implement cooperative learning. **Thank them**.

REFERENCES

Anderson, T., & Armbruster, B. (1982). Reader and text studying strategies. In W. Otto & S. White (Eds.), **Reading expository material.** New York: Academic Press.

Annis, L. (1979). Effect of cognitive style and learning passage organization on study technique effectiveness. **Journal of Educational Psychology, 71,** 620-626.

Armento, B. (1977). Teacher behaviors related to student achievement on a social science concept test. **Journal of Teacher Education, 28,** 46-52.

Aronson, E., Blaney, N., Stephan, C., Sikes, J., & Snapp, M. (1978). **The jigsaw classroom.** Beverly Hills, CA: Sage

Association of American Colleges (1985). **Integrity in the curriculum: A report to the academic community.** Project on redefining the meaning and purpose of baccalaureate degree. Washington, D.C.

Astin, A. (1977). **Four critical years: Effects of college on beliefs, attitudes, and knowledge.** San Francisco: Jossey-Bass.

Astin, A. (1985). **Achieving educational excellence.** San Francisco: Jossey-Bass.

Astin, H., Astin, A., Bisconti, A., & Frankel, H. (1972). **Higher education and the disadvantaged student.** Washington, DC: Human Science Press.

Atkinson, R., & Shiffrin, R. (1971). The control of short-term memory. **Scientific American, 225,** 82-90.

Ausubel, D. (1963). **Psychology of meaningful verbal learning.** New York: Grune & Straton.

Bargh, J., & Schul, Y. (1980). On the cognitive benefits of teaching. **Journal of Educational Psychology, 72,** 593-604.

Barnes, C. (1980). **Questions: The untrapped resource.** Paper presented at the annual meeting of the American Educational Research Association, Boston.

Barnes, C. (1983). Questioning in the college classroom. In C. Ellner and C. Barnes (Eds.), **Studies in college teaching** (pp. 61-81). Lexington, MA: Lexington Books.

Blake, R., & Mouton, J. (1974). Designing change for educational institutions through the D/D Matrix. **Educational and Urban Society, 6,** 179-204.

Blanc, R., Debuhr, L., & Martin, D. (1983). Breaking the attrition cycle: The effects of supplemental instruction on undergraduate performance and attrition. **Journal of Higher Education, 54,** 80-90.

Bligh, D. (1972). **What's the use of lectures.** Harmondsworth, England: Penguin.

Blumberg, A., May, J., & Perry, R. (1974). An inner- city school that changed--and continued to change. **Education and Urban Society, 6,** 222-238.

Bok, E. (1986). **Higher learning.** Cambridge, MA: Harvard University Press.

Bovard, E. (1951a). Group structure and perception. **Journal of Abnormal and Social Psychology, 46,** 398-405.

Bovard, E. (1951b). The experimental production of interpersonal affect. **Journal of Abnormal Psychology, 46,** 521- 528.

Bowers, J. (1986). Classroom communication apprehension: A survey. **Communication Education, 35**(4), 372-378.

Boyer, E. (1987). **College: The undergraduate experience in America.** New York: Harper & Row.

Boyer, E. (1990). **Scholarship reconsidered.** Lawrenceville, NJ: Princeton University Press.

Broadbent, D. (1970). Review lecture. **Proclamations of the Royal Society, 1,** 333-350.

Brown, J., Collins, A., & Duguid, P. (1989). Situated cognition and the culture of learning. **Educational Researcher, 18**(1), 32-42.

Bruner, J. (1960). **The process of education.** Cambridge: Harvard University Press.

Campbell, J. (1965). **The children's crusader: Colonel Francis W. Parker.** PhD dissertation, Teachers College, Columbia University.

Chickering, A., & Gamson, Z. (1987). Seven principles for good practice. **AAHE Bulletin, 39**(7), 3-7.

Cohen, E. (1986). **Designing groupwork.** New York: Teachers College Press.

Collins, B. (1970). **Social Psychology**. Reading, MA: Addison-Wesley.

Cooper, J. (May 1990). Cooperative learning and college teaching: Tips from the trenches. **The Teaching Professor, 4**(5), 1-2.

Costin, F. (January 1972). Lecturing versus other methods of teaching: A review of research. **British Journal of Educational Technology, 3**(1), 4-30.

Daloz, l. (1987). **Effective teaching and mentoring**. San Francisco: Jossey-Bass.

Dansereau, D. (1985). Learning strategy research. In J. Segal, S. Chipman, and R. Glaser (Eds.). **Thinking and Learning Skills (Vol. 1, Relating instruction to research)**. Hillsdale, NJ: Lawrence Erlbaum.

Dansereau, D. (1987). Transfer from cooperative learning to individual studying. **Journal of Reading, 30**, 614- 618.

Davison, M. (1991). Personal communication.

Deutsch, M. (1949). An experimental study of the effects of coopertion and competition upon group processes. **Human Relations, 2**, 199-232.

Deutsch, M. (1958). Trust and suspicion. **Journal of Conflict Resolution, 2**, 25-279.

Deutsch, M. (1960). The effects of motivational orientation upon trust and suspicion. **Human Relations, 13**, 123- 139.

Deutsch, M. (1962). Cooperation and trust: Some theoretical notes. In M. R. Jones (Ed.), **Nebraska symposium on motivation** (pp. 275-319). Lincoln, NE: University of Nebraska Press.

Deutsch, M., & Krauss, R. (1962). Studies of interpersonal bargaining. **Journal of Conflict Resolutions, 6**, 52-76.

DeVries, D., & Edwards, K. (1973). Learning games and student teams: Their effects on classroom process. **American Educational Research Journal, 10**, 307-318.

DeVries, D., & Edwards, K. (1974). Student teams and learning games: Their effects on cross-race and cross-sex interaction. **Journal of Educational Psychology, 66**(5), 741-749.

DeVries, D., Slavin, R., Fennessey, G., Edwards, K., & Lombardo, M. (1980). **Teams-Games-Tournament: The team learning approach**. Englewood Cliffs, NJ: Educational Technology Publications.

DiPardo, A., & Freedman, S. (1988). Peer response groups in the writing classroom: Theoretic foundations and new directions. **Review of Educational Research, 58**, 119-150.

Dishon, D., & O'Leary, P. (1984). **A guidebook for cooperative learning.** Holmes Beach, FL: Learning Publications.

Eble, K. (1983). **The aims of college teaching.** San Francisco: Jossey-Bass.

Eison, J. (1990). Confidence in the college classroom: Ten maxims for new teachers. **College Teaching, 38**(1), 21-25.

Fay, B. (1929). **Benjamin Franklin.** Boston: Little, Brown.

Gabbert, B., Johnson, D. W., & Johnson, R. (1986). Cooperative learning, group-to-individual transfer, process gain and the acquisition of cognitive reasoning strategies. **Journal of Psychology, 120**(3), 265-278.

Gagne, E. (1985). **The cognitive psychology of school learning.** Boston: Little, Brown.

Gibbs, J. (1987). **Tribes.** Santa Rosa, CA: Center Source Publications.

Glasser, W. (1986). **Control theory in the classroom.** New York: Harper & Row.

Goldschmid, M. (1971). The learning cell: An instructional innovation. **Learning and Development, 2**, 1-6.

Good, T., & Brouws, D. (1977). Teaching effects: A process-product study in fourth grade mathematics classrooms. **Journal of Teacher Education, 28**, 49-54.

Guetzkow, H., Kelly, E., & McKeachie, W. (1954). An experimental comparison of recitation, discussion, and tutorial methods in college teaching. **Journal of Educational Psychology, 45,** 193- 209.

Haines, D., & McKeachie, W. (1967). Cooperative versus competitive discussion methods in teaching introductory psychology. **Journal of Educational Psychology, 58**(6), 386-390.

Harkins, S., & Petty, R. (1982). The effects of task difficulty and task uniqueness on social loafing. **Journal of Personality and Social Psychology, 43**, 1214-1229.

Hartley, J., & Marshall, S. (1974). On notes and notetaking. **Universities Quarterly, 28**, 225-235.

Hartup, W. (1976). Peer interaction and the behavioral development of the individual child. In E. Schloper & R. Reicher (Eds.), **Psychology and child development.** New York: Plenum Press.

Helmreich, R. (1982, August). **Pilot selection and training.** Paper presented at the annual meeting of the American Psychological Association, Washington, D.C.

Helmreich, R., Beane, W., Lucker, W., & Spence, J. (1978). Achievement motivation and scientific attainment. **Personality and Social Psychology Bulletin, 4,** 222-226.

Helmreich, R., Sawin, L., & Carsrud, A. (1986). The honeymoon effect in job performance: Temporal increases in the predictive power of achievement motivation. **Journal of Applied Psychology, 71,** 185-188.

Helmreich, R., Spense, J., Beane, W., Lucker, W., & Matthews, K. (1980). Making it in academic psychology: Demographic and personality correlates of attainment. **Journal of Personality and Social Psychology, 39,** 896-908.

Hill, G. (1982). Group versus individual performance: Are N + 1 heads better than one? **Psychological Bulletin, 91,** 517-539.

Hwong, N., Caswell, A., Johnson, D. W., & Johnson, R. (1990). **Effects of cooperative and individualistic learning on prospective elementary teachers' music achievement and attitudes.** University of Minnesota, manuscript submitted for publication.

Ingham, A., Levinger, G., Graves, J., & Peckham, V. (1974). The Ringelmann effect: Studies of group size and group performance. **Journal of Personality and Social Psychology, 10,** 371-384.

Johnson, D. W. (1970). **The social psychology of education.** New York: Holt, Rinehart & Wilson.

Johnson, D. W. (1971). Role reversal: A summary and review of the research. **International Journal of Group Tensions, 111,** 318-334.

Johnson, D. W. (1973a). Communication in conflict situations: A critical review of the research. **International Journal of Group Tensions, 3,** 46-47.

Johnson, D. W. (Ed.) (1973b). **Contemporary Social Psychology.** Philadelphia: Lippincott.

Johnson, D. W. (1974). Communication and the inducement of cooperative behavior in conflicts: A critical review. **Speech Monographs, 41,** 64-78.

Johnson, D. W. (1979). **Educational psychology.** Englewood Cliffs, NJ: Prentice-Hall.

Johnson, D. W. (1980). Constructive peer relationships, social development, and cooperative learning experiences: Implications for the prevention of drug abuse. **Journal of Drug Education, 10**, 7-24.

Johnson, D. W. (1990). **Reaching out: Interpersonal effectiveness and self-actualization** (4th ed.). Englewood Cliffs, NJ: Prentice-Hall.

Johnson, D. W. (1991). **Human relations and your career** (3rd ed.). Englewood Cliffs, NJ: Prentice-Hall.

Johnson, D. W., & Johnson, F. (1991). **Joining together: Group theory and group skills** (4th ed.). Englewood Cliffs, NJ: Prentice-Hall.

Johnson, D. W., & Johnson, R. (1974). Instructional goal structure: Cooperative, competitive, or individualistic. **Review of Educational Research, 44**, 213-240.

Johnson, D. W., & Johnson, R. (Eds.), (1978). Social interdependence in the classroom. **Journal of Research and Development in Education, 12**(1).

Johnson, D. W., & Johnson, R. (1978). Cooperative, competitive, and individualistic learning. **Journal of Research and Development in Education, 12**, 3-15.

Johnson, D. W., & Johnson, R. (1979). Conflict in the classroom: Controversy and learning. **Review of Educational Research, 49**, 51-70.

Johnson, D. W., & Johnson R. (1980). Integrating handicapped students into the mainstream. **Exceptional Children, 46**, 89-98.

Johnson, D. W., & Johnson, R. (1980). **Belonging** (16mm film). Edina, MN: Interaction Book Company.

Johnson, D. W., & Johnson, R. (1981). Effects of cooperative and individualistic learning experiences on interethnic interaction. **Journal of Educational Psychology, 73**(3), 454-459.

Johnson, D. W., & Johnson, R. (1983a). The socialization and achievement crisis: Are cooperative learning experiences the solution? In L. Bickman (Ed.), **Applied Social Psychology Annual 4** (pp. 119-164). Beverly Hills, CA: Sage.

Johnson, D. W., & Johnson, R. (1983b). **Circles of learning** (16mm film). Edina, MN: Interaction Book Company.

Johnson, D. W., & Johnson, R. (1985). The internal dynamics of cooperative learning groups. In Slavin, R., Sharan, S., Kagan, S., Lazarowitz, R., Webb, C., & Schmuck, R. (Eds.). (1985). **Learning to cooperate, cooperating to learn** (pp.103- 124). New York: Plenum.

Johnson, D. W., & Johnson, R. (1985). Classroom conflict: Controversy vs. debate in learning groups. **American Educational Research Journal, 22**, 237-256.

Johnson, D. W., & Johnson, R. (1986). Impact of classroom organization and instructional methods on the effectiveness of mainstreaming. In C. Meisel (Ed.), **Mainstreaming handicapped children: Outcomes, controversies, and new directions.** Hillsdale, NJ: Lawrence Erlbaum.

Johnson, D. W., & Johnson, R. (1987). **Creative Conflict.** Edina, MN: Interaction Book Company.

Johnson, D. W., & Johnson, R. (1989a). **Cooperation and competition: Theory and research.** Edina, MN: Interaction Book Company.

Johnson, D. W., & Johnson, R. (1989b). **Leading the cooperative school.** Edina, MN: Interaction Book Company.

Johnson, D. W., & Johnson, R. (1975/1991). **Learning together and alone: Cooperative, competitive, and individualistic learning.** Englewood Cliffs, NJ: Prentice-Hall.

Johnson, D. W., & Johnson, R. (1991). **Teaching students to be peacemakers.** Edina, MN: Interaction Book Company.

Johnson, D. W., & Johnson, R. (1991). **Active learning: Cooperation in the college classroom.** Edina, MN: Interaction Book Company.

Johnson, D. W., & Johnson, R. (1992). **Creative controversy: Intellectual challenge in the clasroom.** Edina, MN: Interaction Book Company.

Johnson, D. W., Johnson, R., Bartlett, J., & Johnson, L. (1988). **Our cooperactive classroom.** Edina, MN: Interaction Book Company.

Johnson, D. W., Johnson, R., & Holubec, E. (Eds.) (1987). **Structuring cooperative learning: Lesson plans for teachers.** Edina, MN: Interaction Book Company.

Johnson, D. W., Johnson, R., & Holubec, E. (1991). **Cooperation in the classroom** (Revised Ed.). Edina, MN: Interaction Book Company.

Johnson, D. W., Johnson, R., & Holubec, E. (1984/1990). **Circles of learning: Cooperation in the classroom.** Edina, MN: Interaction Book Company.

Johnson, D. W., Johnson, R., & Maruyama, G. (1983). Interdependence and interpersonal attraction among heterogeneous and homogeneous individuals: A theoretical formulation and a meta-analysis of the research. **Review of Educational Research, 53**, 5-54.

Johnson, D. W., Johnson, R., Ortez, A., & Stanne, M. (1990). **Impact of positive goal and resource interdependence on achievement, interaction and attitudes.** University of Minnesota, manuscript submitted for publication.

Johnson, D. W., Johnson, R., & Smith, K. (1986). Academic conflict among students: Controversy and learning. In R. Feldman, (Ed.). **Social psychological applications to education.** New York: Cambridge University Press.

Johnson, D. W., Johnson, R., Stanne, M. & Garibaldi, A. (1990). The impact of leader and member group processing on achievement in cooperative groups. **The Journal of Social Psychology, 130,** 507- 516.

Johnson, D. W., Maruyama, G., Johnson, R, Nelson, D., & Skon, L. (1981). Effects of cooperative, competitive, and individualistic goal structures on achievement: A meta-analysis. **Psychological Bulletin, 89,** 47-62.

Johnson, D. W., & Matross, R. (1977). The interpersonal influence of the psychotherapist. In A. Gurman & A. Razin (Eds.), **The effective therapist: A handbook.** Elmsford, NY: Pergamon Press.

Johnson, D. W., & Noonan, P. (1972). Effects of acceptance and reciprocation of self-disclosures on the development of trust. **Journal of Counseling Psychology, 19**(5), 411-416.

Johnson, D. W., Skon, L., & Johnson, R. (1980). Effects of cooperative, competitive, and individualistic conditions on children's problem-solving performance. **American Educational Research Journal, 17**(1), 83-94.

Kagan, S. (1991). **Cooperative learning.** San Juan Capistrano, CA: Resources for Teachers.

Karp, D., & Yoels, W. (1987). The college classroom: Some observations on the meanings of student participation. **Sociology and Social Research, 60,** 421-439.

Keppel, G., & Underwood, B. (1962). Proactive inhibition in short-term retention of single items. **Journal of Verbal Learning and Verbal Behavior, 1,** 153-161.

Kerr, N., & Bruun, S. (1981). Ringelmann revisited: Alternative explanations for the social loafing effect. **Personality and Social Psychology Bulletin, 7,** 224-231.

Kerr, N. (1983). The dispensability of member effort and group motivation losses: Free-rider effects. **Journal of Personality and Social Psychology, 44,** 78-94.

Kiewra, K. (1985a). Investigating notetaking and review: A depth of processing alternatives. **Educational Psychologist, 20**(1), 23-32.

Kiewra, K. (1985b). Providing the instructor's notes: An effective addition to student learning. **Educational Psychologist, 20**(1), 33-39.

Kiewra, K. (1987). Notetaking and review: The research and its implications. **Instructional Science, 16**, 233- 249.

Kiewra, K., & Benton, S. (1988). The relationship between information-processing ability and notetaking. **Contemporary Educational Psychology, 13**, 33-44.

Kohn, A. (1986). **No contest: the case against competition.** Boston: Houghton-Mifflin.

Kohn, A. (1990). **The brighter side of human nature.** New York: Basic Books.

Kouzes, J., & Posner, B. (1987). **The leadership challenge.** San Francisco: Jossey-Bass.

Kuhn, T. (1962). **The structure of scientific revolutions.** Chicago: University of Chicago Press.

Kulik, J., & Kulik, C.L. (1979). College teaching. In P.L. Peterson & H.J. Walberg (Eds.), **Research on teaching: Concepts, findings, and implications.** Berkeley, CA: McCutcheon.

Lamm, H., & Trommsdorff, G. (1973). Group verses individual performance on tasks requiring ideational proficiency (Brainstorming): A review. **European Journal of Social Psychology, 3**, 361-388.

Langer, E., & Benevento, A. (1978). Self-induced dependence. **Journal of Personality and Social Psychology, 36**, 886-893.

Latane, B., Williams, K., & Harkins, S. (1979). Many hands make light the work: The causes and consequences of social loafing. **Journal of Personality and Social Psychology, 37**, 822- 832.

Lave, J. (1988). **Cognition in practice: Mind, mathematics and culture in everyday life.** Cambridge: Cambridge University Press.

Levin, H., Glass, G., & Meister, G. (1984). **Cost- effectiveness of educational interventions.** Stanford, California: Institute for Research on Educational Finance and Governance.

Lew, M., Mesch, D., Johnson, D. W., & Johnson, R. (1986a). Positive interdependence, academic and collaborative-skills group contingencies and isolated students. **American Educational Research Journal, 23**, 476-488.

Lew, M., Mesch, D., Johnson, D. W., & Johnson, R. (1986b). Components of cooperative learning: Effects of collaborative skills and academic group contingencies on achievement and main streaming. **Contemporary Educational Psychology, 11,** 229-239.

Light, R. (1990). **The Harvard assessment seminars.** Cambridge, MA: Harvard University Press.

Little, J. (1981). **School success and staff development in urban desegregated schools.** Paper presented at the American Educational Research Association, Los Angeles, April.

Mackworth, J. (1970). **Vigilance and habituation.** Harmondsworth, England: Penguin.

Male, M., Johnson, R., Johnson, D. W., & Anderson, M. (1988). **Cooperative learning and computers: An activity guide for teachers.** Santa Cruz, CA: Educational Apple-cat-ions.

Masqud, M. (1980). Effects of personal lecture notes and teacher notes on recall of university students. **British Journal of Educational Psychology, 50,** 289-294.

May, M., & Doob, L. (1937). **Competition and cooperation** (Social Science Research Council Bulletin No. 25). New York: Social Science Research Council.

Mayer, A. (1903). Uber einzel und gesamtleistung des schul kindes. **Archiv fur die Gesamte Psychologie, 1,** 276-416.

McKeachie, W. (1951). Anxiety in the college classroom. **Journal of Educational Research, 45,** 153-160.

McKeachie, W. (1954). Individual conformity to attitudes of classroom groups. **Journal of Abnormal and Social Psychology, 49,** 282-289.

McKeachie, W. (1967). Research in teaching: The gap between theory and practice. In C. Lee (Ed.), **Improving college teaching** (pp 211-239). Washington, D.C.: American Council of Education.

McKeachie, W. (1986). **Teaching Tips: A guidebook for the beginning college teacher** (8th ed.). Boston: D.C. Heath.

McKeachie, W. (1988). Teaching thinking. **Update, 2**(1), 1.

McKeachie, W., & Kulik, J. (1975). Effective college training. In F. Kerlinger (Ed.), **Review of Research in Education.** Itasca, IL: Peacock.

McKeachie, W., Pintrich, P., Yi-Guang, L., & Smith, D. (1986). **Teaching and learning in the college classroom: A review of the research literature.** Ann Arbor, MI: The Regents of the University of Michigan.

Menges, R. (1988). Research on teaching and learning: The relevant and the redundant. **The Review of Higher Education, 11**(3), 259-268.

Mesch, D., Johnson, D. W., & Johnson, R. (1988). Impact of positive interdependence and academic group contingencies on achievement. **Journal of Social Psychology, 128,** 345-352.

Mesch, D., Lew, M., Johnson, D. W., & Johnson, R. (1986). Isolated teenagers, cooperative learning and the training of social skills. **Journal of Psychology, 120,** 323-334.

Moede, W. (1927). Die richtlinien der leistungs- psycholgie. **Industrielle Psychotechnik, 4,** 193-207.

Motley, M. (1988, January). Taking the terror out of talk. **Psychology Today, 22**(1), pp. 46-49.

Murray, F. (1983). **Cognitive benefits of teaching on the teacher.** Paper presented at American Educational Research Association Annual Meeting, Montreal, Quebec.

Murray, H. (1985). Classroom teaching behaviors related to college teaching effectiveness. In J.G. Donald and A.M. Sullivan (Eds.), **Using research to improve teaching** (pp. 21-34). San Francisco: Jossey-Bass.

National Center for Educational Statistics. (1984). **Two years after high school: A capsule description of 1980 seniors.** Washington, DC: U.S. Department of Education.

National Institute of Education. (1984). **Involvement in learning. Study group on the conditions of excellence in higher education.** Washington, DC.

Neer, M. (1987). The development of an instrument to measure classroom apprehension. **Communication Education, 36,** 154-166.

Noel, L. (1985). Increasing student retention: New challenges and potential. In L. Noel, R. Levitz, & D. Saluri (Eds.), **Increasing student retention: Effective programs and practices for reducing the dropout rate** (pp. 1-27). San Francisco: Jossey-Bass.

Pascarella, E. (1980). Student-faculty informal contact and college outcomes. **Review of Educational Research, 50,** 545-595.

Orlick, T. (1982). **Cooperative sports and games book.** New York: Pantheon.

Pelz, D., & Andrews, F. (1976). **Scientists in organizations: Productive climates for research and development.** Ann Arbor: Institute for Social Research, University of Michigan.

Penner, J. (1984). **Why many college teachers cannot lecture.** Springfield, IL: Charles C. Thomas.

Pepitone, E. (1980). **Children in cooperation and competition.** Lexington, MA: Lexington Books.

Petty, R., Harkins, S., Williams, K., & Latane, B. (1977). The effects of group size on cognitive effort and evaluation. **Personality and Social Psychology Bulletin, 3,** 575-578.

Rhoades, J., & McCabe, M. (1988). **The nurturing classroom.** Willits, CA: ITA Publications.

Rosenshine, B. (1968, December). To explain: A review of research. **Educational Leadership, 26,** 303-309.

Rosenshine, B., & Stevens, R. (1986). Teaching functions. In M. Wittrock (Ed), **Handbook of research on teaching** (3rd ed.) (pp. 376-391). New York: Macmillan.

Ruggiero, V. (1988). **Teaching thinking across the curriculum.** New York: Harper & Row.

Ruhl, K., Hughes, C., & Schloss, P. (1987). Using the pause procedure to enhance lecture recall. **Teacher Education and Special Education, 10**(1), 14-18.

Salomon, G. (1981). Communication and education: Social and psychological interactions. **People & Communication, 13,** 9-271.

Schmuck, R., & Schmuck, P. (1983). **Group processes in the classroom.** Dubuque, Iowa: Wm. C. Brown.

Schniedewind, N., & Davidson, E. (1987). **Cooperative learning, cooperative lives.** Dubuque, Iowa: Wm. C. Brown.

Schoenfeld, A. (1985). **Mathematical problem solving.** Orlando: Academic Press.

Schoenfeld, A. (1989). Ideas in the air: Speculations on small group learning, peer interactions, cognitive apprenticeship, quasi-Vygotskean notions of internalization, creativity, problem solving, and mathematical practice. **International Journal of Educational Research,** in press.

Scully, M. (1981, October 21). One million students at U.S. colleges; triple present number seems likely by 1990. **The Chronicle of Higher Education,** p. 1.

Shalaway, L. (1985). Peer coaching...does it work? **R&D Notes**, National Institute of Education (September), 6-7.

Sharan, S. (1980). Cooperative learning in teams: Recent methods and effects on achievement, attitudes, and ethnic relations. **Review of Educational Research, 50**, 241-272.

Sharan, S. & Sharan, Y. (1976). **Small group teaching.** Englewood Cliffs, NJ: Educational Technology Publications.

Sheahan, B. & White, J. (1990). Quo Vadis, undergraduate engineering education? **Engineering Education, 80**(8), 1017-1022.

Sheingold, K., Hawkins, J., & Char, C. (1984). I'm the thinkist, you're the typist: The interaction of technology and the social life of classrooms. **Journal of Social Issues, 40**(3), 49-6.

Skon, L., Johnson, D. W., & Johnson, R. (1981). Cooperative peer interaction versus individual competition and individualistic efforts: Effects on the acquisition of cognitive reasoning strategies. **Journal of Educational Psychology, 73**(1), 83-92.

Slavin, R. (1980). Cooperative learning. **Review of Educational Research, 50**, 315-342.

Slavin, R. (1983). **Cooperative learning.** New York: Longman.

Slavin, R., Leavey, M., & Madden, N. (1982). **Team-assisted individualization: Mathematics teacher's manual.** Johns Hopkins University, Center for Social Organization of Schools.

Slavin, R., Sharan, S., Kagan, S., Lazarowitz, R., Webb, C., & Schmuck, R. (Eds.). (1985). **Learning to cooperate, cooperating to learn.** New York: Plenum.

Smith, D. (1977). College classroom interactions and critical thinking. **Journal of Educational Psychology, 69**, 180-190.

Smith, D. (1980). **Instruction and outcomes in an undergraduate setting.** Paper presented at the annual meeting of the American Educational Research Association, Boston.

Smith, L., & Land, M. (1981). Low-inference verbal behaviors related to teach clarity. **Journal of Classroom Interaction, 17**, 37-42.

Starfield, A., Smith, K., & Bleloch, A. (1990). **How to model it: problem solving for the computer age.** New York: McGraw-Hill.

Stones, E. (1970). Students' attitudes to the size of teaching groups. **Educational Review, 21**(2), 98-108.

Stuart, J., & Rutherford, R. (1978, September). Medical student concentration during lectures. **The Lancet, 2**, 514-516.

Terenzini, P. (1986). **Retention research: Academic and social fit.** Paper presented at the meeting of the Southern Regional Office of the College of Entrance Examination Board, New Orleans.

Tinto, V. (1975). Dropout from higher education: A theoretical synthesis of recent research. **Review of Educational Research, 45**(1), 89-125.

Tinto, V. (1987). **Leaving college: Rethinking the causes and cures for student attrition.** Chicago: University of Chicago Press.

Tjosvold, D. (1986). **Working together to get things done.** Lexington, MA: D. C. Heath.

Tjosvold, D. (1991a). **The conflict-positive organization.** Reading, MA: Addison-Wesley.

Tjosvold, D. (1991b). **Team organization: An enduring competitive advantage.** New York: John Wiley.

Treisman, P. (1985). A study of the mathematics performance of Black students at the University of California, Berkeley. (Doctoral dissertation, University of California, Berkeley, 1986). **Dissertation abstracts international, 47**, 1641-A.

Triplett, N. (1898). The dynamogenic factors in pacemaking and competition. **American Journal of Psychology, 9**, 507-533.

Verner, C., & Dickinson, G. (1967). The lecture: an analysis and review of research. **Adult Education, 17**, 85-100.

Vygotsky, L. (1978). **Mind and society.** Cambridge, MA: Harvard University Press.

Wales, C., & Sager, R. (1978). **The guided design approach.** Englewood Cliffs, NJ: Educational Technology Publications.

Watson, G., & Johnson, D. W. (1972). **Social psychology: Issues and insights.** Philadelphia: Lippincott.

Waugh, N., & Norman, D. (1965). Primary memory. **Psychological Review, 72**, 89-104.

White, R., & Tisher, R. (1986). Research on natural sciences. In M. Whittrock (Ed.), **Handbook of research on teaching** (3rd ed.). New York: Macmillan.

Williams, K. (1981). **The effects of group cohesiveness on social loafing.** Paper presented at the annual meeting of the Midwestern Psychological Association, Detroit.

Williams, K., Harkins, S., & Latane, B. (1981). Identifiability as a deterrent to social loafing. Two cheering experiments. **Journal of Personality and Social Psychology, 40,** 303-311.

Wilson, R. (1987). Toward excellence in teaching. In L. M. Aleamoni (Ed.), **Techniques for evaluating and improving instruction** (pp. 9-24). San Francisco: Jossey-Bass.

Winget, P. (Ed.). (1987). **Integrating the core curriculum through cooperative learning: Lesson plans for teachers.** Sacramento, CA: California State Department of Education.

Workplace basics: The skills employers want. (1988). American Society for Training and Development and U.S. Department of Labor.

Wulff, D., Nyquist, J., & Abbott, R. (1987). Students' perception of large classes. In M. E. Weimer (Ed.), **Teaching large classes well** (pp. 17-30). San Francisco: Jossey-Bass.

Yager, S., Johnson, D., & Johnson, R. (1985). Oral discussion, group-to individual transfer, and achievement in cooperative learning groups. **Journal of Educational Psychology, 77**(1), 60-66.